THE PH❤ENIX MAN

JULIE ANNETTE BENNETT

BALBOA.PRESS
A DIVISION OF HAY HOUSE

Balboa Press books may be ordered through booksellers or by contacting:

Balboa Press
A Division of Hay House
1663 Liberty Drive
Bloomington, IN 47403
www.balboapress.com
844-682-1282

Because of the dynamic nature of the Internet, any web addresses or links contained in this book may have changed since publication and may no longer be valid. The views expressed in this work are solely those of the author and do not necessarily reflect the views of the publisher, and the publisher hereby disclaims any responsibility for them.

The author of this book does not dispense medical advice or prescribe the use of any technique as a form of treatment for physical, emotional, or medical problems without the advice of a physician, either directly or indirectly. The intent of the author is only to offer information of a general nature to help you in your quest for emotional and spiritual well-being. In the event you use any of the information in this book for yourself, which is your constitutional right, the author and the publisher assume no responsibility for your actions.

Any people depicted in stock imagery provided by Getty Images are models, and such images are being used for illustrative purposes only. Certain stock imagery © Getty Images.

Print information available on the last page.

ISBN: 978-1-9822-6871-8 (sc)
ISBN: 978-1-9822-6873-2 (hc)
ISBN: 978-1-9822-6872-5 (e)

Library of Congress Control Number: 2021909606

Balboa Press rev. date: 07/20/2021

In Loving Memory of Scott Joseph Bennett
June 13, 1951 – May 9, 2019

Dedication

To my husband, Scott, my best friend, lover, comforter, listener: you will always be with me in my heart and soul and I will never forget the wonderful times we had together before and after our lives changed.

To my children, Matthew, Jonathan, Charlie (Charlisse), and grandchildren, Killian and Tatum: having each of you in my life has brought many joys, wonder, and beauty that only children and grandchildren can provide.

To all the caregivers that already know the importance of their job in this crazy world, to the caregivers still wondering if it is all worth it, and to all future caregivers needing reassurance that their feelings are legit…they are!

Book Reviews

The Phoenix Man is an amazing story of mutual love expressed by a husband and wife's journey through three debilitating diseases ending with Alzheimer's. As Julie cares for her husband, Scott, she shares intense moments of frustration vs. joy, weariness vs. strength, mixed with humor and lots of hope.

Not only is this book a beautiful love story, it is also a guide to help you become a kinder and gentler caregiver. Each chapter's ending provides suggestions to stay focused on the bigger picture...you and your loved one's needs. Not a caregiver? This story will resonate with anyone who has ever had a hardship that seemed interminable reminding each of us of our humanity.

From caregiver to widowhood, this book gives you permission to feel all the emotions a caregiver goes through on a day to day basis.

Kathi Spork, Caregiver to husband with Primary Progressive Aphasia

In *The Phoenix Man*, Julie gives an intimate portrayal of her caregiving journey with her husband, Scott, through Alzheimer's. Julie weaves in every day wisdoms and practical advice for caregivers among her personal story of love and navigating a complicated medical picture. The way this book is written has you experiencing Julie's journey as a caregiver right alongside of her as she makes every decision.

This 'must read' book will give strength to others on their own caregiving journey while emphasizing, through Julie's example, the importance of celebrating each moment of this life and honoring each other.

Shelley Dombroski, Regional Director, **Lauren Hibdon**, Family Care Specialist, Alzheimer's Association in Northern California and Northern Nevada

Reading *The Phoenix Man* reminded me of when Scott was in the Early Stage Memory Loss Group that I facilitated for the Alzheimer's Association. He spoke openly about his heart transplant, losing his memory, and his appreciation and love for Julie.

Caring for a relative with physical impairment(s) can be very different from caring for a person with memory loss. In *The Phoenix Man*, Julie beautifully outlines the differences for her and Scott before and after his heart transplant and during the years he had dementia, offering readers tips, encouragement, and education during her dual caregiving experiences.

Laurie White, MSW, co-author of Coping with Behavior Change in Dementia *and* Moving a Relative with Memory Loss

Contents

Acknowledgments

First and foremost, I want to thank my husband, Scott Joseph Bennett, for being a wonderful and loving comfort in my life. I hope that in some small way this book pays tribute to his strength and resilience through the many physical hardships he endured over the years, as well as our love and commitment to each other. May your story, my sweet husband, live on to give hope, joy, and comfort to all who read our book.

Matthew Bennett, thank you for all the visits you made to see your dad at the nursing home, even when it seemed like he didn't know who you were at times. I know that was tough to experience, yet I also know that your father now knows of your love and dedication at the end of his life. Being there for your dad meant you were there for me as well, and I will always be thankful for your comfort in those difficult yet loving moments.

Jonathan Weintraub, all the times you gave of yourself to your step-father, you were also giving to me and I thank you. I will always treasure the special moments Scott and I spent with you and your family as you opened your home to us. Scott and you became close and I could see it in the way he reacted each time you walked into the room.

Charlie Weintraub, you are a very special daughter-in-law, not only beautiful on the outside, but your light shines bright on the inside, too. You opened your heart to both Scott and me giving us many loving times with our beautiful grandchildren, Killian and Tatum. The videos and photos you took and shared when they asked for grandma or grandpa always made our day. Thank you for just being you.

Thank you Carol Bennett for being the perfect big sister for Scott. He needed your love and was so thankful each time you opened your home when he needed to go to Kaiser's heart transplant medical offices. You were a driving force in his life and he loved you so much.

Thank you Gil and Cynthia Bennett for always being there for your brother and brother-in-law. Each time you took Scott out to breakfast, Gil, and to play golf, you made his day. He loved you both so much and I am happy to be able to include you in this book.

Janice Mayberry, thank you for always being there for me; thank you for sharing your mom, Olga Lee, and your sister, Karen, with me from the start. Having your family become my family from the time we met in 1982 gave me a safety net through the years. And thank you for always being there for us during all of Scott's illnesses. You are one of my earth angels and I hope this book expresses my continuous love and friendship.

Bill and Marilyn Nasi, Richard Parry-Jones (RPJ), and all the Mayberrys...when Scott and I met, all of you joined together to become our family of friends and you were with us through all the years sharing in good times and difficult ones. All of us could count on each other and who could ask for more in life than the comfort of good friends. Thank you all for helping us survive along the way.

To Anne Basye, my editor, you are a lifesaver. I needed someone to trust and guide me on how to make the book grab people so that they would read it from cover to cover. Your suggestions have given me permission to eliminate the fluff and concentrate on the story itself. Afterall, it is the caregiver who needs to be able to relate to someone who has been through it all so that whatever their story, they feel they are not alone.

Marilyn Nasi and Kathi Spork, thank you both for reading this book chapter to chapter giving me your input and keeping me on track. Your comments and suggestions have enhanced the book and I think you'll both be happy with the outcome. Marti Avery, your suggestions in the first four chapters helped me more than you know giving me visions for the rest of the book.

A big thank you to all the people who sent us supportive emails during each crisis; each one was an enormous comfort to Scott and me. And although I could not include all of your emails in this book, I want to acknowledge those whose emails in some small way contributed to telling our story: Gil Bennett, Gloria Bottaro, Eileen Bill, Pam Chanter, the late Toni Faxon, Deb Hendryx, Kris Howell, the late Ed Matheson, Janice Mayberry, Olga Lee Mayberry, Marilyn Nasi, RPJ (Richard Parry-Jones), Sandy Shults, Doug Taylor, and Larry Wieczorek.

Thank you Bob Evans for all the times you took Scott out to lunch and to play golf, as well as all your many visits to Scott in the nursing home.

Thank you to everyone we met in the Alzheimer's Support Group who listened and gave us both so much support and love. A special thank you to Gloria Brecher and the late Geoffrey Brecher, Diane and John Benjamin, Joan and Dave Crady, and John Zuryk. You were all important parts of our lives and continue to be a part of my life today.

Thank you to Lauren Hibdon and Shelley Dombroski at the Santa Rosa Alzheimer's Association for their awesome book review. And thank you, Laurie White, for your heartfelt book review and invaluable suggestions.

Thank you to all the individuals at Balboa Press who helped to make the presentation of this book so beautiful.

To all the wonderful people that Scott and I were blessed to meet while he was living in the nursing home, my deep thanks. You gave so much of yourselves and I wish that I could have included every single one of you in this book. Just know, though, how much you were and are appreciated. The heart of a person who works in a nursing home is full of caring, love, and joy, giving hope to all whom they touch. Thank you for being our earth angels. I especially want to thank Roberto Huerta for his comfort, touch, and love. And a big thank you to Angie Gatt for the depth of her compassion in a sometimes thankless job.

Thank you to all the residents whose lives touched mine, and whose anecdotes brought so much joy and love to Scott and me every single day. Only a few of you are mentioned in this book, yet I will always be grateful to have had all of you in my life to help me grow into a more gentle, loving, and kind person.

Foreword

I met Scott and Julie in August 1990 soon after they were introduced on a blind date. I had just met my future husband, Bill, who worked with Scott, both as letter carriers for the US Postal Service. All four of us had been previously married. We found that we enjoyed one another's company and began going out to dinner, holding potlucks, and celebrating birthdays and holidays together. Our friends merged to make one big happy family.

All of Julie's work life had been devoted to helping people with their medical insurance needs. One job was with HICAP, Health Insurance Counseling & Advocacy Program, providing free and objective information and counseling about Medicare. Julie was a good listener and communicator during her working years helping people one-on-one and giving presentations on Medicare in six counties in Northern California. Although I am sure Julie never expected to put her professional experience to such personal use during Scott's medical challenges, her awareness of patients' rights made her a fierce advocate for her husband as she accompanied him in doctors' offices, hospitals, and the nursing home. Julie continues to be an advocate for caregivers by volunteering as a group facilitator for the Alzheimer's Association.

The Phoenix Man brought up so many memories with minute details, many of which I had forgotten. Even though I shed some tears, I'm so glad she asked me to read their story. This is a narrative about two people who loved each other immensely, a man who survived all odds again and again, and a spouse who became a caregiver with hardly a moment's notice. *The Phoenix Man* takes you on a journey of sorrow and pain, yet also shows how hardships can bring joy and comfort. Along the way, Julie draws on what she learned as a caregiver to share insights and advice to help other caregivers on their journey. I hope you will find Julie and Scott's experiences helpful in your own lives.

Marilyn Nasi

Scott and I became fast friends in 1988 while we worked at the post office in Santa Rosa. Because I am an extrovert and Scott was an introvert, our personalities worked well together. Each of us could be ourselves. We were roommates for a short time, two bachelors enjoying many pizzas together. Although we were both football and baseball enthusiasts, we especially enjoyed watching the 49ers at Candlestick Park with Scott's cousin, Doug Taylor.

When Marilyn and I were married in May 1991 and Scott and Julie were married that August, we had no idea how our paths and friendship would intertwine as the years rolled by. Life was good for the four of us, until Scott's heart began to die and their medical journey began in 2007. Luckily, Scott's heart transplant saved his life. Life was tough at times for Scott and Julie but there were no complaints from either of them. Scott was a trooper to the very end and I will always be thankful for the good memories we shared. My life will always be better for knowing Scott Bennett.

The Phoenix Man fits Scott to a T as he came back again and again flouting death at every turn. As I watched my good friend suffer through each illness, I was humbled by his strength and endurance. Julie adds her own compassion, growth, and yes, fear as she tells their story from a caregiver's viewpoint. I know what she shares will help other caregivers walk alongside their own loved one on their own individual journey.

Bill Nasi

Introduction

After being married only six months, I found out my husband had a heart condition. As a licensed Life Insurance Agent working for a broker, I applied for life insurance for Scott knowing that at our age, the cost for a policy would be minimal. Imagine my surprise when the underwriter called to say that my new husband was being rated for a heart condition called Idiopathic Hypertrophic Subaortic Stenosis (I.H.S.S.).

In shock, I asked the underwriter to repeat the diagnosis, then asked what the words meant. I stopped listening after hearing the words, "This disease can cause sudden death...." As I hung up the phone, I sat in total disbelief. And when I got home from work that night, I had a little talk—okay, a big talk—with Scott.

"Why didn't you tell me? Were you ever going to tell me? You could just drop dead and I wouldn't have known why!" It crossed my mind that by Scott not disclosing this information a divorce could be easily obtained. But as quick as that thought came into my head, it flew right back out. I loved Scott and was truly scared.

He told me he had known about this condition, but had shrugged it off as he never had any symptoms. He first learned he had a hole in his heart, causing a heart murmur, from the results of his high school sports physical. This meant that Scott was not allowed to play competitive sports. Yet when we met, Scott was playing on the post office softball team and bowling league.

At that time, I was the pitcher on a woman's softball team and could pitch underhand with a rubber arm. Every time Scott came to watch me play, that rubber arm became like Jello, wobbling with no control. If Scott were around, I couldn't concentrate, and my underhand pitch was a flop. Secretly, I think, the way I fell apart around him made him fall in love with me.

We met on a blind date on July 3, 1990. I was 37 and he had just turned 39. I was a single parent to my ten-year old son, Jonathan, and Scott was an every-other-weekend dad to Matthew, who was almost five. Together we ended up parenting two talkative, trying teenagers who considered us totally inept and the worst parents ever. Sound familiar? Many years later they both told us that in hindsight they could see that we were the best and the most normal parents.

I came from a big family and was a shy girl. After moving out of the house at age 18 and while working in the insurance industry, I became more talkative and competitive. Scott, on the other hand, was raised in a small, quiet family household where no one talked at the dinner table. This could explain why he was so quiet, too. A golf pro in his early 20's, Scott then became a USPS letter carrier. I always got a little thrill when I saw Scott in his work uniform and thought of him as my handsome mailman.

Like most relationships, our life together had its ups and downs. I believe my love for Scott to be deeper, more expressive than his was for me, but through the years I believe that his love grew exponentially. About 10 years into our marriage, I finally understood that if I really loved Scott, and God knows I did, then I needed to accept every part of him. This was a real awakening. Now I could let Scott be himself without all the expectations I was putting on him and our relationship. After all, he was the best thing that had ever happened to me.

Jonathan and Scott had a challenging relationship. Scott had little experience raising a child and Jon had never had a father figure living in the house. Through the Big Brother Big Sisters program, Jon had Rod, a huge influence from age seven until his untimely death six years later. Losing this father figure, a beacon in his life, was difficult. I could never get Jon to talk about his feelings of loss, possibly one reason Jon and Scott's relationship was difficult. Eventually, Jonathan realized how much he loved Scott and how much Scott's influence had helped him in life. From that point on their relationship made a complete turnaround, for which I am so thankful.

In 1996, ten-year old Matthew came to live with us. The first year,

Matthew was angry with his dad and let him know. After about a year, he turned that anger towards me. Scott and I almost split up several times as I didn't know how much more of Matthew's resentment I could take. When Bob Kat came to live with us in 2002, she stopped a lot of arguments. When we humans stood in the kitchen arguing, Bob Kat would walk up and meow for us to pay attention to her. Our love for her reminded us of our love for each other.

Every six months, Scott had a check-up with a local cardiologist. When symptoms began in 2005, he was put on heart medication. Soon after, a defibrillator was implanted above his heart. Still, his heart was in and out of rhythm, causing his breathing to be shallow at times. The next two years had him in and out of the hospital for three cardioversions (*a brief procedure where an electrical shock is delivered to the heart*) and a cardiac ablation (*a procedure to scar or destroy tissue in the heart that's allowing incorrect electrical signals to cause an abnormal rhythm*).

Scott continued to work at the post office, but he often came home out of breath. Making love was no longer an option as we were both afraid that he would die if we tried. Little did we know the extent to which our lives were about to change.

From 2005 to 2019, Scott lived through three serious diseases: a dying heart, aspergillus pneumonia, and Alzheimer's. Learning to live with each one while having as normal a life as possible was an ongoing effort, but we did it. Were we perfect? No. Did Scott want to end it? At times, yes. Would we want to go through this again? Hell no! And yet, what we both gained together as husband and wife and best friends will hopefully shine a light for others to see that love endures even through the darkest of times.

The Phoenix Man is a story about two lives that were taken on a journey of chronic illnesses and eventual grief that spanned 2005 to 2021. One spouse would become the patient, the other the caregiver. That caregiver was me. Part One was mostly taken from emails to update family and friends while Scott's uncertain heart issues unfolded; some entries are notes to myself that confess my internal feelings. Most of Part Two was written during moments of sadness and heartache as I witnessed my husband succumb to Alzheimer's.

All of the doctors' names in the book have been changed to protect their privacy. Any errors on medical terminology and medications are all mine. Brand-name medications are capitalized where generics are not.

As you read our story, you will feel Scott's and my love grow, feel the comfort that only good friends can bring, and feel the pain that serious illness will cause. You will also feel the joy, humor, and comfort we shared together.

Scott Joseph Bennett was not a perfect man, nor was our marriage, and yet our life together has been the best part of mine. Scott was quiet, non-combative, a worshiper of the Giants and 49ers, and he loved our girl tabby cat, Bob Kat, immensely. At the end of our journey, I realized how much he loved me and I think he realized it, too. If there's any good to come out of this disease called Alzheimer's, it is the fact that a couple's love for each other can become the most precious thing in their lives.

I loved and still love my husband Scott…completely, fiercely, and with a bit of awe. That's what caregiving did for me; heaven knows what Scott's illnesses did for him.

PART ONE

A Caregiver in the Making

Redwood Boxes

On March 4, 2007, my world changed from one of comfort and predictions to a world of not knowing one day to the next whether my husband would live or die. This day was a typical almost spring Sunday afternoon in Santa Rosa, California. It was 70 degrees and the sun was shining, with a few clouds in the sky to give it a bit of personality. We were shopping at Target for some shadow boxes to put on the newly painted wall in our family room. I was feeling really good about our choice and looking forward to setting them up behind and to the right side of the television set. After all, blank walls are, well, just blank.

On this peaceful sunlit day, Scott seemed fine, with none of the heavy breathing or heart-related issues that happened from time to time. I can remember walking to the car with me in the lead and Scott not too far behind. I was almost to our SUV and had just passed a parked red truck when I noticed in my periphery that Scott had slowed almost to a stop. I glanced behind to see why, thinking a car must be backing out or he saw something else concerning.

I asked Scott what was wrong. He told me he didn't feel quite right then began falling down towards the blacktop right in front of my eyes. Luckily, I was able to help Scott to the ground without hurting him too much. His glasses cut his nose, and something gashed his arm (maybe my wedding ring?). As he collapsed, my heart and soul began screaming,

Oh My God! I'm not ready. Please don't take him yet. Please God, don't let him die!

People were running over asking what was happening and how they could help. Somehow I managed to pull out my cell phone to dial 911, yelling to a woman that his heart must have stopped and to run into Target to call 911 from there. I remembered hearing that calling 911 from a cell phone doesn't always get you to a live person, that sometimes you were put on hold for minutes at a time. But a woman with a comforting voice answered that call, and she, whoever she was, guided me and calmed me until the ambulance arrived approximately five minutes later.

A man came out of nowhere, an off-duty police officer he said. He quickly kneeled down and talked to Scott as he came to. As I spoke to the dispatcher, I didn't realize Scott was awake, never mind alive. This compassionate man asked Scott pertinent questions about his heart condition and kept him alert. Another woman brought over something to put under Scott's head; she and her young son stayed with us until the ambulance took my husband to the hospital. As I watched the paramedics drive out of the parking lot, making a right, then another right, then driving out of sight, I just stood there, feeling alone and unsure about what to do next. After a few minutes, I realized that I needed to get into the SUV, drive to the hospital, and call our sons.

Scott didn't remember falling to the ground and I don't know how I got him down without hitting his head *and* without breaking the redwood boxes I was still holding. It's amazing what we can do in an emergency without any training or warning. I just know that my silent prayer is what kept Scott from leaving the earth that day, to give us more time together.

At the Emergency Room (ER), someone from Medtronic arrived to read Scott's defibrillator. When he collapsed, the device apparently went off, shocking his heart. If the device hadn't gone off, he would have died.

Scott was told he could not drive anymore, so on Monday, March 12, I drove him to Dr. Decker's office. He could hardly walk up the ramp, but fortunately someone happened to be passing by with a wheelchair. As she wheeled him onto the elevator, then to the cardiologist's office, I was starting to wonder what was in store for the rest of our lives.

In his brief exam, Dr. Decker found Scott in a life and death situation. An ambulance was called as the doctor was worried Scott wouldn't make it to the hospital without the assistance of the paddles in the ambulance. Once in the ER, Scott received a sedative through an IV before Dr. Decker performed an electrical cardioversion to shock his heart. It was very strange for me to watch Scott's body jolt up in the air.

Tuesday, March 20, 2007: This afternoon, the defibrillator shocked his heart again. Dr. Decker is concerned that his heart is having two separate problems. Today both occurred at the same time, causing his heart to stop. This is why the device shocked him again.

From March 4 to June 3, Scott had seven doctor visits, five shocks to his heart, one cardioversion, one ablation, numerous lab work, and four ER visits. While Scott was at home living with an uncertain future, I continued to work for HICAP (Health Insurance Counseling and Advocacy Program) giving presentations on Medicare to seniors and the disabled in six counties. It was nerve-racking for me to drive sometimes an hour and a half away. Petrified that something would happen to Scott while I was gone, I called him multiple times a day. I tried to keep our lives as normal as possible by celebrating friends' birthdays, having get togethers for dinner, and other social outings. Working and being available to take Scott to necessary doctor appointments and procedures began to take its toll.

On Memorial Day, our birthday group (our good friends Bill, Marilyn, Olga Lee, Janice, RPJ, and RPJ's wife Christine) came over to our house to celebrate RPJ's 55th birthday. I had baked a homemade chocolate cake and bought a small white cake for Bill, who can't eat chocolate. We were all talking and laughing until the conversation turned around to Scott and what's been happening with his heart and defibrillator. As I was sharing those stories, all of a sudden Scott looked like he was going to pass out. We called 911 and he was taken to Santa Rosa Memorial Hospital. Before Janice and I left to follow the ambulance to the hospital in my car, I told RPJ and Christine to take the chocolate cake home and enjoy.

At the ER, the Medtronic Representative read Scott's device. Using a machine called a programmer, it showed that his heart had *not* been shocked. The ER visit ended quickly and we were ready to leave. As Janice, Scott, and I looked at each other, we realized that there wasn't going to be any decadent chocolate cake with dark fudge frosting waiting for us at home. We wanted some so badly that we decided to drive to RPJ and Christine's house, even if we seemed totally uncouth and rude. I've often wondered what they thought about us showing up unannounced and taking half the cake with us.

A few days later, my son Jonathan came over to talk. Looking quite serious, he asked if we had ever considered a heart transplant. Scott and I looked at each other as we contemplated the idea.

My first thought was, *Hell, no!*

Scott said, "If it would keep me alive."

As I considered the impact of such a huge undertaking, I thought, *A heart transplant? Are you kidding me? What would that entail? Will Scott survive it? OMG!* It sounded scary and eerie all at the same time, like a horror movie with a really bad ending. At this point, though, we didn't know that this would become Scott's only option.

Note to Caregivers:

We are not born caregivers. Mothers and fathers don't think of themselves as such during the years they care for their young children, and yet that is exactly their role. As we get older we may be thrust into the caregiver role for our spouse, parent, or adult child without any warning or training—often after an unexpected MRI or some such test that yields a dire result.

As you become adjusted to the new reality and your new normal, you will go through a lot of emotions: anger that your life is changing, fear of the unknown, frustration that your loved one can't do certain things for themselves anymore, uncertainty about whether you can take some time for yourself or whether friends and family will think you are selfish if you do. All these feelings are legitimate and valid and I am here to say that there are many ways to help you cope. As you continue reading our story, there will be suggestions for ways to adjust so you can have as normal a life as possible. You are not alone, but it is up to you to find and create the support you will need to get through this challenging time. As you go through this journey, remember that this too shall pass for nothing lasts forever.

2

No Juice for the Paddles

I began helping people with health insurance issues when I was hired by an insurance company in Hollywood at the young age of 18 in 1970. Joining the first customer service class in 1974 gave me a feeling of accomplishment and I was good at it. After moving to Santa Rosa in 1980, I continued along that path, working for different brokers and then Health Plan of the Redwoods (HPR). The satisfaction I received from figuring out who to call to fix an issue and comforting someone when there wasn't anything else I could do for them was its own reward. So when a job at the Health Insurance Counseling and Advocacy Program (HICAP) opened up in 2001, it was the right move.

In 2006, Medicare Part D (drug coverage) had just come out and our program manager quit. Not finding a suitable replacement, in April 2007 I was asked to be the program manager. With all the uncertainty happening to Scott, I didn't feel I had it in me. The doctors didn't know how long Scott could survive with his heart the way it was and I didn't want added pressure to my already fragile psyche. We compromised with me as the interim program manager while continuing to look for someone else to fill the position.

Sunday, June 3, 2007: Scott's device went off at 7:30 a.m. So on Monday, back to Dr. Decker's office we went where he practically collapsed in the office just like on March 12. Dr. Decker again called for an ambulance and Scott was taken to the hospital to be admitted. Although he is feeling better just by being in the hospital, his breathing is very shallow. Knowing he was in good hands, I left at five o'clock as my back couldn't handle any more of the uncomfortable hospital chairs.

This evening as I was talking to Scott's sister Carol, Scott called to say his device went off again at 6:00 p.m. Dr. Decker wants to monitor him overnight and possibly send him down to UCSF tomorrow. It doesn't look good and I am scared. Scared of losing Scott and scared about losing my job. But for right now, I need to be with Scott and try not to worry about what I can't foresee.

Tuesday, June 5: Keeping up with phone calls and emails has become a struggle, so I created a group email list to keep our family, friends, and coworkers updated on Scott's condition. Feel free to share these emails.

Dr. Decker came to the hospital around noon today to check on Scott's condition. He looks better than yesterday, but still very pale. Thank goodness his device hasn't gone off today, but when it does, his heart is saying *Enough already!*

The doctor hasn't been able to get hold of anyone at UCSF, and I'm not sure we want to go through with a heart transplant anyway. For those of you who understand the different medications, he was on Coreg and Lotensin. The doctor took him off both as he may be having reactions to these meds. *(Coreg is used to treat heart failure and hypertension. Lotensin is used for hypertension.)*

His heart is stiff and not expanding as it should when it pumps blood. The Echocardiogram (Echo) showed this today. He seems to be in good hands in the hospital and I know he feels safer being there. He will spend the night and then we will see what the doctor says tomorrow. *(An Echocardiogram is a noninvasive test using sound waves to show the heart's size, function, and thickness of the heart muscle.)*

Friday June 8: The waiting game is on to hear back from UCSF. Dr. Decker doesn't like the results of Scott's Echo from one month ago to Tuesday. His heart is enlarging *(hypertrophy)* quickly and not pulsating as it should. Otherwise, his spirits are good and his color looks better. A few friends came by for a visit and it was nice to hear Scott laugh as he seemed to forget for just a moment the severity of his condition.

Scott just called me at home. He will be transported to UCSF in a couple of hours. I am leaving now to go back to the hospital to wait with him.

Saturday, June 9: Last night when Scott was transported from Memorial Hospital to UCSF his device went off three times. The paramedics had to stop at Marin General Hospital in Greenbrae, about three-fourths of the way to San Francisco, as they were worried they wouldn't have enough juice for the paddles. He was stabilized and then transported the rest of the way. It was a harrowing experience for Scott. As I sat by his bedside today, the fear in his eyes was plain to see. It's difficult for me *not* to look like my world is falling apart, but I will try my darndest if it will help keep him alive. Although Scott is on an intravenous medication to keep him from going into arrythmia (abnormal heart rhythm), the doctor said his only option is a heart transplant.

On Monday, Scott is scheduled for a heart catheterization to find out if there are any blockages in the arteries. This is one of the many tests needed to determine if he is a candidate for a heart transplant. Other diagnostic tests that need to be performed include blood and urine testing for HIV antibody, EKG and Chest X-Ray to check the size and position of the heart and lungs, cardiopulmonary stress test on a treadmill to evaluate extent of damage to the heart, cancer screening, testing for neurological issues, and a colonoscopy.

Monday, June 11: The heart catheterization procedure was completed today and so far so good. Now they can proceed with the other tests. Scott's spirits are good as I'm sure he feels there is hope. He has some fluid on the right side of the heart, which they are trying to eliminate with Lasix. This must be why he looks so much better today, besides the fact that his new room has a fantastic view of San Francisco.

We won't know until Thursday what the decision will be for a heart transplant. The UCSF cardiologist Dr. Redig wants to put him at the top of the list, but it is not just his decision. If Scott doesn't qualify, he has one to two months left to live. At least that is what the doctor said yesterday. Jonathan, Matthew, and I will go down tomorrow to talk to the Social Worker.

Tuesday, June 12: The heart transplant coordinator came into Scott's room to explain to me as the caregiver and Scott as the patient what to expect immediately after a heart transplant. As she handed Scott a thick three-ring binder, I believed I was ready to hear what she had to say. I mean, it couldn't be that bad, could it? She said something like this:

"First off, you will need to live in San Francisco with Scott for about four to six weeks. This is for two reasons: first, because of the long drive back and forth to Santa Rosa, there's a risk of injury with the seat belt over the shoulder and chest and we don't want to risk the sutures opening up; second, there are tests and biopsies that need to be done almost every day of the week. We don't schedule tests on the weekends, but if something urgent comes up, you would go to the ER here at UCSF.

"There is risk of rejection to the heart, so we monitor this constantly and adjust medications as needed. Here is a list of the possible medications that Scott will be taking which will change as he adjusts to the new heart. You will need to read this binder front and back for guidelines on what to be aware of while living in San Francisco and when Scott returns home.

"Scott will be immunosuppressed and susceptible to all kinds of viruses, bacteria, etc., and you will need to be vigilant on keeping him safe from exposure to people's germs, mold, mildew, and other things mentioned in the binder. Scott will need to wear sunscreen whenever he goes outside as certain immunosuppressant drugs can cause skin cancer from sun exposure." And on and on she went scaring me half to death. Then she asked if we had any questions.

As I sat there dumbfounded and shaking in my boots, I was thinking, *How the hell can I possibly get through this? I'm already stressed to the max wondering if Scott will live or die, and now all of this? And they still don't know if he will make it through the surgery. How will I find a place to live in San Francisco not knowing when or if he'll get a heart? Help me, Father/Mother to get through these uncertainties!*

After she left, I looked at Scott with my mouth wide open, eyebrows lifted, and ready to scream. Did she really say that we will need to live in San Francisco for a month to six weeks? Are you freaking kidding me? Although I was scared and unsure if I would be able to handle all that was to follow, I wanted what Scott wanted. And Scott wanted to live.

Note to Caregivers:

When the situation is new and all the information being tossed at you has thrown you for a loop, just pause...yes pause. Take the handouts, go home, and find a comfy place to sit and contemplate everything. When you are ready, read the handouts and write out your questions for the doctors and coordinators. Don't expect to remember everything the first time. You won't. Too much data is coming at you all at once. Be diligent when talking to the doctors and, if need be, ask the same question more than once until it all sinks in. After all, a doctor doesn't become a doctor the first day he or she starts medical school.

There are hospital social workers and financial planners who can help guide you to what you need in this moment. If you write down only what needs to be done right now and only concentrate on those issues, you will feel more in control. Worrying about something that may or may not happen in the future is counterproductive, especially when you are already taking on more than you ever thought you could possibly handle. I wish you the best as your journey continues to play out.

3

Don't Leave Us Alone

Wednesday, June 13, 2007: All of your responses to my emails are helping a lot. Thank you so much. I can feel your love, concern, and friendship! Today is Scott's 56th birthday. Happy birthday, my sweet man.

Have you ever been on a roller coaster that you couldn't wait to get off? That up, down, up, down feeling just can't be good for you. Oh, but at the time it's so exhilarating as it gets your adrenaline going. Then you get off and walk around in circles, laughing all the while. Wow…what a thrill!

Well, I'm on a roller coaster and it doesn't seem to want to stop. I've lost the pilot, but maybe there never was one, so I'm on this coaster ride without any directions. Which way should I turn? Can I jump off? Do I turn left or is it a straight away? When will it slow down so I can get off? Please…make it STOP!

I lost it today, but my friends at work and my best friend Janice were right there when I needed them. And did I need them. There is no owner's manual for this kind of stuff, but there are friends, family, and strangers right there, right by your side wondering what they can do for you. And I don't know what you can do for me because I don't know what I need. So just keep those emails coming to help me right now.

Yesterday, Jonathan, Matthew and I visited Scott along with his sister Carol from the San Jose area. About an hour into the visit, Scott started to have an episode, like at the house when the paramedics came.

Everyone except me left the room as the doctor and nurses came in. The episode starts as a tingling in his hands that moves up his arms to his stomach, chest and head. Then he feels almost like he is suffocating and can't catch his breath. At an hour it was the longest yet, so the doctor ordered Ativan. It ended about 10 minutes after the medicine took effect, which is making the doctor think he is having panic attacks. They said his vitals on the heart monitor were fine. After helping Scott eat his lunch we left for home. We didn't want to wear him out.

When I arrived today, I was told he will be discharged tomorrow. I was shocked and confused, especially with what had happened yesterday. First, the heart transplant coordinator came in to ask Scott if he had read the thick binder she left him a day ago. I'm thinking, *Are you kidding me? Of course, he hasn't read it. He's not feeling well!* Then the doctor came in to answer my questions about Scott going home, which of course being unprepared I didn't know what to ask. Like, *Do we get a hospital bed? How will he get around? Will there be a nurse coming to the house to check on him? Don't leave us alone!!!*

It sounds like he is a good candidate for a heart transplant, but there is one test left—a colonoscopy. Those of you who have had one know the prep work is stressful in a normal situation. Well, they want to send him home tomorrow and come back next Tuesday, June 19, for the colonoscopy. They want him to do all of the preparation at home and for us to drive down, a ride that takes an hour and fifteen minutes with no traffic.

Now do you see why I lost it? You would think that because I have helped numerous people in these types of situations for years, it would be easy for me to cope and make logical decisions. But I can't seem to hold it together. After talking to a few coworkers and close friends, I now know what I need to do to request what Scott and I need. And by the way, I asked the doctor what I should do if something happens on the ride home tomorrow. His response…call 911.

This email from RPJ helped to ease our minds for the upcoming colonoscopy. '*YIKES! No wonder it's a roller coaster ride for you two. You will be in my thoughts and I would like to visit the SOB next week if possible. My colonoscopy wasn't too uncomfortable, and I came round in the middle of it, but I was surprisingly calm. YOU CAN DO IT SCOTTIE!*'

(Note: RPJ always called Scott SOB and Scott called Richard RPJ. It was their thing.)

Thursday, June 14: It looks like Scott will be coming home tomorrow. He is doing very well as the medication amiodarone seems to be working. We will meet with the doctors at 10:00 a.m. and go from there. Everything was explained much better today, especially the colonoscopy and how well Scott is doing on this medication. He walked the long way around the hospital, and man, you should have heard the catcalls and whistles while his gown was flapping in the wind. What a sight to behold. *(Maybe that was because it was open in the front. Hey, hey.)*

Speaking of cats, Bob Kat is so happy that she'll see her favorite human companion so soon. Meow!

I figured out what each of you can do for me tomorrow. When you go about your day, watch for the opportunity to be an angel for someone: your partner, your child, your parent, your friend, or someone you don't know and who would least expect it. Then feel that little leap in your heart as you acknowledge that loving feeling.

Responding to my email, Scott's childhood friend, Sandy Shults said, *'Happy to hear that Scott is doing better and the medication is working. I enjoyed reading your email about Scott's catwalk thinking of those sexy legs as he walks the hospital floor.'*

My friend Kris Howell from Bremerton, Washington, thanked me for reminding her to reach out to others, especially to *'show my students that I care and how precious they are...for some, I'm the only person who will show them that.'*

Monday, June 18: Scott came home on Friday and is wiped out. It was a horrendous day, but thanks to Janice who was by our side all the way, we are home. Since a week ago, Scott has been on nine different medications and one injectable. He has a sore throat and is just plain tired.

On Saturday a Home Health Care aide came to the house to go

over all of Scott's medications. He seemed genuinely nice and we felt extremely comfortable with him. We tried to rest as much as possible, but during the night Scott was coughing. He slept so I didn't wake him, but if any of you have tried sleeping with a snorer, you know you just don't sleep well yourself. So to the other bedroom I went.

On Sunday I was alarmed because of the cough and now a fever of 99.8 degrees. The on-call cardiologist at UCSF told me to take him to the ER at Santa Rosa Memorial Hospital, where we were escorted immediately into a room because of his heart condition. The doctor examining Scott felt there was something else going on besides the cough and fever, finding cellulitis (inflammation of the cells) in his right arm. A blood draw was taken twice by a young female technician who remarked that Scott had *beautiful veins*. We both started to laugh, but she was so serious that we had to stop (laughing). Scott had a chest X-ray before being sent home with a prescription for cephalexin to treat the cellulitis. The colonoscopy has been postponed until July 12.

Here's a request to Scott's coworkers at the post office. I'd like to go back to work tomorrow and the rest of the week, but I don't want to leave him alone for any length of time. If anyone is willing to come for a few hours in the morning and someone else a few hours in the afternoon, that would be great. Just call Scott and he'll start a schedule. Bring your favorite movie to share with him. Scott promises to tell you if he gets tired and will go lay down.

Friday, June 22: As I glanced out the upstairs window at the evening sky I noticed an angel cloud. She was the most beautiful soft white cloud formation with her hands outstretched, a little pug nose, and her hair flying in the breeze. As I looked closer, I could see a slight outline of her wings. But what I felt in my heart were her comforting thoughts. What a wondrous sight. I hurried downstairs to get Scott outside to see her before she faded away. Then we took a very slow, very cautious walk down the street.

Yesterday Dr. Decker went over Scott's medications with us, checking for possible side effects and drug interactions. Although Scott looks pale, he is walking around the house as much as possible each day. That was his assignment when he left UCSF. Although he is still on antibiotics for cellulitis and bronchitis, he seems to be on the mend.

Dr. Decker says that Dr. Redig, the UCSF cardiologist, wants to place Scott on the heart transplant list. The other doctors disagree as they feel the new meds are helping him enough. One doctor that treated Scott said to think of this positively, as a heart transplant *is* the last resort. There is a person at UCSF right now recovering from a heart transplant and still in the hospital with complications after 53 days. I'm not sure what would be best, as the stories I've heard about serious complications after a transplant are worrisome.

Scott had many visitors this week, including his good friend, coworker, and golf buddy, Bob Evans, who thankfully took him to see the Employee Assistance Program (EAP) counselor so I could go to work. Because of all the stress Scott has been under, it was good for him to be able to voice his worries to someone besides me. Watching from the sidelines is not the same as living with a death sentence looming over your head. Scott was lucky enough to be able to see the same counselor that we used back when Matthew came to live with us.

(Note: EAP is a voluntary, work-based program that offers free short-term counseling, referrals, and follow-up services to employees with personal or work-related problems. The post office provides this program to their employees.)

Note to Caregivers:

Mental health care is especially important during times of crises and for Scott it proved invaluable. If this is something you or the patient needs, set it up now. Don't wait…just do it. Make that call!

Most diseases have support groups, like the American Diabetes Association, American Heart Association, Alzheimer's Association, American Lung Association, etc. Just go online and type in the name of the disease to find the type of support they provide. Or ask your doctor, family, or friends for referrals for one-on-one counseling. If the first therapist doesn't work out, try someone else.

Another strategy is to talk things out with family and friends. Having someone to talk to helps you to think through the issues and is just plain smart. And it works! For me, writing emails to my group email list and receiving comforting and reassuring responses back from family and friends did the trick. No matter what direction you take, finding your support therapy will help get you through your time of need.

4

Root Beer Freeze Please

Monday, July 9, 2007: Although the medications seem to be having a positive effect, Scott has two appointments with UCSF heart specialists on August 2. At that time, we'll ask all the difficult questions.

Scott's colonoscopy is scheduled for Thursday, July 12. It was confirmed by phone last week. The doctor said he had to stop taking Coumadin four days before the colonoscopy *and* begin giving himself an injectable called Lovenox twice a day. *(Note: Both Coumadin and Lovenox are blood thinners (anticoagulants) used to prevent blood clots. I am sure there was a very good reason the doctors stopped the Coumadin before surgery and prescribed Lovenox, but since I am not a doctor or pharmacist I won't even speculate.)*

Today Scott called UCSF to check on instructions for the GoLYTELY medication used to cleanse the bowel prior to a colonoscopy. He was told that he wasn't scheduled for a colonoscopy and that UCSF wanted us to meet with a gastroenterologist on Monday next week instead. I found all this out when I got home from work and Scott was stressed to the max. After leaving voice mail messages for two people at Health Net, I was stressed beyond limit, too. How much stress can his failing heart handle?

Within an hour, a doctor from UCSF called back. To make a long story short, he apologized for the mix-up, then went right into how Scott needed to learn how to handle his stress better. This from my phone message to someone else. Then he said that Scott needs to meet with a counselor to help him in these types of situations. I told the doctor that Scott was already seeing a therapist through EAP. He was surprised because no one had told him. "No one asked us," I said as I fumed to myself. Then he mentioned that the colonoscopy was being cancelled because it hadn't been approved by Health Net and they didn't want us to be surprised if we had to pay the bill. I told him that no one had told me that, not knowing that this had been explained to Scott.

Needless to say, I think the doctor finally realized that we had every right to be stressed out after I explained all the precautions and phone calls we made before picking up the Lovenox. For Scott to be giving himself injections for the past three days only to be told that the procedure wouldn't be happening was unforgiveable. Can you imagine if Scott had arrived at UCSF after fasting Wednesday night, only to be told it wasn't happening? Thank God Scott called today!

But the story isn't over yet. Health Net had set us up with a Case Manager, who I had met a few weeks ago. I left her an exceptionally long message tonight, as she mentioned that one thing she can do is get approvals for prior authorizations quickly. She is well aware that we are preparing for this colonoscopy and how stressful it is for Scott. So we shall see what happens tomorrow. For anyone going through a similar situation, I hope you have someone to advocate for you.

I love the responses I received from this emotional email. Olga Lee wrote: '*I can't for the life of me understand WHY the insurance company wouldn't authorize approval for a colonoscopy since most doctors say that you should have one after you turn fifty and have a repeat one every ten years after that! So sorry you are having so much trouble and stress added on for no good reason.*'

My wonderful friend Deb Hendryx told me: '*Go ahead, vent anytime. You and Scott deserve that opportunity. Insurance nightmares…I thought they were only in movies of people who had stories to tell; you never think it will hit so close to home.*' No, you don't, yet here we are.

Wednesday, July 11: Thanks to Dr. Guzzo at UCSF and the office of Scott's Primary Care Physician (PCP), Dr. Bartel, the colonoscopy was approved by Tuesday morning. Dr. Guzzo apologized profusely for what we were put through. She said that Health Net had wanted a gastroenterologist to meet with Scott first, then write a letter about the necessity of having the colonoscopy at UCSF. Are you kidding me? The necessity being that a colonoscopy showing no abnormalities is necessary in order for Scott to be placed on the heart transplant list; the urgency being that he is one to two months out from dying from heart failure. Health Net wasn't going to accept the head of UCSF's heart transplant cardiology department's request. But Dr. Guzzo and Dr. Bartel's office pulled through for us, thank goodness.

The next issue was that no one scheduled the correct anesthesiologist for Thursday's colonoscopy, so even with the authorization, it still might have been postponed. I didn't have to wait long before receiving another phone call that it was a go for Thursday.

This morning we left the house at 6:15 as we had to meet with the UCSF Prepare Department to review Scott's medications, check his vitals, take blood, and make sure certain medications were stopped, etc. It was the same man who discharged us from the hospital in June and he remembered us. He told us that Scott looked so much better *and* that he was surprised that Scott was discharged the last time we were there. Man, finally someone confirming my doubts. It wasn't just me questioning the discharge!

Scott's done all the preparation and his spirits are much better than two days ago. Monday night we were both so stressed that we may have gotten 10 hours of sleep combined. We were walking zombies on Tuesday. I will say that all these experiences have given me new direction in my job. When I'm out giving presentations to the seniors on Medicare, I have stories to share that can only help them learn to help themselves.

Now to leave you with something to brighten your day: As Scott and I were watching the last episode of *Six Feet Under* tonight, the phone rang. When Scott doesn't want to talk, he hands me the phone. Since I didn't want to talk either, we let it go to voice mail. It was UCSF reminding us of our appointment for Monday with the gastroenterologist. I guess whoever made the original appointment at UCSF wasn't informed that it needed to be cancelled. It's cancelled now!

Thursday, July 12: I've always hated waking up early. I would sleep in everyday if I could until I woke up on my own. Scott gets so nervous about time, especially with me. Even a few minutes drives him crazy. We left the house at 5:17 a.m., which I felt was pretty darn good, to drive down to UCSF in order to arrive by 7:00. I was driving on adrenaline *(get the pun)* and hoping that I would be able to stay alert the entire way.

The scenery was awesome! As we drove from Cotati down to Petaluma, the fog was low on the hills, tugging gently around the landscape of early morning dew. To the left, the sun was slowly rising and the clouds were a pale pink across the sky. The scene caught our breaths and gave us a feeling of peace and hope. Traffic was consistent and I commented on how so many people wake up this early every day to make this commute. I thanked my lucky stars that I was not one of them.

From Petaluma to the Novato wide, more fog and sleepy cows meandered around the golden brown hills and forest green trees. Then I noticed that all the drivers who like to tailgate were way far ahead, and the next group of cars were 20 or more car lengths back, giving us a feeling of having the road to ourselves. It was great!

We arrived in front of UCSF at 6:25. I dropped Scott off at the patient circle drop off so he could wait in the lounge area, because it is too hard for him to make the trek from the parking garage. After finding Scott, we walked to the Endoscopy waiting room but it was locked. So back down the long corridor to the waiting room until 7:00, then back to Endoscopy where a nurse welcomed us.

Scott wanted me to go with him to check in, which was good because the nurse didn't think we were in the right place. Because of Scott's heart condition, he needed a specialized anesthesiologist (a cardiothoracic anesthesiologist with the expertise for someone with a severe heart condition, I believe). The day before we had been told to go to the fourth floor by one person and the first floor by the last person we saw. So with Scott in a hospital gown, his belongings on his lap, a nurse wheeled him to the operating room (OR) on the fourth floor with me close behind.

Paperwork wasn't complete but was pieced together quickly and efficiently. I stayed with Scott and the nurses so I could help answer questions. When he was taken for the colonoscopy, I went to the waiting room. Exhausted, I read and fell asleep, read and fell asleep, when all of a sudden, I heard someone call my name. There was Scott and a nurse. Scott said the procedure took 10 minutes which made my wait just about an hour. We were on the road again by 8:00 a.m.

As we were heading into Larkspur, Scott asked, "Can we stop at A&W for a root beer freeze please?" Scott slurped that baby all the way home. We both relaxed then slept for four hours. Wow did that feel great. So everything is fine now and we don't have to make that drive again until August 2. Yeah!

From Sandy: *'A root beer freeze…the simple things in life that we enjoy so much. Thank you for sharing the updates on Scott. We can feel the abundance of love in your home that he so well deserves.'*

Sunday, July 22: We drove out to the ocean today. It was a drive to remember. The sun was shining brightly and a slight breeze was moving the yellow and purple wildflowers to-and-fro. At the top of the hill, the fog was barely above the water line, then came in quickly as we got into Bodega Bay. We had lunch at the Tides Wharf Restaurant, where we watched seagulls push each other around as if each needed to be the center of attention. One gull had a long, solid white neck and was quite handsome. I think his name was Jonathan. (In reference to the book *Jonathan Livingston Seagull* by Richard Bach, not my son. A must read!)

As we were pulling out of the parking lot, a car was waiting for the handicap parking spot we occupied. Scott mentioned that the driver gave us a dirty look as I pulled away. I didn't see her face, but I guess she didn't see the handicap placard Scott pulled down from the mirror when we got in the car. Just a reminder for all of us that sometimes we can't see the persons' handicap—and maybe the placard was removed before you pulled up. Oh well, we all have a lot to learn.

Note to Caregivers:

If you or your spouse is disabled, get a disability license plate and placard from your state's Department of Motor Vehicles (DMV). Your doctor will need to verify your disability, but the time spent filling out forms will be worth it. I can't begin to tell you how many times the license plate and placard have come in handy.

Get a disability license plate for the disabled person's vehicle so he or she won't have to remember to put the placard up in the window. The plastic disability placard is for the main caregiver, family, and friends who take their loved one to appointments, grocery shopping, or other necessary errands. This placard can be used in any vehicle that the disabled person rides in so that the driver can legally park in a handicap parking spot.

When Scott received a ticket for forgetting to put the placard up in his car, we got a disability license plate for him. AAA provides this service in Northern California. From that day forward, I didn't have to worry about Scott forgetting to put the placard up. Such a simple thing that saved a lot of anxiety for me and Scott. About the ticket: After I wrote a letter to the DMV about the ticket, it was voided. However, if Scott had gotten a second ticket, we would have had to pay. And tickets are not cheap!

Now We Wait

Thursday, August 2, 2007: Since Scott's discharge from the hospital on June 15, plenty was happening behind the scenes. Not only did Scott have to go through lots of tests to make sure there were no hidden health issues, the doctor(s) had to recommend him as a viable candidate, AND the insurance company had to approve the transplant.

The average cost of a heart transplant in 2007 was $1,000,000, so I wanted to make sure that the representative making this life-or-death decision saw Scott as a person and not just a dollar sign. I contacted Health Net's Transplant Case Manager to present my case for Scott's approval. After creating a beautiful greeting card on my computer, I wrote an imploring story giving her personal information to show Scott's humanness in hopes that would help sway her to approve the heart transplant.

The last two weeks have been hard on Scott both emotionally and physically. This past Monday we went to see Dr. Decker, who asked Scott if he wanted to be admitted to the hospital. He did not. He wanted to wait until our visit to UCSF today. Janice accompanied us down...thank goodness and bless her heart.

First, the heart transplant coordinator went over our questions about the transplant. Compared to our first meeting in June—the one with the thick incomprehensible binder—I felt prepared to ask questions and hear the answers. It didn't seem as overwhelming. And, yes, after a heart transplant we will need to live four to six weeks in San Francisco.

Second, we met with Dr. Redig who put things in motion. Once he examined and spoke to Scott, he decided that it was in Scott's best interest to be admitted right away, if that was what Scott wanted—which it was. While we were waiting for a hospital bed, the social worker Martha came to explain the protocols. Again, we were much better prepared and felt better about what we were hearing. But no matter what, Health Net must approve a heart transplant and then we wait for a donor heart.

Scott got a private room with a limited yet gorgeous view of parts of San Francisco. Janice and I went to the gift shop and bought a word book, chocolate, oatmeal cookies, a chocolate truffle, a pencil for the word book, oh, and did I say chocolate? When we got back to the room, two doctors were talking to Scott and when they saw all the goodies, they told him to make sure the other patients didn't find out about his stash. Scott can have them, but just about everyone else on the floor is on a low-fat diet. The party's in Scott's room later tonight.

When Janice and I arrived in Rohnert Park around 7:00 p.m., we enjoyed dinner at El Torito's Mexican Restaurant with Jonathan, Charlie, and a few of Jon's friends. Because we hadn't eaten much since the morning, we scarfed down our food. I always enjoy being with my son and was fine up until the most loving moment when he touched my shoulder to ask, "Are you okay?" That almost did me in, but like all parents, I did my best to hold my emotions in check so as not to scare him. He then said, "You probably don't know what to feel." *No, I don't.*

Scott and I will be married 16 years tomorrow, so I plan on picking up something special for lunch and driving down to UCSF to spend our anniversary together. And I'll be thankful for this day.

Saturday, August 4: Scott looks and feels better with all the nurses and doctors around, so I am feeling more optimistic.

UCSF received a letter from Health Net that says, *"After a thorough review of provided medical records, Health Net has determined Scott*

Bennett is an appropriate candidate for a heart transplant evaluation." Did you notice the word *evaluation*? We won't know until Monday or Tuesday if he will be placed on the waiting list as they will do another catheterization to check out his heart capacity.

Other than that, I did not go down today as I needed to catch up on grocery shopping and laundry. Sunday I'll be going down again and then will probably make the trip three times a week from here until further developments.

Tuesday, August 7: Yesterday Scott told me that one of the doctors told him that everything the doctors told him last Thursday was off base—meaning that he's not even close to being listed. But I have noticed lately that Scott's take on what is said is almost always different than what I thought had been said. Maybe the heart issue is causing brain fog.

He had the heart catheterization yesterday and was told that his heart looks better than expected. Yesterday it sounded like Scott would be discharged from the hospital soon. Today, however, he tried walking around and his breathing was quite shallow. When the nurse and I walked with him, she agreed with my observation.

I am driving down tomorrow to ask the doctor(s) why no one can seem to agree on his condition. Or does everyone agree on the condition, but not on the transplant? I just don't know. It is obvious to me, as I'm sure it seems obvious to those of you who have visited Scott, that he doesn't look well. The local cardiologist told us he is at end-stage heart failure. So what gives?

Wednesday, August 8: Scott had a stress test today for six minutes on a stationary bike and of course his heart symptoms were visibly clear *and* alarming, to say the least. I did ask to see the doctor and he got there around 1:00 p.m.

Scott insisted that I could ask the hard questions with him present, that these questions don't bother him. What does bother him is if anyone brings up his defibrillator going off or talks about others in the same situation. So with Scott listening, I asked, "Is Scott still considered in end-stage heart failure? If not, what changed? Can you guarantee that he will live without receiving a heart transplant?"

This doctor would not or could not answer the questions. He wants us to talk to the cardiologist. I was trying to find out what had changed between the day he was admitted on August 2 and now. The doctor seems to think that Scott is holding his own on the amiodarone medication for his heart. The big issue they believe is post-traumatic stress syndrome due to his defibrillator going off so many times and so quickly, as it did on the way down to UCSF in June. They put him on Lexapro for depression. A CT scan will be done tomorrow to help the doctors decide on Scott's best option— discharge him from the hospital or place him on the transplant list.

Note to Caregivers:

As caregivers, we wait a lot. Wait for the doctor, wait for the lab result, wait for the patient to walk to the car, you name it, we are waiting. How do you fill in the time during this waiting game? You know how they say the journey is the best part, well...

Once, when Jonathan, Charlie, Matthew, and I were in San Diego for my niece's wedding, we went out to dinner with other family members. Afterwards we took the Red Train back to the hotel. Walking the last couple of blocks, we had to stop and wait at a traffic light. Jonathan would push the pedestrian crossing button and a male voice would say, "Wait...wait...wait." Each wait was one second apart. By the third light, you might say we were all getting a bit annoyed with this voice.

We reached the next traffic light at the same time as a couple with a young son who were walking closely behind. When that voice began, Jonathan, with a silly face and in a deep monotone voice like a DJ or anchorman, said, "Wait...wait...wait," right along with it. The boy started laughing hard as by now Jonathan was playing the childish part as well. The way we laughed brought a beautiful ending to a wonderful day and created a lasting memory. It also made us look forward to the next light.

My advice to help you cope while waiting for your loved one is to keep a packed bag in your trunk with items to keep you occupied: a book, a crossword or sudoku puzzle, a magazine, whatever wets your whistle. Throw in some granola bars, crackers, or other snacks that will not melt sitting in your car. And lastly, bring fresh water for both of you to keep hydrated. And remember, while you wait...find joy and some humor in each moment.

6

It Was a Really
Good Shower

Thursday, August 9, 2007: SCOTT HAS BEEN LISTED today as Status B-2. This is great news even though he's at the bottom of the list. For one, he is feeling less depressed and has something to hope for, and two, he can stay in the hospital for now. If he gets put on an intravenous medication he will be bumped up the list. And apparently there are only two patients listed at UCSF for a heart transplant, so hopefully this will be in Scott's favor.

A heart transplant is not given lightly. Sometimes the quality of life may be better with a person's own heart. But after hearing the doctors talk about Scott's condition, I truly believe Scott's odds for survival will be much greater with a heart transplant. So even though this surgery has many complications, I am starting to feel that a heart transplant will give him the best outcome. This I know from the bottom of my heart, actually within my soul, if you will. Thank you for being with us all this way.

Saturday, August 11: Seven of us celebrated Matthew's birthday last night at Cattlemen's and had a great time. The Bean Girl who walks around filling up your bowl with beans saw the birthday cake and exclaimed that it was her favorite. We decided to give her a piece.

After we arrived at Cattlemen's, I remembered I had forgot the pad that I sit on for my back. As I was walking out to the car, a man about my age was walking towards me. He was handsome with a beautiful, kind smile. As I walked by him, I realized that I hadn't felt sexy for some time and it felt good. But then I started thinking that I should feel guilty to even think that way with Scott in the hospital dying. And then I just told myself that, hey, I am only human and a woman after all.

After we ate, we went outside and called Scott. As we passed the phone around, I realized that the same man had walked outside with either a son or nephew and had looked at me again. Well, at least maybe I'm still attractive to men my age, so that's a good thing.

In bed tonight, I couldn't stop thinking about Scott and couldn't get to sleep. I kept thinking, *Is tonight the night he dies, is it tomorrow, or when?* These thoughts haunt me and I don't know what to do with these feelings of doom. The other night I dreamt that we moved to a different house with lots of rooms. Scott was sick and I couldn't understand why we would move when he was so sick. I was incredibly sad in the dream.

When I finally got out of bed the next morning to call Scott, I was so distraught and he could tell that I was breaking down. He comforted me, telling me everything would be okay and would work out. I asked him if he wanted me to drive down, but he said he was doing fine and that he could wait until Tuesday. I started crying on the phone and seemed to be crying off and on all day.

Janice and I went to the movies to see *Stardust*, a fantasy, but there was also some truth in it. Parts of it reminded me of Scott and our love. It's funny how life changes all the time. And I know that I am being helped by my unseen helpers, but it's getting harder and harder to believe they are with me.

Sunday, August 12: Matthew and I visited Scott on Saturday and received some great news. Scott was bumped up to Status 1B as he was put on dobutamine, an intravenous medication that stimulates heart muscle and improves blood flow by helping the heart pump better. It is usually given after other heart medications have been tried without success. This means he is closer to the top of the list for a heart transplant. As long as he can handle this medication he will remain at Status 1B.

Dr. Angelina (can't remember her last name, but I really like her first name since it has *angel* in it) talked to Matthew and me about what will happen from here. When Scott gets a heart, we will live in S.F. for four to six weeks. I am preparing my mind and body as best I can for this and trying to take each day as it comes.

For those of you who are comfortable doing this, please call or visit Scott. He is getting lonely and needs his friends. Just keep in mind that he tires easily and does *not* want to talk about his defibrillator going off. I am visiting this Tuesday and Thursday, then taking two weeks' vacation so I can stay in San Francisco to be closer and visit longer.

While Matthew and I visited Scott, he mentioned that he had had a shower earlier and that it was really good. The warm running water was soothing and the subtle smell of the soap helped to make him feel normal again.

As a concerned wife, I asked, "Was someone in there with you?"

Then Matthew quipped, "Is that why the shower was so good?" Well, we all burst out laughing as we realized where Matthew was going with this. You just got to laugh, or you'll go crazy.

As we were getting ready to leave Scott's room, I realized that I hadn't put my contact information on the bulletin board. So I wrote Julie Bennett/Spouse, then the home, work, and cell phone numbers, and then *lover*. Matthew wanted me to add *BFF* for best friend forever. And you know, that's exactly how I feel about this man called Scott Bennett.

Monday, August 13: There is a donor problem in the United States. Did you know that even if you check *donor* on your driver's license that your family can decide against it? So make sure you let your family know your wishes…verbally and in writing. Parents of young adults should talk to their sons and daughters to find out their wishes. None of us knows what the future holds, but just knowing our families' wishes ahead of time can save unneeded heartache. A doctor explained this in front of Matthew, suggesting that all young people make their wishes known to their parents. Because let's face it, a young person's organs are in high demand. And you never know when someone's loss can give another person a new life.

A friend emailed the following website where people can signify their donor wishes on a California registry line: www.donateLIFEcalifornia. org. This would be a little broader than just putting a dot on your driver's license.

Scott seems to be doing really well on the dobutamine intravenous medication. He was able to walk to the end of the hall where we sat in a waiting room with a wonderful view of S.F. I got some pictures on my cell phone, but alas, I don't know how to get them onto my computer. Probably need to get another plug of some sort. I'll figure it out.

While perusing the Internet, I realized that there's no guarantee of Scott receiving a heart. One website indicated a 50/50 chance of getting one. Each year about 4,000 people in the U.S. make the waiting list for a new heart, but only 2,000 get one in time. And when a person gets one, there are other complications that go along with it. So, it's a challenge for Scott and craziness for me.

Wednesday, August 22: Scott's still alive and I'm barely functioning. I feel like I'm in limbo and wondering if I can climb out and leave. Do people who believe in a limbo then die get stuck like this for a while? Wow, hopefully they would wake up quickly and go on to the afterlife.

This sucks big time. I try to remind myself of all the good things I have in life, but my mood just won't lift. I feel stuck between feelings— do I mourn or hope he will get a heart?

Also, the drive down to S.F. is depressing and the traffic horrendous. I need to figure out the best time to drive back and forth and keep my sanity. Knowing that we'll have to live in S.F. after a transplant doesn't make me any happier. And then the following happened.

When I arrived at UCSF, there was a young female nurse's aide in Scott's private bathroom ready to help him with a sponge bath. As soon as the aide saw me, she hightailed it out of there. She left us alone in a bathroom with a tub (not shower), plastic bags covering the I.V.'s in both of Scott's arms, and me with my mouth wide open in disbelief. Apparently, she assumed that I could handle the rest.

It was extremely difficult for Scott to get into the bathtub because of the height of the tub when stepping in. He had to face backwards then kneel down because of the way the I.V. stand was hooked up to him as he couldn't reach the bars any other way in order to hold on. So here we are both on our knees with me washing him down in the tub. I was just shocked that this aide didn't ask if I could handle this task. And I hope that anyone reading this who encounters a similar situation will now have the wherewithal to stop, push the call button, and get that hospital aide right back in to finish the job.

I stayed at the Queen Anne Hotel Sunday and Monday night. It was quite nice in an old-fashioned sort of way. The room was cute, the carpet clean, and the toiletries complimentary. The only thing I didn't like was having a tub instead of a shower. The tub was not flat but was lower towards the faucet end making it uncomfortable when taking a shower. Otherwise the bed was comfy enough.

When I visited Scott on Sunday, Monday, and Tuesday my emotions were going back and forth. I feel angry and sad and anxious, all at the same time. I see my husband and wonder how much more he can take. Then I wonder how much more I can take. Not knowing is the hardest part. Will he get a transplant? Will he die? How do I keep going every day not knowing which way the tide will turn? Is there anyone listening to me—like my angels or guides? Can they help me figure this all out so I can *let go and let God*?

After visiting Scott the first night, I walked down to Fillmore Street and ate dinner at Harry's Bar. I had a glass of pinot noir with my mushroom burger then walked to a Starbuck's for a latte. Passing neon signs in a window for a psychic, I decided to stop in for a reading.

She was not a psychic! I've been told that a true psychic does not let you share anything about yourself. But this person wanted me to tell her everything. She said that she did *not* see a heart coming through for Scott, but she didn't see him dying anytime soon either. No matter what, her reading did not jibe.

The next day while Scott was sleeping, I walked up and down the San Francisco hills. I visited the Carl Hotel on Carl Street. It seemed reasonably priced, but there was graffiti on the building. I did find a few nice restaurants around this hotel and it is close to UCSF. I also visited

Laurel Inn, which seemed nice enough, but the hills around it would be difficult for Scott. The Great Highway Inn sits along the ocean front, but it was very depressing with derelicts hanging out on the corners. But I'm not giving up. When Scott gets a heart, I'll find a nice enough place to live for the time we need to be in S.F.

Wednesday, August 22: It's amazing, the will to live. Scott has it and it is keeping him alive while the doctors have him on medication to keep his heart pumping. His goals are different than yours or mine. When he wakes up each morning his objective is to see how many times he can walk around the hospital floor without tiring. When he first arrived on August 2, he could only walk about 20 feet on a good day. Now he does 12 laps around the 10th floor every day. Of course, this mile is broken up as he walks one lap at a time and much slower than most people can move.

After checking out places to stay when the time comes, I'll be honest that living in San Francisco doesn't look appealing. The hospital provides a list of motels, hotels, and apartments that may or may not give discounts for UCSF patients. If anyone has information on housing within San Francisco, please send it my way. We are looking for a furnished one bedroom with a small kitchen, microwave, and stove.

Friday, August 31: Scott and I had a nice visit yesterday. A nurse had brought Scott playing cards from Las Vegas so we played gin rummy while I learned the rules of the game. I'm sure you will be glad to hear that Scott won in the end, but not without me giving him a bit of competition. Hey, gotta do what I gotta do, as competitive as I am having been raised in a family of nine kids that played canasta and all sorts of poker games.

The waiting game is on and Scott is holding up well. Thank you for your visits, calls, and uplifting cards. They really help keep his mind positive for what is to come. I've sent out emails to lots of places to rent and have received a lot of great information for the surrounding area. I'm less nervous about staying in S.F. once Scott receives his new heart. I feel that whenever it happens, we will find the perfect place for the perfect price.

Continue to keep Scott in your loving thoughts. The waiting is the hard part, but all of your caring helps to keep Scott and me going. Have a wonderful Labor Day weekend.

Sunday, September 2: Matthew and I had a good visit with Scott today, but it was too short for me. Matthew can only handle a few hours, so we arrived around 11:45 a.m. and left by 2:00 p.m. Actually, it was probably for the best as we hit heavy traffic on the bridge.

I wanted to take Scott home with me and I'm sure he wanted to go. Scott and I laughed about removing the I.V.'s, hooking them up to Matthew, and leaving Matthew tied up in the bathroom in order to get Scott out of the hospital. Okay, so I laughed at the thought, knowing it wouldn't really happen. We played cards and that was fun.

Note to Caregivers, Family Members, and Friends:
Taking care of someone is challenging. Most health care professionals don't take the caregiver into consideration. They just assume that he/she will be there to do anything asked. Well, it doesn't work that way. Caregivers, including me, are human beings with feelings and our own fragilities, and we are the most important part of the team. I've read that often the caregiver dies before the sick spouse because of the strain he/she is under. So this is my goal, to bring more awareness to caregivers and the medical community so that together we can help each other take better care of the patient and the caregiver.

One key question for a caregiver is *What Do I Need?* Every moment you are taking care of someone else you are adjusting to *their* needs. And yet, taking care of yourself is essential, too, as well as being flexible, which is not always easy to do. In order to keep from falling apart, find ways you can just be, just breathe. That may mean you hire a caregiver to give you a break, ask a family member or friend to step in, meditate, or go in the other room to rant and rave…then meditate. If you are able to leave the patient alone, go for a walk, a drive, or do what I did—go wine tasting!

After Scott had been in the hospital for two weeks, I gave myself permission to take a day off from driving down to UCSF. On a whim, I decided I needed to be outdoors and close to home. Then it hit me that there were wineries along rustic country roads not too far from our house. I was by myself and had the best day reenergizing. I'm not sure if I tasted any wine, but I did check out the gift shops and found a cool sweatshirt to lift my spirits. Remember, you do have some control, just not as much as you once had. Wherever you are right now, just stop, think good thoughts, play a song that you love…and breathe.

7

A Wee Bit Slaphappy

Sunday, September 2, 2007: HE'S GOT A HEART!!! It's 9:00 p.m. and Scott just called. He will get a heart transplant tomorrow morning around 3:00 a.m. Please start those prayers. Not just for Scott, though. Please pray for the family and friends who lost a loved one and then pray as hard as you can that everything goes smoothly and Scott heals quickly.

This reaction from my friend Gloria Bottaro is priceless: *'My first response was, "HOLY SH*T!!!" But it was meant in a good way, obviously! WOW! I will indeed send lots of prayers and thanks and gratitude. May this be the perfect fit for him and may he heal very rapidly!'*

Monday, September 3: What a day to celebrate! The heart transplant went so well that Scott was out of the Operating Room and into Recovery by 7:30 this morning. Then into Intensive Cardiac Care Unit (ICCU) at 10:30 a.m. Gil, Scott's brother, waited patiently outside from 6:00 a.m. until 10:30 a.m. but had to leave for work before he could see Scott. He'll see him tomorrow.

When Janice and I first went into ICCU, I was absolutely shocked and scared to death. I didn't expect all the tubes and other apparatus hooked up to my husband. And I couldn't wrap my head around the fact that someone can receive another person's heart—and live. Scott was still groggy and his chest was moving up and down, so we knew he was breathing on his own. His arms were immobilized to prevent the medical equipment from being pulled out. He could look at us but with a tube down his throat, couldn't say a word. (Wow, I missed my chance to speak my mind without him talking back.) Looking directly at me, I could tell there was something he wanted, but I just couldn't nod it out of him.

Around 3:30 p.m., the anesthesiologist came in to remove the breathing tube. His explanation of what he was going to do and what he wanted Scott to do couldn't have been clearer. It all went smoothly, and when I tried to assist Scott, he wouldn't let me. Bravo for him!

Once the tube was out and the anesthesiologist cleared the mouth passageway, he asked Scott to say something. I'm thinking, *Please say something, anything!!!* Timidly, and with a weak shaky voice, Scott says, "Hello?"

That's it? His big chance to say something prophetic and *Hello* is all he can come up with? That had us all in stitches, if you will allow me the pun.

Can you tell I'm feeling a wee bit slaphappy? Anyway, just wanted you all to know that he is expected to be out of ICCU within three days. I'll let you know when he can have visitors outside the family and when we've got a place set up in San Francisco.

I just have to share some more responses. From my friend Olga Lee: *'You have a lot of people praying for you two and for the donor family, too. I called several of my friends today to tell them the good news and one of them said it made her day to hear about Scott's heart transplant. I am so happy for my favorite (honorary) son-in-law! I am positive the next few days will show a vast improvement once all the anesthesia and trauma to his body is healing. Hang in there, sweetie, because he is going to be an extremely healthy guy in a few months.'*

My sweet coworker, Ed Matheson, made these reassuring comments to our good news: *'Happy for you and Scott. You went through lots of up and downs, but you managed to remain positive. It is the special belief you have in life that held you together. I look forward to seeing Scott very soon. I picture him the day he came to take you to lunch. I can see him in my office doorway. That was some time back, but that is the picture I have of him in my mind. As time passes, he will once again come by to take you to lunch. Meanwhile, I send good thoughts and my love to both of you.'*

Wednesday, September 5: By Tuesday much progress had been made. Scott walked around ICCU about four times. Gil visited, along with Jonathan and me. We talked about how amazing it all is and listened to the nurses and doctors tell their stories. I had forgotten the day before to thank the surgeon, Dr. Haagen, so yesterday I made sure he knew how thankful I was for his wonderful ability. How modest he was, not wanting any credit, yet how amazing that he can heal someone this way.

Today Scott was moved into a regular hospital room. His throat is sore from the breathing tube, but almost all of the other medical apparatus has been removed. Except, of course, for intravenous medication. No one is babying him, which means even I am not supposed to. We've been given many booklets that we need to read to prepare ourselves for leaving the hospital.

Speaking of which...I located a great place. Once we move in, I would think visitors for short periods of time will be very welcomed by both of us. If you feel sick, have a sore throat or cold, please don't visit.

We were given another thick binder with forms for keeping track of medications and appointments and lots of sunscreen samples in the back. Organ recipients like Scott have to take immunosuppressive drugs for the rest of their life. These drugs keep the person alive and well but also make him or her more susceptible to skin cancer. So when he gets back to playing golf, I'm hoping all you golf buddies will make sure he is covered from head to toe—even if he has to wear a sombrero!

When I arrived in the lobby today, a man with a white coat and badge was walking very quickly out of the hospital with a blue cooler. My heart skipped a beat thinking someone somewhere was going to get a heart, kidney, liver, or other body part. Then a second person came out of a door by the elevators and he too had a blue cooler, walking quickly towards another private elevator in the hospital. How excited I felt for those people waiting for a donor, at the same time realizing how hard it will be for the family who has just lost a loved one. What a difficult and painful decision a family must make, and very quickly. It was explained to us that the brain of the deceased is dead, but the body must be kept alive while the organs are removed for transplanting.

Keep up the prayers for Scott to heal quickly and for me to keep up my strength for what's yet to come.

Thursday, September 6: As I was driving down to S.F. today, I really needed to use the restroom. I decided to drive nonstop, park, and head to the...well, head when I got to Scott's room. When I walked in, I was stunned, shocked, and elated all at the same time. Scott looked just like he did on March 3, the day before his defibrillator, implanted in January 2005, went off for the very first time. Please send a prayer out right now that everything goes well tomorrow when they remove the defibrillator.

Scott was sitting up in bed eating by himself, no one helping, just him. He looked so good, clear eyes, normal complexion, sitting like nothing in the world had happened. Quickly opening the bathroom door, I said, "Hi, give me a sec," and got into the head just in time. As I sat there, I thought, *Wow, he looks so good.* Then I thought, *How could he have gone through all of this and now look so good?* And then I was thinking that I just wanted to slap him silly and tell him, *DO YOU KNOW WHAT I JUST WENT THROUGH? I didn't know if you were going to live or die? How could you do this to me and now look so good.* Of course, in a loving tone, but my gosh, I've gone from *When will he leave me?* to *Now he'll be with me for how much longer?*

We spent three full hours with two different people on the transplant team learning all about his medications and what we can and cannot do around people. So if someone ever tells you they can't shake your hand, don't be surprised if it is a transplant patient protecting themselves. Once Scott gets out into the world again, I think he will probably put his hands behind his back and say, "Sorry, heart transplant patient," instead of wearing a sign around his neck—well maybe a cutesy sign.

I think Janice summarized the whole situation up perfectly on Monday. As we were driving down to UCSF she elegantly observed,

"Now Scott can honestly say I left my heart in San Francisco, and it will be true!" So true.

Everywhere I go it is so hard not to shout out, *My husband just got a heart transplant*. Driving down to San Francisco I kept thinking that I needed to put a sign on the back of my car. I just wanted to scream and shout, but alas, what will people think. Actually...I DON'T CARE!

The apartment I found is just a block down from the Stonestown Galleria and should be perfect for the time we'll be living here. Another bit of good news is that Scott will probably walk out of the UCSF hospital on September 11 without his hospital gown blowin' in the wind.

I've read all of your emails and appreciate your thoughts and feel your loving wishes. They keep me going and that is what I have to do right now...keep going!

This email from Janice expressed the awesomeness of it all: *'It's absolutely amazing and beyond my wildest dreams that Scott already looks better than he did on March 3.'*

When I responded, I mentioned how now that Scott has had a heart transplant, Matthew and I are having a difficult time dealing with the fact that he almost died and now he's well. A nurse we spoke to yesterday said these feelings are quite normal. She told us that when you are preparing for the worst and then a sort of miracle happens, your body and spirit doesn't know how to process it. Making a quick 180-degree turn from expecting the worst to trying to live with the good news is very hard.

Since Matthew was going to help me move clothes and miscellaneous stuff into the apartment on Sunday, I asked Janice and Olga Lee if they could follow us down to help. We could get done sooner and have a longer visit with Scott.

Sunday, September 9: The two-car caravan wound its way from sunny Santa Rosa through the cities of Rohnert Park and Petaluma, past the Novato narrow. With the cows *mooing* and the horses *neighing*, we drove onward through Marin County with one minor stop and go. Stopping briefly at the Golden Gate Bridge toll booth, we headed down

19th Avenue to our new temporary home at the Villas at Parkmerced. I didn't realize this before but it is right next to the University of San Francisco. Matthew's first comment was that we were in party land. Oh no! But we are on the second floor, so at least we won't have to worry about anyone walking around above us.

We unloaded our few belongings from the cars into the one-bedroom apartment. Thank goodness the place is fully furnished, which includes kitchen items like dishes, silverware, glasses, etc. The rent includes a maid once a week…and I don't mean me.

Janice, Olga Lee, Matthew, and I found Scott sitting in a chair looking as calm as can be. No tubes hangin' around, no I.V.'s, thank you very much. We did notice that the hospital gown's pattern compared to the pants he was wearing didn't quite match. What a relief to find out that Scott was well aware of the contrast. I mean, you never know who picked out this ensemble.

My Aunt Rose Anne and Uncle Jim were already visiting with Scott and stayed another hour. It had been so long since we had seen them, so it was a wonderful time together.

Scott has been working with the Physical Therapist (PT) who is showing him how to stand up from a sitting position while protecting his chest in order to get up and down stairs easily. For the first month he needs to make sure the incision that goes from his neck down his chest does not open. Dr. Haagen told Scott that he should be careful, but Dr. Haagen would take the blame if it were to open up as he would feel that he didn't do his job properly. Scott's worst fear is getting in and out of the car, so he'll hold a pillow to his chest as he gets up and down from any position.

My biggest concern has been getting a cold or some bug. What do we do? Margaret, the nurse, explained that we can only do so much. If I wear a mask around Scott when I'm sick and wash hands constantly, that's the best we can do. The rest is up to divine intervention.

Scott will have his first biopsy on Tuesday morning to make sure his body is not rejecting the new heart. If all goes well, Scott will be discharged from the hospital.

Monday, September 17: Scott was released from the hospital on

Wednesday, September 12, and *released* is the correct word. I'm sure it has felt like confinement since August 2.

He is doing GREAT! We have lab in the wee hours of the morning on Mondays, Wednesdays, and Fridays. Biopsies are on Tuesdays, clinic is usually Thursday, with an I.V. scheduled on one of the days (don't have my calendar with me). And they are all early mornings, which is hard on me, but would be harder if we had to drive down from Santa Rosa. Oh, and a Home Health Care person has come out twice now. I think after a month of this we'll be able to go home. We really miss our little girl, Bob Kat—oh, and our sons Jonathan and Matthew, too.

I located the laundry room and did some today. While out walking last night, I found an easier way in and out of the Villas, plus Lake Merced is only a few blocks away.

After lab today, I was able to get some pictures of St. Anne's and St. Cecilia Catholic Churches. Really cool buildings. I'm trying to stay upbeat about living in a strange area and so far it's working. Met a neighbor's kitty cat and an area for Scott to walk around that's somewhat level. Scott's goal is to be able to walk to the park and lake before we go home. His heart is young, but when they performed the heart transplant surgery, they collapsed his lungs. This is what is keeping him from being able to walk fast or up inclines right now. Then when they took his defibrillator out on Friday, September 7, they collapsed his lungs again. But very soon he should be running around me, jumping up and down, and telling me to speed it up a bit. Yeah, we'll see how far he gets with that!

We found a Trader Joe's, Safeway, and Starbucks within two miles, and many other stores just a bit further. That's in addition to Stonestown Mall, right down the street. And the apartment has everything we need.

Saturday, September 22: We've had plenty of visitors to our humble abode here in San Francisco and we really enjoy seeing our friends and family.

Have you ever felt trapped somewhere, held back for some reason from being where you really want to be? Well, that's what this feels like to me. Santa Rosa has been my home since 1980 and I love it. I raised Jonathan on my own from eight months to ten years, met Scott, and together we raised Jonathan and Matthew and met our wonderful friends who have become like family, all in Santa Rosa. So being away, even though not that far away, feels like I'm forbidden to go home. If it sounds like I am whining, please allow me this brief moment to complain, and then these feelings shall pass.

Scott is acing all of his labs, biopsies, and other tests with flying colors. Only a few meds have been adjusted, with one more added. He doesn't have any side effects, for which we are thankful. I spoke to another caregiver yesterday who was ready to scream at her husband who had a heart transplant six days after Scott. He is having severe mood swings. One minute he's crying, the next he's yelling. I am blessed that none of this is happening to Scott. He really is the best patient.

Thanks to suggestions from friends, we are finding lots of places to visit in S.F. that we've never seen before. I had never been to the Legion of Honor and was overwhelmed with the paintings. But within an hour, Scott was wiped out. After getting him back in the car we drove up Scenic Route 49 stopping to take photos along the way. We came across a cute fox that had trapped a little animal and was intent on finishing it up. It reminded me of our Bob Kat when she's trapped a fly or little bug. Animals, like children, are so much fun to watch.

Next week will be the hardest as far as doctor, lab, and biopsy visits. Most days we have two appointments, and we can be waiting four to five hours depending on the test/visit. The biopsy was supposed to be ninety minutes, but I was still waiting at five hours. The plus side is that everything is coming up roses, so I'm not complaining about the wait. The doctors, nurses, and staff are the best—very caring and understanding but pushed for time.

Okay, I think I've reached my limit. So go out and enjoy your day. Thank goodness for the sunny days we've been able to enjoy while here.

Friday, September 28: Last night as we drove up past the Novato narrow, we were welcomed by the sweet sight of California cows pasturing alongside the road. What a beautiful, and might I say, awesome sight to behold. I missed those darn cows! As we headed up the hill past Petaluma into Rohnert Park, the sun was setting. A light blue hue outlined the forest green trees showing off a dazzling vision that calmed my soul. Scott was definitely in seventh heaven watching as the terrain changed with each passing moment. And me? I was going home.

We had just finished a full day that started with early morning labs at 8:00 a.m., clinic at 9:00 a.m., then a doctor's appointment from 1:45 p.m. to 4:00 p.m. We were too late to see Matthew at a cross country meet that just happened to be at Golden Gate Park. Instead, we drove back to the apartment to collect what we needed to bring home for the weekend.

Right before they told us we could go home, we learned that labs would still have to be done in S.F. for a while. I understand they need the results right away in case the meds have to be changed, but for a moment I was stunned and angry that I'd still need to drive Scott down almost three times a week. After I had my little outburst, the transplant coordinator said that I was allowed to let my emotions out. And although she's never been through something like this, she could totally understand my feelings. So once I calmed down and remembered that this is a temporary inconvenience, I was back to normal...whatever that is now.

It was great watching the doctor listen to Scott's heart yesterday, then say, "What a beautiful sound! You've got one healthy heart." Thank you, mystery heart donor person. You are our hero!

Before the Nasis came down for a visit last Saturday, Marilyn and I were talking on the phone. She was thinking about bringing food down for lunch. I couldn't figure out why she would want to do that since anyone who comes to S.F. would definitely want to go out to a fancy restaurant. Then it dawned on me that she didn't think we could go out to eat because of the transplant. "Marilyn," I said, "you know we can go out to eat, right?" But unless you are living the situation, you don't realize how quickly things change. When Bill and Marilyn arrived at the apartment, they were surprised when Scott opened the door on his own. I forget that everyone still thinks Scott is sick.

On Sunday, Jonathan called to see if he and his girlfriend Charlie could visit. Of course, I was ecstatic. The four of us drove over to the De Young Museum. From the top of the building, we could see UCSF on top of the hill where just days before we had looked down at the De

Young Museum from UCSF. Had to take pictures of UCSF for nostalgic purposes. Had to!

Scott had his mask on in the elevator and a young man asked him if he had sores. Scott replied that he had just had a heart transplant and was protecting himself from germs. Did this man's tune change! People are just amazed to meet someone walking around with someone else's heart inside…beating for his/her survival. It *is* incredible.

Since Scott needs to wear sunscreen whenever he is out in the sun, we bought some at Trader Joe's. Before Jon and Charlie arrived, he lathered it on in copious amounts. I was just thinking that he looked almost jaundiced and beginning to get stressed out that maybe he had another bug when Jon arrived and queried, "Why does your face look so pale and drawn?" Almost simultaneously we each realized that Scott wasn't rubbing the lotion into his face. We had a good laugh and I was relieved that it was nothing serious.

After Scott's biopsy on Tuesday morning we explored Mission Dolores. This historical mission brought out many feelings from my Catholic childhood. A picture of the Pope in the Basilica reminded me of my Uncle Johnny, Father John Houle, a Jesuit priest. A few years ago, one of Jonathan's friends came over to our house and asked in a snickering sort of way, "Why do you have a picture of the Pope in your living room?"

My casual response was, "It's actually a picture of my Uncle Johnny *with* the Pope." Was he surprised!

That afternoon, Gil and Cynthia, Scott's brother and sister-in-law, visited us at the apartment making a full and enjoyable day.

Wednesday, we ended up with no appointments, so we visited Grace Cathedral for me, then Harding Park Golf Course for Scott. Gotta keep it equal.

And now back to our drive home. Exiting the freeway, Scott and I had tears running down our cheeks. As we drove down Piner Road, we held hands lost in our own thoughts. What would it feel like to drive down *our* street and park in *our* garage? A garage instead of a carport. Wow! And a washer and dryer in the house, not outside through the carport and down a few paths. And then, of course, the moment we were both waiting for…seeing our girl, Bob Kat. She sat looking at two strangers, or so she thought, but wait...maybe not. Smell, sniff, watch, wait, smell some more. Then some *meows* for food, and she was letting us pet and kiss, pet and kiss her while she ate to her heart's content.

We'll go back to S.F. on Sunday for one more week, then leave San Francisco for good on Monday, October 8. Have a great weekend everyone! I know we will.

Expressing my sentiments exactly, Janice exclaimed via email: *'It's simply marvelous that you two are home for the weekend for the first time since what must seem like forever! Mom and I would love to see you sometime on Saturday or Sunday before you head back to San Francisco.'*

And my coworker Eileen responded with gratitude: *'Thanks for all of your updates and especially this one. WELCOME HOME! May you have some peaceful and restful times in your own abode.'*

Monday, October 1: We are back at the apartment and I'm in a bitchy mood. I feel so tired and dejected about everything. Scott made a comment last night that hurt me to the core. He had been talking to his friend, Mike, on the phone and then came into the bedroom. Accusingly, he said, "We ruined their plans for next Sunday."

"Whose plans?" I asked hesitantly.

"Mike and Jim for golf. They were going to come down and play at Harding Park, but we'll be home."

We were allowed to go home again this coming weekend and I was thrilled. Yet to hear Scott blame me for supposedly ruining his friends' plans pained my heart.

"We'll be back here on Sunday afternoon," I responded in a resentful voice.

"Oh, that's right. I'll call Mike back."

But *ruined their plans* had already hit me the wrong way. For the past eight months, I could make *no* plans of my own. I've been either working, running Scott to the doctors, grocery shopping, or visiting Scott in the hospital, all the while not knowing what the day held for me or Scott. And I was ruining *their* plans???

So today I'm feeling sorry for myself...crying, wondering how many more times I'll have to go to UCSF, wondering when my life can start again. And knowing that these questions have no answers. I tried napping twice, but couldn't sleep. Finally, I started fixing dinner. Scott and I started talking and my mood lifted. I was Julie again…whoever *Julie* is now.

Wednesday, October 10: We're home and does it feel great! We still have plenty of doctors' appointments coming up, but at least we can live at home and come and go as we please.

Our last night in the S.F. apartment, I set the alarm for 7:00 a.m. in order to get Scott to the lab by 8:30. We also had to load the car with the remaining clothes, food, and other miscellaneous stuff that everyone needs to live comfortably. I took my shower and finished my makeup while Scott (yes, he can do this now) packed up the remaining items to be brought down to the car.

As I was adjusting the blinds in the kitchen around 8:00, I wondered why it was still dark outside. When I asked Scott, he replied, "Because it's not 8:00, it's 7:00."

"What????" I yelled, wondering if I could go back in time for that extra hour of sleep. "Did you know I got up an hour earlier than I originally said I would?"

"I just thought you decided to get up earlier, so we'd have more time to get things done." At this point, I realized that it was futile to be upset, especially since I was the one who set the alarm clock. I began to think there must be a good reason for my blunder.

After loading up the car, we drove over to UCSF where I dropped Scott off in front. Coming back from the parking garage, I noticed two other heart transplant patients waiting along with him. I told Scott I would be back in a few minutes and left for Starbucks. That's when I saw the spouses sitting further away for privacy. Aha! No wonder we had to get there early. The three of us hadn't shared addresses and phone numbers. Also, it was one of the only times we three caregivers could compare notes. As we visited, we vented our frustrations on the enormity of our spouse's health issues, understanding each other completely. I believe out of the three I've been blessed with the easiest and sweetest patient, and of course, the best looking and youngest.

My brother Larry's response to my latest email was unexpected. *'Besides Father John Houle, Scott is the only other person I know who had a miracle bestowed upon them!'*

Feeling ecstatic about Scott's new heart, I jokingly responded, *'I've never thought about Scott's heart transplant being a miracle, but miracles do happen every day. You just need to be aware of them. Driving back to Sonoma County yesterday, I saw hundreds of miracles. We call them cows. See?'*

That reminded me that my Uncle Johnny, Father John Houle, received a medical miracle on behalf of Blessed Claude La Colombiere on January 23, 1990. On this day, while Larry, my sister Mary Lou, and I were standing outside Uncle Johnny's hospital room expecting him to pass away, Father Parish told us he was going to pray over our Uncle with a relic of Blessed Claude. The three of us looked at each other skeptically, but within days our Uncle was sitting up in bed eating an apple with no signs of a lung disease. This was the third miracle needed for Blessed Claude to be canonized a Saint by Pope John Paul II at St. Peter's Basilica on May 31, 1992, with Uncle Johnny and Father Parish as witnesses. We were blessed to have Uncle Johnny with us for many more years.

Note to Caregivers, Patients, and Health Care Providers:

When Scott's golf buddies were visiting us in S.F., they asked him when he'd be able to play golf again. I quipped, "When he starts doing the dishes, he can play golf." I was sort of joking and sort of serious, as for the last seven months I had been handling everything on my own.

The next day, Scott stood in the kitchen of the apartment looking down at the dirty dishes sitting in the sink. I was watching him from the dining room table where I was writing out checks for utility bills wondering what he was thinking. I believed he was contemplating whether or not he could actually wash those dishes. I could almost see that lightbulb moment when he realized that he was indeed capable of doing this simple chore. And then he did—he washed the dishes.

A patient who is on the mend needs to be nudged by the doctors and staff into remembering to start doing things independently and not stay dependent on the caregiver. My husband was great after this little reminder, but other caregivers I spoke to were still expected to cook, clean, and handle all chores for their spouse/patient. This is a terrible disservice to the patient and caregiver, but especially to the caregiver who is already giving so much. You've all heard the saying, Physician, heal thyself? Let's make sure the patient knows he or she can do this, too.

8

Someone's in the Closet

Once we got home from San Francisco after Scott's heart transplant, Scott began figuring out what to do with the rest of his life. He was now retired from the post office and bored. While I worked fulltime, Scott was recuperating and getting a bit stronger every day.

Sunday, November 18, 2007: In today's email, Kris said: *'It sounds like things are going great and I'm so happy for your family. You are all very strong. It would be cool if our guys could get out for a round of golf while we talked all day. Keep me posted.'*

At the time I received this email, Scott was fighting a minor bug that he picked up somewhere. Believing he was on the mend, I gave Kris this update: *'We are doing great. Scott's getting over a bug, though. He is learning NOT to shake hands or hug people. The virus ended up going into his sinuses and chest. He's on the antibiotic azithromycin with one left tomorrow. He was wheezing too, which he's never done before, so he'll have to watch it this winter.'*

Monday, November 19: Scott is still coughing and wheezing. A chest X-ray has been ordered for tomorrow morning and I am starting to get nervous. The handouts from UCSF don't seem to give enough information on what, besides thrush, to watch for.

Not wanting to cook this year for Thanksgiving, we are considering going to *The Sizzler* for dinner with Jonathan, Charlie, and Matthew. Sounds weird, I know, but I just don't have the energy to do much else this year.

Monday, November 26: Scott's back at UCSF with pneumonia. Please start praying for a quick and easy recovery. He has been fighting a cold for four weeks that progressed into a sinus infection and cough that won't go away with antibiotics or steroids. I'll keep you all posted as I can, but will be trying to work some, too.

Trying to keep me in a positive mode, Larry replied: *'I had a cough almost two years ago that lasted a month and a half. Scott's cough is, unfortunately, more extreme than mine and I'm sorry to hear. There are more and more viruses around now that seem immune to antibiotics. I hope the scientists are prepared for the future with these super germs emerging. Our individual lives seem trite when we hear or know of a Scott, just trying to make it to another day. Hang in there; prayer is a powerful tool. Remember you have some pull with The Big Guy upstairs.'* And as I read this last sentence, I was praying The Big Guy was listening.

Tuesday, November 27: Scott has been fighting a darn cold since October 28. His sinuses have been inflamed, but nothing the doctor prescribes seems to be helping. He also has a cough that hasn't gotten better with antibiotics, first Septra *(sulfamethoxazole and trimethoprim)* then Zithromax *(azithromycin)*, but it keeps coming back. Scott had a chest X-ray last Tuesday, then saw his PCP Dr. Bartel the next day. There was no sign of a bacterial infection in the lung. Dr. Bartel increased the dosage for prednisone (which he is already taking for his new heart), gave him a nasal steroid and an inhaler with steroids. I am nervous about this, but nothing else is helping so what can I say.

Throughout this time, I've been in contact with the heart transplant case manager at UCSF wondering if we should come down. The case manager kept telling us to see Scott's PCP, but he had never treated a patient with a heart transplant.

This past Sunday, Scott started running a low-grade fever off and on. By Monday morning his fever was 101 degrees and he was getting chills. I called UCSF and was finally told to bring Scott down to the ER where a chest X-ray showed he had pneumonia. He was put on an intravenous antibiotic while we spent the day in the ER waiting for a bed.

While waiting, someone came in to tell us that our insurance card was coming up as inactive, which of course stressed me. At 2:00 p.m. I decided to walk over to Crepe's on Cole for lunch and called the insurance carrier. The representative told me that Scott was showing active in their system and to have UCSF's financial department try the card again.

Today I gave a presentation at the Santa Rosa Senior Center, then drove down to UCSF. Since lunch was fish and Scott doesn't like fish, I went to Subway to get him a tuna sandwich (yes, I know, tuna's a fish). When I got back, he had spilled water on himself and the bed, so I helped him get into another gown and the nurse changed the sheets. Then I had the strongest urge to get up and go home. I never did talk to a doctor or nurse to find out what antibiotic he is now on. When I called Scott later tonight he did *not* sound very good. He told me they are moving him to Long Hospital 10th floor.

Wednesday, November 28: I just got home tonight from a long day at UCSF. Scott was delirious most of the day, which was causing me a lot of concern. He was talking to himself and people I couldn't see. Finally, the nurse and doctor came in around 5:00 p.m. to check on him. I thought that the nurse understood how his condition had been deteriorating as she and the attendant had to lift him from the toilet to a chair then to his bed around 3:00. He was like dead weight and kept falling asleep. Wondering if and when I should alert someone to his worsening condition, I thought that the nurse must know what she's doing. Wrong!

So when Dr. Redig walked in at 5:00 p.m. I was so thankful, as I was scared. I had never seen Dr. Redig raise his voice before, but when he saw that Scott's condition had deteriorated so quickly, he was incensed with the nurse. I had maybe two or three short conversations with Scott in the seven hours I was with him, even asking if he knew who I was. Thank goodness he did. At one point, he picked up the TV remote pushing the button when I asked, "Honey, what are you trying to do?"

"I'm trying to turn the TV off," Scott replied.

"It's already off, honey," and he drifted back to sleep.

They put him on intravenous feedings as he hasn't eaten since yesterday afternoon. They are giving him two new medications: vancomycin and cefepime. In researching these two drugs on the Internet just now, I did not like what I found. Not that they can't work well together, but that a person who is put on cefepime is apparently not responding to typical antibiotics for pneumonia. These are the antibiotics when nothing else is working. Dr. Redig said that when Scott came in on Monday, he thought by putting him on levofloxacin *(an antibiotic that fights bacteria in the body)* he would be sent home on Tuesday. That didn't happen as the levofloxacin stopped working after a day.

Please pray as you never have before and then whatever will be will be. I do know he is in the best hands, not just the doctors, but God/Goddess who I like to call *love*. And for those of you doing my job at work, thank you from the bottom of my heart.

Friday, November 30: The doctors at UCSF told me that Scott was exposed to the aspergillus mold (over 185 species), a common fungus found outdoors and indoors. He is currently in ICU with the best hospital personnel looking after him. The Infectious Disease Unit is watching him closely and questioning us about where we've been, what we've been doing. During the night, I realized that he must have been exposed to aspergillus after our gardener put wet leaves into the garbage can.

Because of the seriousness of this pneumonia and because his heart is doing weird things, the heart transplant team has taken the lead on his care. The next three to four days will tell how things will go for him. Please keep us in your prayers. No one should ever have to go through a disease like this.

He is hallucinating and saying things like, "When I saw your face, you had a long tongue."

When Scott said, "Someone's in the closet," I asked him to describe the person and he said, "It's a little boy hiding."

Another time he said, "The curtain came really close to me."

When the nurse came in, Scott asked him, "Are you going to drill for very long?"

He isn't freaked out by this, just telling me what he sees. Needless to say, these comments are disturbing and I am terrified.

To lighten the mood, though, here's a heartwarming story: On Tuesday morning as I was waiting for the elevator, a petite older gentleman and his slightly shorter wife exited the *down* elevator. He was cute as a button...just darling. With his head down, he walked slowly, making sure every step was paced exactly right. When he raised his head and saw all the people standing around, he asked, "Are you all waiting for me?" Well, that got everyone laughing and to me it felt like in that moment we realized that we were one with everything. We were whole in spirit and I felt like this is what life is all about, making each other happy and helping each other heal our hearts. For one special moment, those of us waiting for an elevator to take us to our loved ones, we could send our worries off to the ethers. And we did.

Note to Caregivers:

There is nothing more powerful than the love that you feel for your spouse, mother, father, and child(ren). And though being a caregiver is lonely at times, wham, out of the blue, here comes an Earth Angel needing to make an impact in your life. They may only be with you a short time, but they are here to guide and comfort you through this journey. When you encounter these Earth Angels, just know that they are being sent to give you hope. And someday in the future, you will be that Earth Angel giving hope to someone else.

As the caregiver, you have more control over your life than the patient does. And so, while you go about your day remember to laugh, watch for the Earth Angels, and then share the joy with your loved one. And if you want to be uplifted, listen to *Angels Among Us* by Alabama. The words will give you comfort, feelings of love, joy, and most of all, hope.

9

It's Got to Come
from Here

Saturday, **December 1, 2007:** Scott's condition is critical and I'm not one to sugar coat things. The last two days have been simply horrible, with the pulmonary specialists trying to get the pneumonia up and out of his lungs. Scott's been saying the strangest things to me, but when the doctors or nurses come in it seems like he is trying to be on his best behavior—as if he says the wrong thing, they'll put him away.

He hasn't been eating much, partly because they wouldn't let him eat until last night. They were waiting to see if he would need a breathing tube. So far, not needed. When I was trying to get him to drink a 600-calorie chocolate shake, he told me he shouldn't because of the milk. Then I remembered that after he first got sick I suggested he stop eating and drinking milk products since they cause mucus. Once I explained that he needed the calories and it was okay for him to drink it, he drank it down fast. At dinnertime he pushed around the sorry-looking beef stew and rice, so I told him if he could eat the fruit, roll, and salad, it would make me happy.

He looked at me and softly said, "Then I'll be a good boy?"

"Yes, sweetie, then you'll have been a good boy," I responded with all my love.

Today, Janice and her friend Carmen Paredes visited Scott. They came to take me to dinner and provided some much-needed comfort. Janice thought he looked better than what she expected *and* he knew her name. After Janice and Carmen left, the nurses sat Scott up to massage his back so he would cough more stuff up. Once they were done, he laid on the bed looking exhausted and spent.

I was looking out at the gorgeous view of the city when a new and awesome reality hit me. I really felt love for Scott like I never had before. I felt so grateful for having had him in my life all these years, even during the difficult times that all marriages go through. In moments like these you can really look at someone without judgment, and realize that your life has meaning because of this person, or that person, and even the ones you don't necessarily like.

I felt like I should leave because he seemed to be trying to stay awake for me. He looked at me with doleful eyes then said, "I love you." It shocked me to hear him say those words, considering lately I haven't been sure that he knows who I am.

Monday, December 3: Scott has continued to hallucinate. These are some of the strangest things he has said:

"Come here. I've got a postage stamp on my leg. It's square. Now it's fading away."

I asked Scott if he knew where we were and he replied, "At our house with my wife, Julie. I'd like to live here a few more years." Then he said, "It's got to come from here," points to my heart and says, "Not just the boob." I had to keep from bursting out laughing.

Scott thought we were at the barber shop when the Certified Nursing Assistant (CNA) gave Scott a shave, then trimmed and combed his hair. Scott looked at me and asked, "Do you have any money?" He wanted me to pay the CNA for the haircut.

Scott asked, "Where's the girl?" Who? I asked. "Bob Kat. I haven't seen her all day."

Since I was too emotional to call, I emailed Janice and Olga Lee about visiting on Wednesday or Thursday. Marilyn and Bill may visit

Scott on Friday or Saturday. RPJ is coming down tomorrow in the morning, Carol in the afternoon.

He's getting worse as far as knowing what is going on around him. Tonight he asked, "Why didn't you call anyone?"

"Who do you want me to call?" I asked.

"To tell everyone that I passed on...oh no, I guess I didn't," he replied.

This was the scariest remark of all. Tomorrow I think I'm ready to ask what his chances are and I think I'm ready to hear.

Tuesday, December 4: Today was difficult. As I was getting ready to head down to UCSF this morning, I got a call that Scott had had three seizures and I should ask everyone who would want to say goodbye to come as quickly as possible. And they did.

The short of it is that the pneumonia keeps spreading, but only in the lungs. Because the doctors are not really sure that he has aspergillus, they gave Scott a spinal tap, which took two full hours. The results also take time, especially if it is a fungus. Meningitis or a bacterial infection may be easier to detect.

Dr. Safavi has been amazing at keeping me informed. Tonight, looking exhausted, he explained the non-findings. I feel for all the doctors involved as they scramble to figure out what it is they are dealing with. I know that they are doing the best they can.

Scott was not coherent at all today, so I was only able to hold his hand and say a few words of love and comfort. He knows you are all praying for him and I thank you for your comforting words, poems, or sayings that you've emailed. I have wanted to share them with Scott, but each day he's slipping a little further away from reality. Keep us in your loving thoughts and prayers. It's not over yet! Miracles do happen.

As I drove home from UCSF tonight, I was desperate and crying out loud, "It's okay, Scott, for you to go home. I love you." A peace filled my heart that everything was just as it should be.

Note to Caregivers:

When your loved one is in critical condition and you don't know which way the tide will turn, you need honesty from the doctors and comfort from family and friends. Even when it appears the worst-case scenario will happen, something wonderful can materialize. I feel that when God wants us to truly know something, even if we can't hear it or hold onto that faith ourselves, He/She sends us someone who can deliver those calming and knowing words.

One day when Scott was in the worst of the aspergillus pneumonia, one of the male nurses in ICU approached me. "I don't normally tell a family member this because I don't want to give false hope, but I have the strongest feeling that Scott is going to make it through this ordeal," he confided. "I can't say why I feel this way, but I do." We hugged and I thanked him for sharing these words of comfort.

Days later when I didn't know how much more uncertainty I could take, I came home to find an email from my brother Larry letting me know that he felt strongly that Scott would survive. With all that Scott had already been through, I still couldn't imagine a positive outcome, but if Larry and this nurse believed, then maybe there was hope after all. Those two exchanges helped me to trust that no matter what, there is something or someone more powerful than little ol' me. They were good reminders to leave this situation in God's hands.

10

Today Was a Good Day

Wednesday, December 5, 2007: The last two days Scott has been unable to talk because of the breathing tube down his throat. He has slept through most everything, which is a blessing. It's hard watching Scott go through all these tests yet I know they are necessary if he is to get better. I've asked myself a few times when to say enough is enough, but until the doctor tells me there is nothing else they can do or Scott tells me he's done fighting, I'll continue to do my part and be here for Scott.

Today a biopsy on his new heart showed he was rejecting it. It took them a good few hours to get his rhythm to a normal level. I was told that Dr. D'Amato did a high five to Scott's nurse when his rhythm was stabilized. It's so hard wondering day to day what will happen, but just know that today was a good day. And my trooper, Janice, was with me every moment.

I held Scott's hand when he woke up and talked to him to keep him from getting scared. The nurse's voice is so soothing that whenever she spoke Scott fell right back to sleep. Carol visited and even though he couldn't respond, I know Scott was happy having her here. Please continue those prayers as we're not out of the woods yet, but we are better than we were.

This email from RPJ comforted me: '*Today was a good day. That's so good to hear. With all the people who are pulling for Scott, perhaps it really is helping. You seem to be so strong and I am impressed.*'

Friday, December 7: Scott did *NOT* reject his new heart as the doctors originally thought. He was having arrhythmias (irregular heartbeats) and has been put on amiodarone to control it. Since the breathing tube means he cannot talk, he uses his index finger to try to tell us something, and if we guess correctly, he'll shake his head *yes* and give a thumbs-up if we've really got it down. Luckily, he just needs help with simple things and hasn't given anyone the finger yet. (Gotta lighten this up some.)

He hasn't been out of bed since Tuesday when he had the seizures. They still don't know why he had them. He is very weak but determined to fight this bug. He seems aware of what is going on, but I don't know if he is still hallucinating since he can't talk.

Yesterday Dr. Safavi said, "Scott, look who's here," pointing to me. "Is it your sister?" Scott shook his head *no*. "Is it your wife?" and Scott nodded *yes*. So that's one way to make sure he knows who we are and that his responses are matching reality. Before Janice and I left the hospital tonight, I asked Dr. Safavi if he could tell me how they will know that Scott has made a turn for the better. Unfortunately, because of the seriousness of his condition they won't know until they see this fungus leave his body for good.

Sunday, December 9: Yesterday Scott frantically wanted to write something, and when he finally did it was to me. He wanted to know if I lied about the house. I can't for the life of me figure out what he means, but then he wrote the word *trust*. The nurse asked him if he trusted me to do whatever needs to be done at the house, and he nodded his head. So until he gets the breathing tube out, I'm at a loss about what is going on inside his head.

Dr. Safavi says the next step may be to remove a portion of his right lung. The aspergillus appears to be attacking the lung and this operation may be the only way to keep it from spreading. The left lung is also affected, but as of yesterday seems to be clearing up.

I took today off to get some shopping done, attempting to relax and just breathe. But first I spoke to Scott while the nurse held the phone up to his ear. He responded favorably to me not coming in, although the nurse told me he hesitated a bit. She was the one who suggested that I sleep in, then call when I got up to get the status. If I was needed, she would call me.

I have a request for those of you who would like to do something for Scott. If you are able to send a Christmas, half birthday, or get well card with a crisp dollar bill tucked inside, that would lift his spirits immensely. He loves receiving cash in cards and I think this would give him joy.

It's a little scary that I know the UCSF address by heart and even more unnerving to walk around UCSF saying *Hi* to people I've gotten to know. Never thought that would happen. Thank you ahead of time for the cards; I'll continue to update as I can.

Wednesday, December 12: Thank you all for the cards! To see Scott's face when I open one and there's a dollar bill inside is precious. I'm not sure what he's thinking as to why he's getting all these cards and dollar bills, but he looks amazed.

He was more aware today, but still tires quickly so we didn't talk for long. He does seem to understand what is going on and wants me to tell him if it gets to the point where nothing will help. The breathing treatments from last night have helped somewhat. It's all the coughing that gets to him and yet coughing up the pneumonia is what will keep him alive. At least the breathing treatments can help to give his body a rest.

A CT scan was done this afternoon, but the results were not in when I left tonight. An X-ray showed that the pneumonia is compacted down in the lower part of the right lung. He may have to have surgery, but Dr. Haagen said that wouldn't happen for a few weeks. Every day the prognosis changes, so no one really knows day to day.

I guess for now all I can say is that he is hanging on and that's a good thing. Dr. Redig told me how strong Scott is, and you know, I would never have thought he'd have it in him to fight like this. But to see how he is holding on through the worst possible illness is an amazing and humbling experience. It's what keeps me driving back and forth each day to make sure he knows how much he is loved.

Thursday, December 13: Scott received seven cards yesterday and four today. The nurses believe Scott is their most popular patient. Even though I have to read the cards to him, I can see how much they lift his spirits. I explained about the dollar bill in the cards and he gave me a look that said, *Now what did you do?*

Scott is so tired, sleeping almost all of the time. The doctors still seem optimistic, but if you could see Scott each day as I do, you would wonder. It takes every muscle in my body not to stop hospital staff from poking and prodding him during the day. But I keep reminding myself that if there is still hope, then the doctors, nurses, and pulmonologists must keep trying.

Today one of the heart transplant doctors made an incision on his right side (sorry if I'm causing anyone to feel faint) to put in a tube to drain the build-up of fluid around the lung. Another X-ray was taken (which makes me wonder how much radiation he is being exposed to) and the results should be available tomorrow. He has been eating a popsicle every day, which is a big improvement from practically nothing. He is receiving liquids and food (in liquid form) through a feeding tube in his nose that provides carbohydrates, protein, and fats to his body.

I held Scott's hand while they put the incision and tube in his side. He didn't feel a thing. Later, when the pulmonologist came in to drain fluid from his nasal passages, she told me I should probably leave the room. Scott's nurse Melanie piped up saying, "I believe Julie can handle this since she was in the room for the surgical procedure." I guess nothing fazes me anymore.

Friday, December 14: When Gil called this morning to tell me that Scott looked and sounded better, I thought, *Yeah, let me just wait to see for myself.* And he does look better. He's talking more, staying awake longer, and even tried eating some soup tonight. The CNA did one heck of a job washing his hair, washing him down in all the right places (oops, did I say that?), and giving him a shave.

The cards keep on coming. Five today with three from the Annex alone. There were zero from the downtown post office, so maybe a little competition is in order. And if downtown has already mailed some cards, well hey, I guess the cards are in the mail. Can you tell I'm feeling a little bit happier tonight?

This morning before I left Santa Rosa, I stopped at Whole Foods to get some sundries and a sandwich from the deli. The one I bought, with turkey, bacon, sundried tomatoes, and avocados, was called, I kid you not, The Golden Gate. How apropos is that!!!

Thanks again for all the prayers, prayer lists, prayer groups, post office groups, as all of your loving thoughts are showing positive results. And just so you know, I plan to double whatever monies show up in the cards. There's a Toys for Tots bin by the elevator begging for toys for kids in the hospital; I'm looking forward to putting a few in there.

Monday, December 17: Scott is an amazing man. I've been married to him for 16 years and to see what he has had to endure brings me down (or is it up) to a new level of respect, understanding, and love. The cards are really having a positive and loving effect on Scott. I read all of them to him each day before I hang them up on the wall in his room with red and green ribbons. It's beginning to look a lot like Christmas!

The hospital room looks out on the Golden Gate Bridge, the bay, S.F. State, and all the tall buildings in this awesome city called San Francisco. We couldn't have asked for a better room. At night, the buildings are lit up with holiday lights and just awesome to behold.

Now back to Scott. Over the weekend he seemed more alert and awake for longer periods of time. On Saturday I told Dr. Nacar that I was concerned about the swelling in his arms. An ultrasound was done on both arms today and the results should be in tomorrow.

According to Dr. Nacar, Scott's white blood cell count is up again, so they have put him back on two antibiotics they had stopped early on. They had to remove and replace his nasal feeding tube today which was curling up in his stomach. Two X-rays made sure it was placed correctly because he has been having a hard time keeping water and regular food down. He hadn't been fed liquid food for 24 hours, which may be why he seemed so tired.

While I visit Scott, I try to keep the nurses, doctors, and physical therapists at bay so that Scott can sleep. If you can, imagine falling into a deep sleep when someone shakes your arm every 10 minutes for another test. It was really pissing me off a few days ago, so I've spoken up. They are really watching it now, at least while I am there. He was sound asleep when they wheeled him off in the hospital bed for the CT scan around 4:30 p.m. and asleep when they brought him back at 5:00, so hopefully he just slept through that ordeal.

I was going to keep this email short and sweet, like all the other emails I've written (yeah, right), but for some reason once I start typing, I just can't stop. Writing emails really is therapeutic for me. I am truly thankful for your concern and caring, and for forwarding my emails on to others. I think Scott is on every prayer list on the West coast.

RPJ's last email jested that, *'IT'S SUPERSCOTT—no more SOB! He seems to be heading in the right direction. I hope he can get all the sleep and nourishment to aid his recovery.'*

Wednesday, December 19: The last two days Scott has been sleeping almost all the time. His white blood cell count is high *(usually indicates the immune system is working to destroy an infection)* and his red blood cell count is low *(causing anemia resulting in fatigue and shortness of breath).* They have held off giving him a blood transfusion until absolutely necessary, so now I guess it's crucial. Hopefully, this will give him the *oomph* he needs.

The other concern right now is that he is unable to swallow food or water without it coming back up. Tomorrow he is scheduled for a swallowing test while an X-ray is taken of his esophagus and throat. This entire situation has been so stressful, as you can imagine, but to see him so tired just breaks my heart. I know that the doctors are doing and considering everything they can to keep him going. All I can do is sit back to watch, wait, pray, and know that whatever happens is meant to be.

Janice and Olga Lee are going down tomorrow in my place so that I can have a day off. And then on Saturday, Scott's cousin Doug and sister Carol will fill in. Hopefully, my replacements will email a status report to keep us all updated.

Please keep on praying. I haven't been able to read any of your cards to Scott the last two days, as he hasn't been awake long enough to enjoy them. And so you know, three large stuffed animals found their way into the Toys for Tots bin at the hospital thanks to all of you.

Thursday, December 20: After Janice and Olga Lee's visit with Scott, Janice emailed this update:

The respiratory therapist was there when Mom and I arrived at 2:40 p.m. Scott was sitting in a chair receiving a treatment that continued for a few more minutes. Scott looked up seeming to recognize us then raised his hand. His eyes looked so tired and his head was bent. We told him we loved him very much. As he held his hand out to me, I took it and held it for a few minutes.

We were told that Scott had an x-ray at 1:00 p.m. because anything he had been swallowing had been going into his lungs instead of his stomach. At 3:45 a staff person came in to do an ultrasound of his abdomen. We left the room. When we came back at 4:20 Scott was resting, but he woke up briefly, lifted his head from his pillow and said, "Hi." We again told him we loved him and touched his arms very gently suggesting he go back to sleep. He seemed to be resting more easily than he was earlier.

At 4:40 Scott began coughing and I asked a nurse to come in to see him. With the nurse's assistance, he was able to cough up quite a bit through the suction. Scott asked where you were and we assured him that you loved him very much, but that you needed to stay home today to rest. He understood. We let him know several times that you would be back tomorrow to see him.

At one point Scott asked, "Could you steal a little water for me?" We told him that we would love to but couldn't because his doctors said he couldn't have any right now. His nurse did put Blistex on his lips and cleaned his face up a little bit, though.

I think Dr. Gransee the ENT specialist, came in to talk with Scott about 5:15. He explained that because the swallowing test showed that Scott was having trouble swallowing his own saliva, he was at high risk of developing another type of pneumonia (I believe). The doctors all believe that a tracheotomy could be immensely helpful. They would insert a surgical breathing tube (tracheostomy) in Scott's neck so he doesn't have to be intubated. While the balloon in the device was inflated, he wouldn't be able to talk. This wouldn't be permanent and there would be minimal risks involved, although he would be left with a small scar on his neck.

Dr. Gransee asked Scott whether he would consider having this procedure. Scott very clearly said, and this was as clear and loud as we heard him all day, "I would like to give it a try." Dr. Gransee said that they might be able to do the procedure tomorrow, or they would have to wait until after Christmas.

At 6:30 his nurse came in to check his blood sugar. She pricked his thumb to do the test and his reading was 216. She gave him 6 units of insulin. His nurse checked his chart and said that he did NOT get a blood transfusion. You may want to ask more about this tomorrow.

Gil came in to see Scott right afterwards. We talked with Gil briefly and then left the hospital.

Friday, December 21: Dr. Gransee called me yesterday at home to explain and obtain permission for the tracheotomy procedure. I was emphatic that Scott be told exactly what was to be done and if he agreed to keep trying, he had my blessings. When I arrived today, they were preparing Scott for this procedure. *(Tracheotomy is a surgical procedure that creates an opening in the neck in order to place a Tracheostomy tube into a person's windpipe. This replaces the breathing tube.)*

I wrote a letter to Dr. Haagen with a copy to Dr. D'Amato with suggestions to possibly help patients before and after a transplant. One is a newsletter, which I've been told Dr. D'Amato is already working on and is soon to be released. The second is that the transplant coordinators arrange for someone from the Infectious Disease Unit to go out to patients' homes before or immediately after a transplant to go over vital information with the patient, spouse, and caregivers so they know what to be aware of and prepared for. In fact, they should have follow-up visits three months and even six months later. I am trying to take positive steps to make sure that no one else has to go through this terrible disease. Besides, this hospitalization must be costing the insurance company a bundle, so it would be a win-win for everyone. *(It did cost a bundle…$3,000,000 in 2007.)*

Back in his room after the surgery, Scott slept until the nurse woke him up around 6:00 p.m. She wanted to make sure he would respond.

After she left I told him to go back to sleep, which he did. Sometimes I think if I wasn't in the room with him he would be awakened several more times during the day. I've noticed different technicians coming by the room ready to slip in. When they see me they stop, turn around, and leave. Hey, I'm just trying to protect my sweet guy and can you blame me?

And the cards just keep on coming!

Reading the following email from Larry reminded me that home is where your heart is and my heart is with Scott. *'I cringe on every email and don't know how you are staying afloat, staying positive. Scott must feel like a pin cushion. He definitely is a fighter, I'll give him that! I'm praying Scott will be home for Christmas but then I realize that with you and your loved ones at the hospital comforting him, even a hospital can be home.'*

Sunday, December 23: Great News! Scott seems to be getting better. But he does seem upset about the whole situation. And can anyone blame him? He asked the doctor today if he was dying—must have mouthed the words as he can't talk right now. The nurse said that Dr. Haagen told him if he had asked two weeks ago he wouldn't have known what to say. But today he could honestly tell him that he believes the worst is behind him. Of course, time will tell, but this is good news.

It's so hard watching Scott go through a disease this difficult and distressing. There have been times that I've wanted to say, *He can't take any more of this! Stop everything!* But thank goodness it didn't come to that and I kept my cool somehow. He is much more alert these last few days, which is probably why Gil and I thought he looked so mad. When we asked if he was angry, Scott shook his head, *No.* But I know that look. I've seen it many a time.

More tests keep being done. And when the pulmonologist attempts to bring up more pneumonia out of his lungs, it wears him out completely. But over all I can say he's come a long way. I am optimistic that he's on the road to recovery.

This email from Marilyn and Bill reminded me that our friends are also having a difficult time with Scott's dire situation: *'We feel so powerless and wish that our prayers would be heard. Sounds like Scott is getting stronger, though, so that's good news. We hope that we can all get together soon for a real celebration!*

Wednesday, December 26: It was a quiet Christmas at UCSF. Jonathan, Matthew, Carol, and I spent an uneventful yet peaceful time in the ICU with Scott. He can't talk because of the tracheostomy, so I put together a typed sheet of words and phrases he could point to for things that he might need in the moment. This seemed to work wonders and helped Matthew and Jonathan see that their dad was getting back to normal.

The list includes: *This sucks; I'm too tired right now; Come back later; I'm angry; Is this going to hurt?* Scott liked it, but wanted it to be in alphabetical order and include just simple things that he needs like *bed pan, nausea med.* We worked on this together and now the doctors think it's a great idea for the entire unit. A great suggestion by one of the female nurses.

The boys opened their gifts from us and Jonathan surprised us with first class stamps with a picture of Bob Kat. Now if only he'd return all of Bob Kat's photos that he took from me. And Matthew told me tonight that he hadn't been able to shop yet but was going to this weekend for both of us. Wow, finally our parenting is paying off.

After the boys and Carol left, Scott and I spent time alone. I'm not good at lip reading, but luckily most of the nurses seem to be. Scott can write somewhat but his handwriting is a bit shaky and hard to read. The nurse and I finally figured out that he wanted me to tell him everything that had transpired from the time he got into the hospital. So I went through the weeks since November 26 as best I could and told him my emails would have the rest of the information.

He was mouthing off to me again...what I mean is he was trying to tell me something and I finally had him write it down, which took another minute to decipher.

He wanted a mirror! Man, I never knew how vain he is and thought it was cute, but there are no mirrors to be found in ICU. Luckily I had a tiny pill box in my purse with a mirror on the inside. So try to picture Scott with the pulse oximeter attached to his finger trying to hold this itsy-bitsy mirror up to his face. It was comical and difficult for him to do. I guess he thought he looked just frightful, which would be keeping right up with Christmas, *The weather outside is frightful*—just in case you didn't know where I was going with this. And luckily, he actually looks pretty good right now. His color is back and the CNA has kept him shaved and bathed, so I think he's feeling a bit more human today.

Although Scott is more aware of his surroundings, he didn't remember Jonathan telling him yesterday, *Thank you for being the best father a son could have.* I'm glad that I asked Scott if he had heard Jon yesterday, as it meant the world to me and I know Scott feels the same.

Today as we played blackjack, I'm happy to say that I was in the lead. I held up Scott's cards for him to read. He would then gesture for another card or shake his head *No* if he didn't want one. I also read off clues and the number of letters of crossword puzzles. He would mouth the answer if he knew it. I figured this would help me learn to read his lips and help him to think of something besides being in the hospital.

Isn't life crazy? One day you're up, then down, then back up again. If there's a lesson to be had, I wish it would just jump up and bite me already. But maybe it's just to remember that it's all good, it's life, and it never really ends anyway. Staying focused on the important stuff, like love, now that's the lesson.

Note to Caregivers:

It is all about love. I wouldn't say it if it wasn't true…in fact it's the only truth we really know. How you treat your loved one is especially important. If you ever wonder if caregiving is worth it, ask yourself: If you could do anything, anything at all in this world right now, what would it be?

For me, it was being there for Scott. I will never regret the time I spent with him, helping him (within my limits, as after all I am still human), driving down to San Francisco as I could, and just being there when he woke up. There may be things I wish I hadn't said or done, but I will never regret the time I took to care for my guy. I hope that when you look back at the caregiving season of your life, you will feel satisfied that you did good and did it in the name of love.

11

Get a Grip

Monday, December 31, 2007: Scott is doing much better, but he is still very, very sick. Now that he is more aware, I can see the uneasiness in his face. I asked him what he wanted done in case he makes another turn for the worse. His answer is to take him off all life support. I don't blame him one bit as aspergillus pneumonia is a horrible life-threatening infection to go through.

Dr. Haagen told us today that he will not operate to remove the bottom right lobe of the lung until either Scott gets much better or gets much worse. I asked Dr. Haagen if this surgery, compared to the heart transplant, is relatively free and easy. He admitted that this surgery is just as serious, if not more so. The good part is that Scott now has a healthy heart. The bad part is that he is immunosuppressed and during surgery, fungus will be free to roam his body. This surgery is not taken lightly, so please pray for the perfect outcome.

Wednesday, January 2, 2008: Caregiving sucks! And yet I am sure that being sick like Scott is much worse.

While Scott has been pretty much comatose since November 28, I've been at the hospital most days making sure he gets what he needs. Some days after he was moved back to bed I needed to place the nurse's call button and TV remote close by his hand, and the suction for mucous build up in his other hand.

Other ways of helping are questioning the doctors about what they are doing and why, and trying to keep people away to let him sleep when something can wait. Yet more ways are trimming fingernails, rubbing lotion on his arms and legs, and giving him a swab of water or an ice chip. Doesn't sound like a lot, but it does help the nurses and gives me something to do. And then while he's sleeping, I can slip out to get something to eat, read, work a crossword puzzle, go to the restroom, make a phone call, scream, laugh, cry...GET A GRIP.

Not only are these emails beneficial for me, but maybe one of them will help guide you in a positive way in the future. I'm telling you these things because you might become a caregiver someday (unless your spouse, mom, dad, or child goes very quickly), and my suggestions may help you and your loved one. Most important, I want you to know that as a caregiver, you will have to go through some things alone. Here's my advice:

1. If you ask questions, be aware that you may be frowned upon by the medical community and made to feel like a pariah.
2. When the nurses and doctors are trying to do things in the room with the patient, make yourself as small as possible, or you will be made to feel like a pariah.
3. If you attempt to go somewhere trying to have a normal day, you may not feel welcomed as it's a downer to have someone around who is going through something like this and you will be made to feel like a pariah.
4. As your loved one becomes aware of his/her surroundings and starts feeling a little normal, he/she will wonder why you are second guessing everything and everyone in the room. You will look like you are butting in where you shouldn't and you will be made to feel like...well you get the picture.

No one, not even your spouse, has a clue about what you have been going through, which includes the fact that you thought your loved one was going to die—again, and again, and again. This roller coaster just keeps on going. It seems and feels interminable. You can rationalize that all of this must end at some point, but in the middle of the situation it sure doesn't feel that way. So now I'll tell you Scott's condition and I can try to be in my normal mode after I finish this email.

Scott has been in the hospital bedridden since November 26 and in ICU since November 28. It takes two big men or four female nurses to move him from the bed to a chair. He has been somewhat lucid for the last five days, although yesterday he could not remember sitting up in a chair for three hours while Paul the physical therapist worked his magic. Scott is off the respirator during the day, so he's been able to talk for two days now—and he is mad! "I sure hope this is all going to be worth it," he grumbled.

He doesn't say much, but he's never been a big talker. He complained to the doctor yesterday that his nose was clogged up, but the doctor told him that he couldn't give him any decongestant because of his heart. Today, looking closely at his face, I noticed snot oozing out of his nose. The doctor had never looked in his nose! I knew this at the time but I was trying to let Scott handle this on his own. So today I had a nurse immediately clean out his nose. It doesn't make sense that I would even have to suggest this to anyone.

I've been trying to bow out a little and not be the middle-woman since Scott had indicated that I kind of take over when I'm in the room. Of course that upset me. I asked what he wanted me to do about it. He shook his head to indicate it was just who I am, and I believe he meant this in a nice way. What he doesn't realize, though, and maybe no one at UCSF realizes, is that I, the caregiver, have been the constant in this scenario.

Each day brings a different nurse and the doctors are in the room maybe three to five minutes tops each day. Imagine coming in today and finding my husband sitting in a chair with his hospital gown half-way covering his body, fuming because he can't get himself back to bed… and the nurse is busy with someone else. Then I find out that she didn't realize how weak he is and that it takes several strong people to get him into bed. Once in bed, he was shivering from head to toe. We had to cover him up with three blankets and turn up the heat.

If I sound a bit annoyed tonight, I hope you can understand why. And again, if any of this can help someone else during their time of crisis, then this email was worth it. Now I'll close and maybe sleep better tonight after getting some of my frustrations out of my system.

The email responses from everyone were amazing. They gave me permission to feel what I feel.

From my childhood friend Deb: '*I feel your frustrations. I'm with you. You wonder why people in the medical field can't find ways to communicate with each other AND ICU is Intensive Care Unit so why would someone not know how weak and ill Scott is. Thanks for sharing as I know it will help someone in the future.*'

From my friend Gloria Bottaro: '*Wow, you really needed to vent. Don't EVER worry that you are complaining as caregiving is frustrating. You feel alternately rebellious, like you don't want to do it, but then you realize that if you don't do it nobody will. And then you feel guilty for wanting to be free and live your own life, followed by feelings of compassion and understanding. And when you step in to make things right, you DO feel like a pariah! My thoughts and heart are with you.*'

From my friend Toni Faxon: '*I'm sending you a giant hug and you are right…caregiving sucks, bigtime! You have done and still are doing a tremendous job. I'm not sure any of us can understand entirely what you must be going through. Emails are a good way for you to vent your frustrations and you should by all means LET IT OUT!*'

Thursday, January 3: Matthew read the following update before I hit send because I wasn't sure I should. Not only did he want me to send it, but he also wanted more detail. I told him that I couldn't make an email *that* long or no one would read it. So here's my update with Matthew's stamp of approval.

When I arrived today, Scott's face was pale and his eyes had the hollow look they had when he first became sick. As we talked, I could see that while his mental acuity was intact, he was weary of everything, and that was getting to him. He agreed that we needed to talk to Martha the social worker. Worried that he may make a turn for the worse, I wanted as many people as possible to know his desires from this point on. I don't want to be put into the position to say, *Enough is enough.*

First a speech pathologist came by to tell us that Scott would be getting a swallowing test on Tuesday. She was in and out so quickly that we didn't think of what to ask. Like, why are we waiting until Tuesday as Scott hasn't been able to eat or drink anything for almost five weeks? But when I walked out to the hallway—quick as lightning—she was gone. I had Dr. Nacar paged.

The speech pathologist must have been called as she was back very quickly. Out in the hallway, she explained that she was concerned that Scott would fail the test and have to wait another week to take it. Okay, that made sense, so I had her go into the room to explain this to Scott. She said she would try to get him on Monday's schedule.

Meanwhile, Martha came by to listen to our concerns. Scott expressed his wishes about end of life issues and I explained my concerns about not wanting to make this decision if it came down to it. We went over the Advance Healthcare Directive and gave Martha a photocopy to place in Scott's medical records. She came back to tell us the directive was official.

While we were talking to Martha, Dr. Nacar arrived to talk about the nurses' responsibilities. I was emphatic that all the nurses know to check his nasal passages, be aware that Scott can't get up on his own, and remember to place the nurse's button, remote, and suction by his hands at all times.

A few days ago, Dr. Nacar suggested that depression is the reason Scott wants to call it quits. He wasn't getting that this life Scott is living is not a life and that depression is not the real issue. Besides, who wouldn't be depressed in this situation? Martha brought this up with Dr. Nacar and I reiterated that I did *not* want the term depression used to make Scott feel guilty or as the reason he may want to call it quits. I believe that Dr. Nacar finally got it, then mentioned that we needed to talk to Dr. Haagen so that everyone knows Scott's wishes from here on out.

Scott was supposed to have a biopsy today for his heart, but since two staff members have colds, Dr. Nacar rescheduled it for Monday. After Martha and Dr. Nacar left the room, I got all comfy and started working a crossword puzzle when it dawned on me that two very tiring tests had been scheduled on the same day. Dr. Nacar was outside our room with the interns, so I quickly wrote him a note saying to cancel the biopsy and keep the swallowing test on Monday per Scott. In 10 minutes, Dr. Nacar was back to say that the biopsy would be done tomorrow by other staff members.

What a day! When the physical therapist came in, Scott was able to sit up on the side of the bed with no one supporting him. She had him raising his arms and doing stretches, which was exhausting for him. When she left the room for a moment, Scott said, "She's not going away unless I do this, huh?"

Did I mention that we played gin rummy yesterday *AND* Scott was able to hold the cards on his own? Today we were back playing blackjack, but I'm bringing the rules tomorrow as we couldn't agree on most of them.

Thanks for listening, and remember, no one is required to read these emails. There is always the delete button, but, hey, if you've already gotten this far, well...I won. (Told you I'm competitive!)

Emails like this help me cope. From Deb: *'I am going to have to stop reading your updates so early in the morning and so glad I have waterproof mascara on. You are awesome. Keep on doing what you're doing.'*

And Marilyn reminds me that we are not alone: *'Well, I read the other night's email to Bill and neither one of us knew what to reply. We feel that both of you are going through Hell right now and we don't know how we can be of any help. We just want you to know that we are here for you.'*

In December, when Scott became mindful of what was happening to him, he told me he was surprised that I didn't let him die. I explained I had asked him three different times if what was happening was becoming too much for him. Each time he assured me that he wanted to continue to try. Now I understand that he couldn't have made any decision in the first month of this illness, because he wasn't cognizant of his dire situation. So although it may sound like I was pushing the issue of Scott calling it quits, it was Scott expressing his wishes to me. I just wanted everyone to hear his concerns and know what to do if he became comatose again.

Monday, January 7: Watching Scott learn to walk and move his arms again is heartbreaking. Thanks to Paul, though, today he was able to walk over to a chair with a walker. His spirits are at an all-time low, so I've suggested that we see if he can get counseling with Martha or someone else.

A CT scan was done tonight to see how his liver and lungs look, especially the lower right lobe. Concerned that Vfend (brand-name for voriconazole) is causing liver damage, the doctors may switch Scott to Noxafil (brand-name for posaconazole). *(Voriconazole and posaconazole are drugs that treat aspergillus pneumonia. Scott ended up taking posaconazole for the rest of his life.)*

Scott asked that one of the nurses be taken off his watch. This nurse has been with him from day one and I haven't felt comfortable with her from the beginning. Back in November, when I realized she would be his main nurse, especially while he was unaware of what was happening, I decided to be extra cautious and not make waves. After all, she was caring for my husband.

One day this nurse complained to me, the wife for goodness sakes, that Dr. Haagen had been in suggesting that Scott's mouth needed attention (mucous buildup). This was her job and she was complaining to me? If I noticed the mucous buildup myself, I would suction him. This was when Scott was unable to move his arms up to his mouth. In fact he couldn't move them much at all. So again, I sort of bit my tongue and hoped that she wouldn't be there the following day. Well, she was Scott's nurse on the Friday I didn't drive down due to the worst storm of the last two years. Whatever happened caused him to talk to someone on Sunday to make sure she never came back. Guess it wasn't just me.

I feel like I've become an outcast at UCSF. Oh, everyone is nice to me, but I can feel the phoniness. I guess being outspoken, even though it's all been on Scott's behalf, is frowned upon by the medical community. I've been trying to get answers to how he contracted the aspergillus pneumonia, but I am getting nowhere. The doctors, nurses, respiratory therapists, and even an infectious disease person talk about what will happen from here on out, but no one can tell me how to make sure he doesn't get this again. I've ordered four books about heart transplants, from *The Ethics of Organ Transplants* to *Memoirs of a Transplant Surgeon*. Hopefully they will help me answer my questions.

I was really feeling defeated driving home tonight thinking: *Why can't we all get along? Don't most people want the same things? Like love, truth, and a good night's sleep? Isn't putting the patient's welfare first, along with quality of care, the best outcome for all concerned? If there is a way to prevent something as serious as aspergillus pneumonia, where's the information? Why did it take so long for the heart transplant team to get Scott tested for this when he first developed the cold and cough? He was only two months out from the transplant surgery and we were calling down to UCSF two to three times a week in the month of November. Why, why, why?*

Note to Caregivers:

As a caregiver you have the right to ask questions. You have the right to be your loved one's advocate and if you have been chosen by your loved one to be the Health Care Agent, you have the right to make decisions when your loved one cannot. The only thing you don't want to be responsible for is deciding when to stop all lifesaving support. That is why it is so important for you and your loved one to put in writing the lifesaving treatments you want or don't want before a serious health condition becomes apparent. You do not want to be put into the position of making a life or death decision for someone else. Trust me, you don't.

If you don't have a will and trust in place, contact a lawyer to set this up. Besides the will and trust, our lawyer had us complete the Five Wishes Living Will form, which is the same as an Advance Healthcare Directive. Copies were then given to our Primary Care Physicians (PCPs) and all other doctors we saw regularly. Before you designate someone as your Health Care Agent, talk to that person to find out how they feel about life and death situations. Talk about this designation and make sure the person you choose agrees to respect and follow your wishes.

In California and many other states, the Physician's Order for Life Sustaining Treatment (POLST) form is a medical order that gives seriously ill patients more control over their care by specifying the type of medical treatment a patient wishes to receive at the end of life. It includes a Do Not Resuscitate (DNR) option. The California Emergency Medical Services Authority (EMSA) website's link for the DNR and POLST forms is: emsa.ca.gov/dnr_and_polst_forms/. Check out your state's website for their form.

12

Guard Spouse on Duty

uesday, January 8, 2008: He sat in a hospital chair with a high
back. His arms and shoulders scrunched to the right with
a big machine holding him in place. As I watched from the
window, she gave him fluid to swallow. The X-ray machine showed
about one-fourth of the liquid escaping into the larynx and trachea
causing pulmonary aspiration (fluid into his lungs). A thicker liquid
was given, one with honey, she said. This time most of it went down
the esophagus but again he aspirated. Next was Jello with fruit. Once
more he aspirated. I was ready to leap to his rescue should something
unforeseeable happen.

She came around the glass partition and talked to me and her
coworker. The good news was that he did at least 70 percent better
than last time. The bad news was that he shouldn't eat regular food for
another two weeks. Listening to her, I could see Scott looked dejected.
Over I went to put my arms around him, patting and kissing his head.
We both started to cry as I held him as best I could. One or maybe both
nurses gasped as they watched us, feeling our pain. *Good*, I thought to
myself, *they need to see how hard this is for him...for us.* And they need
to see the love, true love, of two people just wanting him to get well and
come home. There was no shame in our tears, only a release of our last
six weeks—no—the past year of emotional ups and downs.

Scott did *not* pass the swallowing test today. This was emotional in itself, but coming back to his room and watching the respiratory therapist wreak havoc with his chest to bring up more pneumonia, it took all I could to keep my hands off her face. It takes so much energy for him to go through this treatment and then he's just spent. But that doesn't stop other therapists, nurses, and doctors from attempting other therapies they tell us will help him get better. When Scott told Paul that he couldn't do any more physical therapy today, I was so thankful. He was too emotionally drained and looked like he was ready to throw in the towel. What does a spouse do but silently watch and glare at the next person who walks in to awaken your sleeping spouse. Okay, I didn't really glare, but I was ready to lunge at that next person. Instead I silently, quietly, and urgently pushed each one out the door before they woke him.

If anyone knows how to help Scott see the bigger picture without preaching, or to concentrate on something else, please email me some suggestions. I've thought of just bringing him a cheeseburger and root beer float, which he really wants, but that would risk another round of pneumonia. So come on out there…how can I raise his spirits? Surely there must be something. All suggestions welcome. I just can't think of anything.

Thursday, January 10: Here's a snapshot of Scott's day:

"Good morning, Mr. Bennett, I'm your nurse today. I'll be the one putting meds in your PICC line."

"Good morning, Mr. Bennett, I'll be your physical therapist for the day. Ready to walk from your bed to the computer room?"

"Good morning, Mr. Bennett, I'm your respiratory therapist. I'll be suctioning you to cough up this nasty pneumonia."

By the time I arrived today Scott was fuming. Dina, the nurse for today, explained that he had just fallen asleep when a doctor walked in. Not only did this doctor *NOT* wake Scott gently, but he reached right in to remove Scott's tracheostomy tube so he could insert a new one. Scott woke up to this doctor, in a sense, manhandling him without so much as an *Excuse me, Mr. Bennett, I need to change your tube.* And we like this doctor.

About a half hour later, Paul came in for physical therapy. He was very considerate, talking to Scott first to make sure he was up for some exercise. Scott stood up with a walker, walked over to the computer area and walked back. It took about four minutes, but he was able to do this mostly on his own. Paul was right by his side to catch him if he faltered. After this, Scott sat in a chair and fell asleep in 10 minutes. I had the nurses put him back to bed.

Scott's nurse the last two days was a young woman with a lovely English accent. She was wonderful except that even though she had asked about the back brace I was wearing, she asked for my help hoisting Scott up on the bed. As I write this I'm wondering whether it's even a good idea for a nurse to ask a family member to help lift a patient. Aren't risks of lawsuits involved, especially when the nurse knows this family member already has a compromising condition? I do help out a lot, and I did feel her frustration when in a nice way I refused to do this one thing. She even said that I should be paid for all that I do.

About an hour later, the nurse came in and woke Scott up. He looked at me as if to kill. I asked if it was because she woke him up, and of course it was. So I asked her to finish up anything she needed to do for a few hours. Once she left, I put a sign on the glass door that said: "Shhhhhh... Sleeping until 4:00 p.m.—Guard spouse on duty." No one came in the room, except one man to fill the medication cabinet. He tiptoed in and wheeled the cabinet out without a sound, leaving it in front of Scott's room. It felt powerful to be able to help Scott get some sleep.

Yesterday I should have counted the number of people who walked over towards the door, saw the note, then left. I told Scott I thought it was hundreds, but it was at least 20 in less than two hours...okay, maybe ten. So I put the *Come back after 4:00 p.m.* sign up again today. The nurse was in Scott's room right at 4:00 and he was still asleep. Oh well, I'm doing my best. He slept off and on until around 5:00. We were just going to start a game of cards when the respiratory therapist came in.

"Hello, Mr. Bennett. I just want to give you a breathing treatment and suction you. I'll make it quick. Okay?" Well, this time I was annoyed, or was I feeling Scott's annoyance at the intrusion and sympathizing with him? Either way, I felt his frustration at the system that is trying to make him better.

I was really drained tonight driving home and was *not* going to go online but am so glad I did. Thanks to all of the emails I received, my spirit has been uplifted. One day when Scott is ready, he will read all my emails and yours, and these messages will help him see and feel all the love and caring that was just for him.

P.S. Other signs for the door:
- 4 out of 5 doctors recommend SLEEP for their patients…I'd love to find that 5th doctor.
- Needs SLEEP! Shhhh
- Catnap in Progress! (with photo of Bob Kat)
- Come back later to poke and prod!

This email from my sweet friend Toni predicted this book way before I ever considered it: *I'm glad you're saving all your emails because you'll need them in case you or Scott ever decide to write a book about your experience. And even if you don't ever write a book, it will help you to see what a wonderful job you're doing to encourage and love him and keep his spirits up which will certainly help save his life. YOU GO GIRL!!*

Saturday, January 12: Martha the social worker met with Scott yesterday to give him some moral support and when I arrived today I found out he broke down and cried. I am feeling so helpless right now because I know that he wanted me there. How do I satisfy his needs and take care of myself too? I suggested that he pray or talk to whomever he believes in, asking for what he wants and then to concentrate on that outcome as often as possible. I know each of us has our own paths to live, so I think I'm finding solace in the fact that for some reason Scott needs to go through this illness. And for whatever reason, I'm here by his side on my own path. That's what is keeping me going right now.

After Janice and Olga Lee left this afternoon, Scott cried, then started coughing so hard that it took two nurses to help calm him down. He is so depressed. I don't know how to help him.

Monday, January 14: Remember when I mentioned that I had typed up a chart so Scott could point to words and phrases for what he needed?

As I was revising my chart with Scott the other day, a nurse from the 14th floor (we're on the 10th) who was helping out mentioned that there was already something similar that the nurses use. I was dumbfounded *and* furious, as it was the nurse that Scott dismissed last week who suggested I create this chart. So this nurse on duty locates this chart and shows it to me. Low and behold there it was…the perfect chart. The alphabet and numbers I was just about to add to my chart were already on the hospital chart. Plus it listed all the words and phrases on my chart, plus a skeleton so the patient could point to the place of pain.

Now do you see why I get so frustrated? Why wasn't this chart given to Scott as soon as he had the tracheotomy procedure? And then this young nurse says to me, "But if you need something to do in your spare time."

SPARE TIME…WHAT SPARE TIME??? I thought trying to keep myself calm.

Scott has been increasingly depressed and understandably so. When he coughs, the pulmonologist suctions him. When he attempts to walk down the hallway, he is exhausted after just a few steps. Since he is too weak to use the toilet on his own, a bedpan and urinal hang on the side of the bed. It's depressing and heart wrenching and I'm just watching.

The other night while driving home, I had a light-bulb moment: get one of the doctors to tell Scott what would happen should he decide to stop all meds and medical treatments. If he decided that he couldn't do it anymore, how long would he live and what would his quality of life be like. And then on the other hand, how long do they expect him to be in the hospital from this point on? The next day Scott agreed that this was *exactly* what he needed. I called the transplant team and a doctor arrived in half an hour.

After Dr. Kaatz understood what Scott wanted to know, she explained, in a calm voice, "First, we would send you home with hospice services so you are not alone. Second, once all of your medications are stopped, you would live maybe two days to one week. Hospice would make you as comfortable as possible on morphine and you would go easily and quickly."

She then told us that if he survives, there is no way for anyone to say how long his recovery will be. She also explained what will happen if they need to remove his right lower lobe of the lung. I prompted Scott to tell her in what circumstances he would want to stop medical treatments and start comfort care from this point on.

We talked about the lobectomy surgery and when to draw the line during and post-surgery. We talked about his heart and whether he wants to be resuscitated if his heart stops. He does not. Dr. Kaatz asked if we had spoken to anybody else about this. "Yes, we've already spoken to Martha and Dr. Nacar, just not about his option of stopping all life support," I replied. Dr. Kaatz then asked if we'd like to talk to the palliative care team doctor. Well of course Scott said yes as he wanted to find out more information about how this team may be able to help him through this debilitating illness. Thirty minutes later in walked Dr. Atchison.

Dr. Atchison explained how a hospice team consisting of a doctor, nurse, aide, volunteers, and chaplain would assist us at home if Scott decided to stop life support. She also went over Scott's depression and other medical complaints to see if there were other ways to help him cope. She made suggestions about ways to relieve his dry mouth, handle the pain when he talks because of the tracheostomy tube, and other things that should have been addressed already.

Is it just me or is something missing here? Was there a reason why palliative care wasn't suggested weeks ago? Instead, the focus has been on depression when all along the discomfort has been causing it. Why do the simplest things that can help a patient thrive seem to be avoided at all costs? Isn't it cheaper for all concerned to treat the patient like he or she would like to be treated instead of worrying about the cost? What a concept!

After Dr. Atchison left, the respiratory therapist came in. For the first time in months Scott actually smiled. Now that he knows his options, maybe he'll feel he has some control over his life, and won't feel so hopeless. Thankfully, there will be some added comforts to aid Scott in his recovery.

Wednesday, January 16: After Doug visited Scott today, he sent this update:

When I arrived around 2:30 p.m., Scott's sister Carol and my sister Nancy were already visiting. They had gotten a Pebble Beach calendar and put up pictures of the golf course that Scott liked best. While we were all there Scott ate a full container of yogurt, which pleased the nurse. She told Scott that she wasn't going to schedule another swallowing test until next Tuesday, adding that he was doing very well and to keep doing his swallowing exercises.

Scott was then prepared for a walk. He made it all the way to the entry doors and back with only one rest. He recovered quite quickly and said that he had to stop about three times. The staff were encouraging and said he was on the right track. He asked for and received pain medication for his throat around 3:00. He didn't take a nap after his walk, which was noted as getting better because he wasn't as exhausted as in the past.

He seemed in pretty good spirits. We all joked and brought him up to speed about what's going on with us. He laughed and added a few witty comments. When the nurse asked if he was in any pain, he said his throat still hurt, so they gave him another dose. The staff seemed to be very attentive and Scott acknowledged that he liked this group too.

I told him that he had made a tremendous improvement since Christmas and that he needed to stay strong so we could play golf. He responded that it wouldn't be soon, so I said we would plan for next year. He nodded yes and I left at 6:45, after his evening meds.

Note to Caregivers and the Medical Community:

Our experiences show the need for one-on-one care from our medical community so that a patient's needs are addressed with each new issue, especially for those hospitalized long-term. In Scott's case, he was NOT depressed because of a psychiatric issue, he was depressed because he was in discomfort: sleep deprived, miserable because his throat hurt, disappointed that he couldn't eat real food, and continuously coughing up pneumonia. What Scott needed was hope.

Sure, everyone was doing their job, but whose job is it to make sure the patient feels secure and safe? No one could tell Scott if he would survive this ordeal. Yet all it took to make him feel better was to have someone take his struggles seriously and make immediate positive changes.

When Scott said in Chapter 9, "It's got to come from here, not just the boob", he was pointing to my heart (okay, my boob, too). He was hallucinating, but he was right. It *does* have to come from your heart. Even if you are in the middle of your own misfortune, you can still make a positive impact on those around you and feel uplifted in the process. Until health insurance stops ruling medical care and human kindness prevails, try to show love and compassion to those you meet, whether you are the caregiver, a medical health worker, or the patient. After all, that's how we all want to be treated!

13

Best-Worst Case Scenario

Thursday, January 17, 2008: On Wednesday, Scott was in better spirits and awake the entire time. We played cards. I was ahead in the beginning, but at the end he slaughtered me. And being the good sportswoman that I am, I took it all in my stride and I swear I did NOT walk out saying *52-CARD PICKUP.*

Yesterday Dr. Safavi talked about the possible lung surgery. He mentioned removing both the lower and middle lobes when I piped up, "I thought it was only the lower lobe." This is when Dr. Safavi said that both lobes were filled with aspergillus. Whether they told Scott when I wasn't there or Dr. Safavi wasn't aware that no one had told us, I'm not sure.

Then he said something to the effect that contacting the heart transplant team was important whenever symptoms occurred. I looked at him like he was from Mars while he waited for me to respond. I finally said that we *had* been in contact with the heart transplant team a month before this happened.

"Yes, I heard," he said.

So I said, "We called again...and again...and again." He just stood there looking at me and then laughed. I'm sure it was a nervous laugh. Then he said something ridiculous about Scott just getting through this ordeal. I bet you know what I was thinking then!

This morning I drove Jonathan and Charlie down to the S.F. airport, stopping at UCSF first so they could visit Scott. When we arrived at

10:00, Scott was already exhausted. He hadn't walked yet and was looking so fragile and thin. I also noticed his jowls seemed swollen again. We left at 10:45 so they would get to the airport on time.

When I got back to the hospital, I encountered Dr. Haagen and Dr. D'Amato observing Scott as Paul walked him around the hospital corridors. Both doctors ignored me while acknowledging Scott and his progress. The only two reasons I can think of are that they think I am going to sue them or because I called in Dr. Atchison from palliative care. It couldn't be that they would think that I want Scott to call it quits, could they? Could they? I'm feeling abandoned by the staff at UCSF.

The following response from Larry expresses my sentiments exactly: *Wow, there seems to be a problem, not only with Scott's recovery, but with the medical staff as well. Insensitive doesn't do justice to the way you've been treated. The most important thing right now, though, is to rectify Scott's condition in the most personal and reasonable way for him.*

Thursday, January 24: Eight weeks ago Monday Scott was admitted for aspergillus pneumonia. Even though he has stabilized, he still has a long road ahead. The nurses have been much more talkative lately, but I believe the workload has been less stressful for them overall. I feel like I am a fixture now at the hospital, waving *Hi* to people as I walk about.

Yesterday Scott had the swallowing test. Although I missed the test, I was there in time to review the results.

He did pass...sort of. He'll be able to eat one meal a day, at lunch, and I'll be bringing it from home. Jill, the speech-language pathologist, will meet with Scott daily at 1:00 p.m. to teach him how to strengthen the muscles that allow him to swallow properly while eating, thus allowing me time to get to the hospital with the food. Even though Scott hasn't eaten a meal in more than six weeks, he still won't eat UCSF's hospital food. His first meal was macaroni and cheese and he ate more than I thought he would. For tomorrow, he's requested an egg salad sandwich. At least these are easy to prepare and can be kept cold on the drive down.

Scott coughed a lot yesterday, which makes me feel desperate inside...like he's going to backtrack. But today he was somewhat better.

The last few days the doctors and nurses have been talking to him about getting out to the floor. The *floor* meaning out of ICU and back with the regular patients. He's very nervous about this because he still needs to be suctioned and still can't walk around well on his own. But this may be what he needs to start being more independent. I'm sure that they will move him right back to ICU if it's too much for him.

Yesterday, Dr. Angelina came in and hugged me. I hadn't seen her in a while and that hug was precious. She and Dr. Nacar talked to both of us about getting Scott back onto the floor. When they were done, I repeated something they had said earlier, "Yeah, Scott, we don't want to rush you to the floor, take your time." Then I pointed out the door and said, "But just so you know, the moving guys are right outside ready to go."

As they laughed, Scott said, "My own wife is pushing me."

Last week I decided that my attitude about UCSF needed to change or I would go crazy. This week I've been trying to feel the love instead of picking things apart. It's working. I'm finding everyone much more friendly and helpful. People say *Hi* on the elevator and I feel much less anxious. I also realized that I need to stay focused on what is important and that is to work in concert with the doctors to educate everyone about *aspergillus*. Since changing my thoughts around, I've been feeling much more connected and better able to concentrate on Scott and his recovery. We still don't know the outcome, but hey, none of us knows what each day will bring.

We've been playing cards a lot. I was winning for a few days, but now Scott is back in the lead. Whoever has the most points on the day he goes home for good wins $50. *(Scott won!)*

I can't help but chuckle at Ed's reaction to my email: *You are back to your positive self and you did it after you unloaded all that negative baggage. Happy for you and great that Scott can eat people food again, no matter how much. Has to make him feel good.*

Saturday, January 26: Aspergillus pneumonia is deadly, especially in immunosuppressed patients. It's much worse than his heart symptoms.

Yesterday, Scott noticed that his left arm was swollen again. Today I found out an ultrasound revealed a blood clot, which can be profoundly serious. They removed the chest tube that was inserted yesterday to drain more fluid around his left lung and will need to remove the PICC line that has been in his left arm for some time. *(The PICC line makes it easier for intravenous medications so they don't have to keep poking him with needles.)*

Scott is so tired of coughing up pneumonia and very weary of this entire ordeal. So if you're wondering, yes, he is improving. It's just that so much can still go wrong. I don't know when they will be performing the lobectomy, which carries its own set of problems. If I sound pessimistic, it's because I am trying to prepare myself for the best and the worst-case scenario. How do you prepare? I wish I knew, as so far it has been a tremendous emotional roller coaster.

Wednesday, January 30: Have you ever heard the word *Sisyphus*? In the book *Intensive Care*, John Murray, M.D., uses Sisyphus to describe a person who can't seem to get out of the Intensive Care Unit (ICU). I asked Dr. Safavi whether this term would apply to Scott. *(Sisyphus was a figure of Greek mythology who was condemned to repeat forever the same meaningless task of pushing a rock up a mountain, only to see it roll down again. A Sisyphus just never gets ahead of the game.)* Dr. Safavi said Scott would be more like the Phoenix, the mythical bird that dies in the flames and is reborn from the ashes. Now you know why I am calling Scott *The Phoenix Man*.

It was such a joy for me to go into the office today to see all my coworkers. I didn't realize how much I miss everyone, and my job, too. I am looking forward to the day when I walk through that door to be with my friends and continue helping people on Medicare.

No big news except that Scott is eating a little. Today we tried penne pasta, but it was not the right type of food for him to chew and digest. Tomorrow Jill is bringing black beans and I'll bring yogurt. We're staying with soft chews for now.

Dr. Haagen keeps postponing the lobectomy and I am starting to believe this may be a good thing. Since this surgery would create a whole new set of problems, I am now hoping it won't happen.

One of the nurses, Ron, has taken Scott on what he calls *Road Trips* to the nurses' building across campus. I keep telling Ron not to put Scott's heart through too much, but he takes him anyway. (I really think this is more for Ron than Scott, but hey, who am I to say.) It takes Ron more time getting Scott ready—helping him into the wheelchair, hooking him up to oxygen, wrapping him in blankets—than the actual trip takes. But if Ron wants to do this for Scott, it makes my heart happy, and it gives Scott a distraction.

Ron is the only nurse who keeps the door closed consistently, making it hot in the room. I just turn the temperature down, so we can appease him. We can adjust to Ron's little quirks, like his putting a towel under everything, as his sense of humor and outlook on life really benefit Scott's morale. Each nurse is so different, but I think we've adjusted pretty well to all of them by now. And everyone is pushing for Scott to get better and go home.

It was good to hear my friend Pam Chanter's encouraging remark: *We are happy to hear of Scott's progress and believe that Scott will be a Phoenix rather than Sisyphus. Camus wrote of Sisyphus in one of his books which is still vivid in my memory as a visceral feeling after over 35 years, so I don't wish that image on anyone ever. Go Scott go!*

Sunday, February 3: Scott was transferred out of ICU to Long Hospital Room 1018 on Friday night. Since Matthew was going to visit, I decided not to drive down that day. Scott was suctioned on the left lung to pull out as much aspergillus as possible—at least this is what Scott told me. He was exhausted afterwards.

Heavy rain all the way home last night sounded like a hundred golf balls hitting the roof. But that didn't keep me from stopping for some much-needed food at Trader Joe's. Driving down today wasn't any better. Driving is tiring on a good day, but this torrential rainfall is the pits.

Just when Scott is improving, wham, something else pops up. Last night, he became sweaty after his meds were inserted into the I.V. The description he gave to Dr. Redig and a male nurse made it sound like hot flashes. After receiving his morning meds today, he had diarrhea. Since he didn't have these issues in ICU, I'm thinking a new medication must be behind these annoying side effects.

I try hard not to get discouraged, but alas, sometimes I feel like there is nothing to look forward to anymore. If Scott gets well, when is the next emergency? Can I keep driving down to S.F. all the time? It's just too much, and I can't lose my job.

Thursday, February 7: Last Friday, Scott had a bronchoscopy (a test that allows the doctor to examine his airways) and five other miscellaneous tests on Tuesday. Dr. Nacar said that his right lung is looking better and now they are just biding their time to see if he really needs the surgery. According to Dr. Nacar, Scott is one of the few heart transplant patients who has developed aspergillosis *and* lived through it. So they are proceeding cautiously. Another bronchoscopy will be done soon and hopefully we'll know more by the end of this week.

Scott is back to not eating anything because it hurts his throat— probably because he has a feeding tube down his nose and a tracheostomy tube. That's a big drawback, as they really wanted him eating and moving around better than he can right now. He still needs people to pull him up in the bed and he needs two people with a wheelchair behind him when he walks in case his legs buckle.

Note to Caregivers:

After re-reading these emails, I wish I had had a talk with both doctors when I felt snubbed. I don't mean telling them off, but asking what caused the distance. I should have voiced my concern about the doctors being worried that I would sue them or the hospital. They might not have opened up, but together we might have been able to figure out how NOT to be wary of each other and to focus on Scott, who needed us on the same page.

All I wanted was honesty about the disease and more information to educate myself about aspergillus and the new medication he was now needing to take for the rest of his life. It's too bad that doctors have to worry about lawsuits, but maybe UCSF could have offered an intermediary to eliminate any bad feelings. Then we could have all concentrated on getting Scott the care he needed.

If you are in a similar situation, before you talk to the doctor(s), write out the questions and needs you and your loved ones have. What are you missing from the medical community that would be helpful? Give a copy of your list to the doctor to read before you meet. Most, if not all, hospitals have a Patient Advocate. Many times this is a social worker who assists patients and their families with communication with the medical team, helps families and patients understand why procedures are ordered, helps families with discharge planning, and so much more.

Be prepared to take notes, and if you can, bring a family member or friend along to hear those answers, because as you know, two sets of ears are better than one. (I know the saying is *two heads are better than one*, but you get my drift.)

14

Who Would You Call?

Sunday, February 10, 2008: Scott seems stronger every day, but we still don't know if or when the lobectomy will be done. The good news is no new fungus is growing.

On Friday, I was out walking to get some lunch. I had been having some dizzy spells for about a week and a half. Several times a day the room seems to spin. I still had a few more blocks to get to the bottom of the parking lot, up the elevator to Parnassus, and another elevator to the 10th floor. I really felt like I was going to pass out, so I sat down on a bench when I got to Parnassus. I was thinking, *If I can just make it to the 10th floor, I'll be okay.*

As I got off the elevator, my palms were getting clammy and I wasn't sure I could make it to Scott's room. I told Paul, the Physical Therapist, that I wasn't feeling very well. He felt my hands and walked me slowly to a side room. He sat me down and swung into action. My blood pressure read 138/69, which was high for me. My heart rate was fluctuating between 107 and 110. After Paul found a wheelchair, he let Scott know he was taking me to the ER. After the triage nurse found my EKG normal, she wheeled me into the waiting room. This was about 3:45 p.m. and I was all alone. Who do I call? You got it…Janice, who drove down with her friend Carmen. This turned out to be a great idea as I wasn't able to drive my car home.

The room was spinning constantly while I waited in the ER for another two hours. My mind was racing. Whatever could be going on? When Janice and Carmen arrived, Carmen had us laughing hysterically for most of our wait. I wonder how many patients and family members were annoyed by our loudness, as I swear we probably sounded like teenage girls.

The ER doctor diagnosed vertigo and I promised to see my regular doctor as soon as possible. It was 10:00 p.m. by the time we walked into Scott's room to collect my personal items and make sure he was set for the night.

Because I can't drive myself down to San Francisco right now, Scott is alone all day long. If anyone can visit, please call him on his cell phone. If you are ever in a similar predicament, I hope you have wonderful friends who will drop everything to be with you.

My PCP agrees with the diagnosis of vertigo. He prescribed meclizine and I've taken three doses so far. Although I don't feel much better, I didn't have the spinning sensation last night in bed when I turned on my left side.

Wednesday, February 13: Scott was transferred to a new room with a view of the Golden Gate Bridge. Thank goodness as the other room had no view *and* was always uncomfortably warm.

Dr. Haagen and the cardiology team want to perform the lobectomy at the end of this week. When the doctors realized Monday was a holiday, the surgery was postponed until next week. I believe this is because people with the necessary expertise will be taking the weekend off. Because I'm nervous about this surgery, I am thankful and relieved that it has been postponed. Once the lobectomy is rescheduled, I'll ask all of you to get those prayers and positive thoughts working double time.

Since reporting my diagnosis of vertigo, I've heard from so many people about their own issues with this condition. My only symptoms are feeling off balance and the room spinning when I lie down on my left side in bed. Stress may be the cause of this malady, but I do handle stress pretty well. Anyway, hopefully this will clear up very soon and I will not feel like I'm spinning out of control, at least not from vertigo.

Tuesday, February 19: The lobectomy has been postponed again, which is a good thing. Health Net is pushing the doctors to get him out of the hospital and into a rehabilitation facility by Friday. Kentfield Rehab in Marin County is their choice—an easier commute than driving into San Francisco. Scott will have a biopsy and other tests before the decision is final.

Janice, Olga Lee, and I drove down to spend four hours with Scott. Martha the social worker went over information about the transfer. Hopefully, Scott will have a private room, but this is all being negotiated between UCSF, Health Net, and the rehab hospital. There is talk of inserting a PEG Line into Scott's stomach, then removing the feeding tube in his nose.

We all agreed that Scott looked very well and his spirits were high. He slaughtered me playing gin rummy, but I beat him on Sunday. I guess I have to let him win once in a while. Or is it the other way around?

My vertigo seems to be waning. While I was playing cards, my head wasn't spinning around like it was on Sunday. And no it wasn't spinning around like in the movie *The Exorcist* and I wasn't spouting out curses. Although I did feel that Janice and Olga Lee might have put a little spell on me while I was playing cards—which is probably why I was losing the entire time.

Sunday, February 24: There is no room at the Kentfield Rehab Center, so UCSF is looking at rehabs in S.F. Because of our insurance, we are unable to use Santa Rosa Memorial Hospital's Rehab Center.

On the bright side, Scott's tracheostomy tube was removed yesterday. While Jonathan, Matthew, and I were visiting, Dr. Haagen walked in and just took that baby out. It was over within 15 minutes. Jonathan and Matthew watched the doctor, but I had to turn away. After all the medical trauma I've witnessed these past 12 months, this surprised me.

The most amazing phenomenon was that the hole in his throat was closing within half an hour. It apparently hurt, but not bad enough for Scott to ask for pain medication.

Note to Caregivers:

What do you do when you are a caregiver and find yourself in the midst of your own health issues? Call on your friends and family. For the most part, people want to help other people, especially in times of need. I was lucky that my sons, friends, Scott's relatives, and coworkers stepped in to help or visit.

If you don't have this support or even if you do, most health insurance policies (including Medicare and Medicare Advantage Plans) cover inpatient care in the hospital, short-term inpatient care in a skilled nursing facility (SNF), home health care (HHC), physical therapy (PT), and hospice. Be persistent in asking the doctor for what is needed. Your loved one and you have the right to get the care and help you both require.

Call a local HHC agency for referrals to hire a caregiver for help in the home. If the insurance company doesn't cover it and you can't afford this care, you may qualify for low-income health coverage through your state's Medicaid program (Medi-Cal in California). Medi-Cal covers the In-Home Supportive Services (IHSS) program that will help pay for care so you can remain safely in your own home. Medicaid/Medi-Cal is a joint federal and state program that helps pay for health care costs if you have limited income and resources and meet other requirements. The California Department of Social Services' website for adult services is www.cdss.ca.gov. Other states should provide a similar program.

If you are a veteran or a spouse of a veteran, be sure to check out the U.S. Department of Veterans Affairs (www.va.gov) for home health and nursing home care, as well as many other benefits.

Also check out grants through local and nationwide agencies, such as the Redwood Caregiver Resource Center (www.redwoodcrc.org) and the Alzheimer's Association (www.alz.org), as some may pay up to $1,000 or more for HHC services. There is help out there, so ask around. You don't want to be left alone feeling vulnerable!

15

First Stop…A&W Root Beer

Thursday February 28, 2008: Just a quick email to let you know that Scott has been approved to be transferred to Santa Rosa Memorial Hospital's acute facility. The problem now is that he has an infection. Scott told me it was staph, but in the hallway Paul said that they still didn't know what it was. So I'll wait until I hear it from the doctors.

Scott had his first turkey and tomato Subway sandwich today (he ate half and I ate the rest). He did pretty well up until the last few bites, so his swallowing has improved quite a bit. While he ate, I said, "Wow, your first meal in almost three months; I should have brought my camera!" Since I was holding the feeding tube in his nose against the side of his mouth so he could chew, Scott didn't think a photo would be such a great idea.

A few days later, Scott and I had just returned to his room after taking a walk around the hospital floor. He was so proud of being able to walk so far and we were both happy that he was finally on the mend. All of a sudden, Scott had a funny look on his face. I couldn't fathom what had happened and then I saw. The feeding tube in his nose had come out and landed on the floor. We both laughed and decided we were *NOT* going to tell anyone but just let them figure it out on their own. This was a good day! And he never did get another feeding tube.

Monday, March 3: Tomorrow is one year since Scott collapsed in the Target parking lot. He was to be transferred up to Santa Rosa today, but the hot flashes and stomach problems that started in February are still occurring. All the medications, CT scans, X-rays, and poking and prodding Scott's body endures is so difficult, so it's no surprise that different side effects keep creeping up on him. Saying a prayer that this new development subsides and he'll be up here on Wednesday. *(Note: We found out later that the flushing or hot flashes were being caused by Niaspan, a medicine that increases good cholesterol (HDL) and lowers bad cholesterol (LDL) and fats (triglycerides) in your blood.)*

Thursday, March 6: Yesterday, Scott had his first shower in over three months. He exclaimed that the best part was how the water felt when he was washing his hair. It was wonderful watching him walk to the bathroom on his own using a cane instead of a walker. For some reason, though, he doesn't remember to cover himself up when he gets out of bed or up from the chair. He's still wearing the classic hospital gown. Sometimes I have to remind him that there's a little too much showing. Then he blushes and covers up. I guess when the nurses and doctors have seen every single part of you, after a while, who cares. Talk about *Southern Exposure*!

There's talk that Scott may be discharged to come home as early as next week. A few weeks ago, I would not have been comfortable about this, but now I think it is doable. Hopefully I'll be emailing all of you with the good news that a new era of our life has begun. For me it starts next Monday when I return to my job. I'll close for now in hopes that my next email will bring you the best news ever.

When Toni heard the good news that Scott was soon to be discharged, she said: *If the only thing you're worried about is that he doesn't remember to cover himself up, then you've got it made! Please wrap him in bubble wrap or something like that so he'll stay healthy and well!*

Tuesday, March 11: He's HOME!!! We didn't leave UCSF until 3:00 this afternoon. So many specialists had to give us tips on what he should eat (pretty much anything fatty right now), the medication list (ugh!), and anything anyone else could think of to support us. There were many goodbye hugs and well wishes from the staff. Jill couldn't hug Scott, though, as she was getting over laryngitis. And we didn't get to say goodbye to Paul, who was off this week.

As we drove off into the sunset (okay, so it wasn't quite sunset) we were flying high. Our first stop—you guessed it—A&W Root beer for that root beer freeze and a cheeseburger. Although my chicken sandwich was gone in 15 minutes, it took the rest of the drive home for Scott to finish his food and drink.

Our second stop was to my office to pick up a commode that my boss doesn't need anymore. Now I'm probably giving you more information than you wanted, right? While my coworker Yani helped get it into the trunk, Ed, Eileen and I had a wonderful short visit. Then we went on to our third stop...home.

Scott had forgotten Bob Kat's feeding routine, so while I was out at the grocery store stocking up on all the fattening foods that Scott can eat and I certainly can't, Bob Kat wheedled him into an extra helping of her canned food. What a little beggar and of course Scott's a pushover.

So I'll close for now and send little updates for a short while as I can. I'm back to work tomorrow.

Wednesday, March 26: I think we've finally made at-home adjustments with medications, meals, showers, exercising, and me back at work. I do believe that Scott is ready for more visitors, so if you haven't called yet, please feel free to. Of course, we don't want a large group at once, but a few here and there to lift Scott's spirits would be wonderful, especially during the week when he is home alone and could use the company. A short visit will do wonders and brighten his day. And remember not to visit if you have any inkling of a virus, sore throat, cold, or contagious germs.

Friday, April 11: I am back to working, grocery shopping, and making pharmacy runs. And it feels good!

Today was my first real day with someone other than Scott...my

92-year-old friend. We go to Denny's for lunch, where she has a favorite waitress that simply dotes on her. She gets a breakfast on the 55+ menu and I get the mushroom Swiss burger. Weird that I can get something on that menu now too.

Scott is healing quickly. He's able to walk up the stairs at home now, but we are going to wait a week before we move his bed back upstairs. Right now the bed is in the family room and he's taking showers downstairs. Having him home is so amazing and I'm not feeling so stressed out about everything. I'm going to close and take a shower as our favorite TV show is coming on. I don't check emails very often anymore, so if you don't hear from me, well, that's a good thing.

Note to Caregivers:

After you have gone through a difficult situation as the caregiver for your loved one, how do you get back to your normal life? Since I had to go right back to work, trying to find time to just *be* wasn't always an option.

When Scott first came home from his 107-day ordeal at UCSF, it was up to me to work, grocery shop, cook, clean, pick up and dole out prescriptions, and do anything else required to run a household. Time just for me was hard to come by. Until I was able to adjust to our new normal, the best I could do was limit phone calls and weekend visitors to family and friends. Since I was in a constant state of worry every time I left the house to work, it was a blessed relief when Scott's friends came over during the week to keep him company.

I guess the best I can say is KNOW YOUR LIMITS and stick to them. After all, you can only do so much, you're only human, and you do NOT want to reach your breaking point. After Scott had been home a few weeks and I had caught up on sleep, I was able to welcome our friends with open arms, realizing that no one expected me to entertain them. For that I was so thankful.

PART TWO

Caring for Someone with Alzheimer's

16

The Power of Drugs

As Scott and I adjusted to our new normal, I was on edge every moment—at work, at home, or at the grocery store. I couldn't seem to let go and let God take care of our lives when I never knew if or when the next big health issue would hit. I realized that changes were needed for me to continue working *and* be there for him during emergencies.

Before March 4, 2007, we both worked full time. In the evening, I would fix dinner and we would eat together, mostly in silence. Scott wasn't a talker so I would talk about my day while Scott listened—at least I think he was listening. After dinner, Scott would watch TV while I read emails, played solitaire, and read in bed before I fell asleep.

Scott's return home after his long hospitalization was the perfect opportunity to change things up a bit. Matthew had moved out in July 2008, so it was just the three of us—Scott, me, and Bob Kat. Now when I came home from work, Scott helped me with dinner. When the meal was ready, we would sit down in front of the TV with our food laid out on the TV trays. Scott taped the shows ahead of time so we could watch them whenever we wanted and fast forward through the commercials. We would bet with each other (okay, I would get Scott to bet) on things like who killed whom. I really am competitive and like to win. Many times Scott wouldn't bet because he didn't feel he had a grasp on whodunit. And many a time I lost a bet because I really thought I knew whodunit.

When the first TV show was over, we did the dishes together. I washed and he dried. These times were special for both of us and helped Scott feel useful. Watching favorite TV shows gave us quality time together and something to talk about. We especially loved *The Mentalist* and *Medium*.

Of course, Bob Kat was part of our ritual. After we ate dinner, she would get on Scott's lap for some love time. She would look up at him with such adoration that I should have been jealous, but I wasn't. I enjoyed watching her give him all that attention knowing my turn was next.

Bob Kat and I would play hide and seek or have a boxing match. I would sit on the floor with my legs crossed, and she would plop down right in front of me. When we were both ready, I would hold my palms up. She would move her eyes to the right and left, then swat at one of my palms as hard as she could. Sometimes she got a little carried away and I would have to reel her in, but I loved being her play thing.

Around 10:00 each night, Bob Kat would saunter into whatever room I was in and sit facing me until I noticed her. When her stare made me glance around, I'd exclaim in my high pitch baby voice, "Oh, sweetie girl, I forgot your treats!" As soon as I said the word *treats* she'd run to her food bowl waiting for those tasty morsels.

The second part of life that needed to change was my sleep pattern. I stopped sleeping well after my son Jonathan developed asthma at three years old keeping me constantly on edge. When Scott and I moved in together, my sleep difficulties grew even worse. As the years went by, Scott's snoring became unbearable and then he began jerking in his sleep every 30 seconds or so. He could sleep right through it all, but I couldn't. Almost every night had one of us downstairs sleeping on the couch.

Since 2006, I had been relying on Xanax (brand-name for alprazolam) to help me sleep at night. But after Scott came home from UCSF, I began having strange reactions, beginning with an episode while I was driving on a lunch break. I could still drive, do errands, and work, but something was wrong. Thinking I might be experiencing a drug interaction between Xanax and the allergy medicine I had been taking, I stopped taking both. The strange feeling came and went for a few weeks, then went away completely. But I still wasn't sleeping well. Three months later I was back on Xanax.

At the time we were spending over $10,000 a year on health insurance through Scott's disability retirement. Watching Scott's pension dwindle, I wasn't certain how much longer we could afford the horrendous premium. The copayments for his medications kept rising as well. The nonprofit I worked for paid a minimal wage and health insurance was not offered. Neither one of us would qualify for an individual policy due to the strict pre-existing medical condition clause.

When I started researching other medical plans offered through his retirement, Kaiser seemed to be the best option. But Scott would have to change all of his doctors *and* drive an extra hour to Santa Clara for his heart transplant appointments. On the other hand, Scott's sister Carol lived a mile from the Santa Clara Kaiser, so he would have a place to stay the night. As I vacillated, I kept thinking, *He'll never have another heart transplant, so why am I so worried?* We decided to make the switch.

July 1, 2011 was the effective date of our Kaiser plan, as well as Scott's first appointment with his new Primary Care Physician (PCP), Dr. Thorburn. Since we had already taken a tour of the hospital and medical buildings to familiarize ourselves with the layout, Scott knew exactly where to park and how to get to Dr. Thorburn's office. When I saw Scott that night, he gave rave reviews of the new doctor who eased his mind that all his medications had been ordered. The referral to the heart transplant team in Santa Clara made for a smooth transition, which took a lot of pressure off me.

When I met my new PCP on July 18, I explained that I wanted to stop taking Xanax and asked if there was anything else I could take to help me sleep. She suggested Trazadone. That night, I took half a tab, and ended up feeling weird and a bit scared. With this odd reaction, I switched from Trazadone back to Xanax, plus I was taking Allegra for allergies. Off and on for the next week I felt strange, so I stopped taking Allegra but continued taking Xanax at night.

On July 27 I took a few sips of a two-shot nonfat latte as I began giving a Medicare presentation to about 20 seniors—just as I had done for years. All of a sudden, I couldn't think or remember what I had been talking about. In the past when I would lose my train of thought, I would ask the audience to remind me where I had left off. Someone would call out the answer and I would make a joke about being a senior.

This time was different. I really couldn't concentrate. My face and hands were clammy and I was probably white as a ghost. Not knowing what to do, I asked the HICAP volunteer in the front row to continue with the presentation. As she began to talk, I sat down at a table in front of the audience. After about 10 minutes, the volunteer noticed how pale I looked and asked if I was okay. When I told her no, she asked whether I wanted them to call an ambulance. For me to say *Yes* meant I was not okay.

The ER doctor seemed to believe that it had to do with the medications. After three hours of inconclusive tests, he sent me home. He didn't want me to drive, so I called Janice. Thank goodness she and Olga Lee both came so one of them could drive my car home.

For the next few weeks, I visited or called my PCP often. Even though I was never admitted to the hospital, I considered myself bedridden. I couldn't stand up for any length of time, my blood pressure was all over the place, and weird new symptoms kept appearing. When I realized that my coffee drink was also a drug, I quit my two-shot lattes.

Just after midnight on August 3 I jerked awake, my body shaking uncontrollably. I was so scared. Jonathan took me to the ER, where the shaking stopped. I was sent home with instructions to seek care if I didn't start feeling better within two days.

My PCP referred me to a neurologist who told me to go back on Xanax. I had already taken myself off both Xanax and Allegra because I just knew the interaction of these meds plus the one dose of Trazadone was behind my symptoms. I said yes to Xanax again because I just couldn't sleep.

Homebound with a husband who didn't know how to help, I would lie in bed for hours wondering if Scott would come upstairs to check on me. Dragging myself downstairs to fix a sandwich, I could barely hold my head up to eat. To get back to bed, I crawled up the stairs. Luckily, our friends drove me to doctor appointments and took Scott grocery shopping.

I was so disappointed that I couldn't attend my soon to be

daughter-in-law Charlie's wedding shower. Although I was upset about missing it, I knew I couldn't have sat very long—and certainly didn't want to put a damper on the party.

On August 17 my PCP reviewed a blood draw and prescribed Florinef Acetate, although I can't remember why. I took one tablet each day for two days and ended up back in the ER with another bout of uncontrollable shaking. The ER doctor wanted me to hold my Xanax dose steady and take half a tab of the Florinef for two days, then stop and meet with an endocrinologist.

I was at my wit's end. Each new doctor had the same answer: more drugs. One doctor told me that Xanax is highly addictive, yet didn't try to help me wean off it. Determined that I would be Xanax free within a two-week period, I found an article online that explained how to do this. And I did!

In October, I was able to go back to work part-time, but my symptoms did *not* go away. I wasn't sleeping well and although I was giving presentations, many times I couldn't concentrate on what I was saying. The weird sensations would come and go at the most inopportune times. Old symptoms went away and new ones appeared. Eventually I went back to work full-time.

In November, I started taking Tylenol for pain in my left arm. At 5:00 a.m. on February 8, 2012, I started shaking uncontrollably again. Scott called an ambulance. As soon as the paramedics got me to the ER, the shaking stopped. By the time the ER doctor came in to see me, I looked pretty normal. Explaining my previous issue with Xanax and Trazadone, as well as how long I had been taking Tylenol, I suggested I was having another severe reaction.

After a quick examination, his demeanor implied that it was all in my head. "I'm writing you a prescription and you can go home," he said.

"Can I ask what you are prescribing and why? I questioned.

"Ativan," he said, with no explanation.

"No, I don't want any drugs," I exclaimed. Surprised, he had no other suggestion but to see my PCP. Instead, I saw my chiropractor later that morning. While she adjusted me, she could feel me shaking. At least she believed me and I stopped taking Tylenol.

Two nights later, I woke up shaking again. The Tylenol wasn't completely out of my system. I didn't want to go to the ER again, because I was tired of being made to feel like a loony toon. I woke Scott up and asked him to hold me. "If I look like I'm not breathing or start shaking really hard, call an ambulance." He held me while I shook for 45 minutes. It happened a few nights later for 15 minutes, so I felt the Tylenol was almost out of my system. Since then I have taken one, maybe two Tylenols, each time with a reaction. Otherwise my body has been drug free.

A month or so later, my PCP suggested that my symptoms might be due to a mental problem—even though one of the meds she put me on caused the shaking. I stood my ground. "I am open to any suggestions and even thought of this myself, but I know my mind and body," I said. "I've always had sensitivities to medications. So, no, these symptoms have nothing to do with a mental issue, but a chemical imbalance from interactions with medications."

Plenty of people out there are having these same issues but don't have the gumption to question medication interactions with their doctors. Hey, it's not easy for me either. If there was anything I had learned during Scott's heart transplant and aspergillus ordeal, it was that I needed to stand up for myself as well as for Scott. It was daunting, to be sure, but I wasn't going to let a doctor or drugs ruin my body and the rest of my life.

Take this for that, take that for this, and before you know it, you are up to 10 medications and each one has their own side effects. Doctors really need to be able to help those of us who have serious side effects without bringing up the mental card. They also should at least consider that the patient knows and understands his/her body better than anyone else.

A doctor who can't treat this issue should own up to it and help the patient find someone who treats medication interactions. It has taken me years of taking no medications (except for hypothyroidism) to start feeling normal again. And I did it pretty much all on my own, listening to my body and taking copious notes along the way. In looking back at my life today, I am so thankful that I followed my intuition as I needed to be as healthy as possible in order to be there for Scott.

Note to Caregivers:

I don't mean to scare you about medications, but I do want to remind you that medications can profoundly affect your body. Caregivers are only human. If you aren't careful, you can become dependent on drugs that may have serious side effects the longer you take them. I am not talking about drugs for chronic illnesses like diabetes or heart disease. These medications are needed to keep something more serious from happening, and even with side effects may be needed for your overall health *and* to keep you alive. Scott was on a slew of medications and was lucky that the only side effect he ever really had was flushing from Niaspan. The power of drugs can be magnificent and alarming all at the same time.

No, I am talking about medications you don't need to take. If you feel you are having side effects or have become addicted, I hope you will find and talk to a doctor who will guide you to a better solution. And remember that alcohol, marijuana, and caffeine are also drugs. Being a caregiver is the most difficult job you will ever have. It tests your limits and causes stress and anxiety that no one understands unless they have been through it themselves. You have enough on your plate, so listen and be kind to your body, because your life matters, too.

17

Acts of Kindness

In 2014, both Scott and I started noticing serious memory loss. Learning the ropes on a new job, I was exhausted every night, usually falling asleep before 10:00. Still, I noticed Scott doing and saying the strangest things, forgetting where he put his wallet or phone, and crying about things he did or did not do.

He had also been complaining that he couldn't see very well, even with glasses. An ophthalmologist confirmed that he had cataracts, and operated on Scott's right eye in early January 2015. Four weeks later came surgery on the left eye.

About the same time, I was laid off. At age 62, I was finding a very real discrimination for older workers and feeling more vulnerable than ever. But I was grateful to be home, as Scott was unable to follow instructions on how and when to take the three different eye drops pre- and post-surgery. Even with his confusion, it still wasn't registering that something more serious was developing. Once the cataract surgeries were over, we talked about what might be wrong.

When the movie *I'm Still Alice* came out in theaters, we decided to see it, wondering if Scott could have Alzheimer's. As we walked out of the theater he said, "I think this is what's wrong with me." We were both distressed and scared contemplating what this meant to each of us. Scott was probably wondering how this would all end. I was wondering what new caregiving roles I would need to play. During Scott's aspergillus pneumonia, I had many talks with God. I asked Him/Her that whatever happened from this point on, to please let my body and spirit be able to handle it. My biggest fear was that the caregiving at home would require me to lift, and I knew my body—especially my back—could not handle that.

On March 17, 2015, Scott's PCP listened to our concerns and referred us to a Memory Care Class about dementia. On June 2, we met with the memory doctor and a social worker. Dr. Canby, a geriatrician and the director of the memory clinic, took Scott into a room to ask questions, assess his responses, and give him a verbal and written test. Meanwhile I met with the social worker to find out where to get support as a caregiver. Once the doctor was done with Scott, the three of us met to discuss her findings, and she set up an appointment with a neuropsychologist for more testing.

On July 16 we heard for the very first time that Scott had Alzheimer's. Even though the neuropsychologist confirmed what we already believed to be true, it was still devastating to hear. Scott was told he could no longer drive and I was torn by the 'what now' quandary. How much more could either of us take? Why Scott? Why us? It didn't seem fair. We both cried and held hands as we walked out of the medical building.

From this point on, Scott was a patient with the memory clinic, who along with the PCP stayed in close contact as the disease progressed. After talking to the heart transplant doctors in Santa Clara, we decided to see a Santa Rosa cardiologist for all further tests related to Scott's heart. This doctor would be our go between with the Santa Clara heart transplant office. The two of us also agreed he would *not* be put on any Alzheimer's related meds. Adding another drug to his already fragile body did not seem like a good idea.

Now I could see that the decision to change to Kaiser back in 2011 was one of the best decisions I had ever made. Kaiser had protocols in place for determining what was causing a patient's memory loss and ensuring that the diagnosis is as accurate as possible.

When Scott and I found out he had Alzheimer's, I had begun working for Catholic Charities just a couple of months before. This was the happiest I had ever been at any job. Everyone, from the CEO to the management team to my immediate supervisor, showed ethics and an integrity that I had never found in any other work setting. And even better, Catholic Charities sponsored an adult daycare program, the Shaw Center for Memory Care. The compassion we were shown by my coworkers after receiving Scott's Alzheimer's diagnosis gave us a feeling of hope. We knew we were not alone.

Note to Caregivers:

Next time you think it can't get worse, that life is getting you down, and you can't seem to get out from under it, remember that it's not about what's happening—it's about the people that are there helping you get through what's happening. And when your current situation has ended (no matter what the outcome), remember the blessings you received and share them with others.

We aren't meant to go it alone, we are here to help and guide each other. Sometimes you are the giver, sometimes the receiver. Life is a give and take. Through all the ups and downs that Scott and I went through, we were always encountering acts of kindness. From the doctors and nurses to our sons, family, friends, and people we met along the way, we received compassion and thoughtfulness in our time of need. As you read the next chapters, I hope that you will feel the power and benevolence of these earth angels that appeared time and time again. And just know that by asking for what you need, you will receive the comfort, love, and hope to help you along the way. You only need to believe.

*(Note: The following organizations offer tips for caregivers and families of people with dementia, facts about the forms of dementia, resources, and more: the Alzheimer's Association at **www.alz.org** or call **1-800-272-3900** for local offices and support groups; the U.S. Department of Health and Human Services (HHS) at **www.Alzheimers.gov**; and the National Institute on Aging at **www.NIA.nih.gov**.)*

18

The Shoe Is on the Other Foot

Monday, August 10, 2015: While coming to grips with Scott's new diagnosis and trying to live in the moment, I was afraid for the future. What would this new normal have in store for me and what, pray tell, was the good in this for Scott? How would we find hope and joy through these next years of our lives? Where would we find support and solace? How would I live each day as I watch my husband change?

Most of the time, Scott seemed perfectly normal. Then out of the blue, something he said or did reminded me that he wasn't.

Over breakfast, Scott told me, "Our trash can was pushed over and I had to put everything back into the can. I put it away with the recycle bin."

"Why didn't you leave it out so the garbage collectors could pick it up?" I questioned.

With confidence he said, "It's the same truck that picks up both cans."

I didn't think this was true, but thought, *What do I know?* When he claimed to have put our next door neighbor's cans away, too, I started to wonder. We walked outside to find all four cans still out in front. As we walked back into the kitchen, I felt sad for both of us.

This afternoon, I called Kaiser to make an appointment with my PCP to talk about my thyroid symptoms. The representative asked for my address. As I rattled it off, I saw Scott look up at me. After I hung up, he asked, "What's our address?" I repeated the number and the street when he said, "No, it's 2015." I explained that our address is 2014 and that the year was 2015. "Oh, yeah," he said, looking quite embarrassed.

Friday, August 14: I took Scott to his PCP for a referral to the chiropractor. After the exam, Dr. Thorburn suggested that Scott get an X-Ray since Scott mentioned his back had been hurting for five months. This surprised me as he never told me he was having back pain.

As we were standing in line at the radiology imaging department waiting to check Scott in for the X-ray, Scott asked, "So I guess I'll go sit down and wait for you?"

Perplexed, I said, "No, the X-ray is for you and you need to stay in line with me to check in."

Looking surprised and confused, he asked, "It's for *me*?"

Saturday, September 5: Yesterday, Scott went for a bike ride while I went to see my PCP for a check-up. When I got home, Scott was walking around mumbling and seemed really upset. He couldn't find his wallet and cell phone. After calming him down, I used my cell to call his phone. I could hear a faint ringing in the garage. Both the phone and wallet were sitting on top of his SUV. He was relieved and I was thankful that they didn't get into the wrong hands. As we hugged, Scott was crying softly. Trying to comfort him, I murmured, "It's okay, honey, it's just the disease and we'll get through this together. I am *not* going anywhere."

Tonight Scott barbecued six turkey burgers and veggies. I prepped the food, got it on foil and sprinkled the veggies with herbs and spices. We really were a team now: fixing dinner together, setting up the TV trays, and a TV show to watch. When everything was cooked, Scott brought the food inside to dish out. After serving myself, I sat down in the family room and turned on the TV to find the latest *Medium* TV show.

After Scott sat down, I glanced at his plate. Something seemed odd, though. All the veggies were on one side and *all* five remaining turkey burgers were piled one on top of the other. I was blown away.

"Scott?" I asked softly.

"What?"

"I don't think you can eat that many burgers." He didn't laugh so I didn't laugh, although I thought it was a cute faux pas. I knew he was confused so I didn't want to make a big deal about it, yet I could see that he was annoyed with himself. *(Note: In looking back, I find it baffling that Scott could actually cook the burgers, yet couldn't grasp that he had put too many on his plate.)*

Monday, September 7: This is getting scary. Tonight at 6:00, I fixed chicken breast, baked potato, and a salad for Scott. I had eaten while he was napping. At 9:00 p.m., I went to use the microwave finding Scott's dinner still inside. When I asked him about it, he said he thought he had eaten it earlier. Luckily, he had eaten the salad.

Did I confuse him when I gave him the salad, which is why he forgot to go back to the microwave to get the main course? Should I be monitoring him better? I just don't know.

Wednesday, September 9: While shaving my legs last night, I pulled my back really bad. It was the worst pain ever and I was afraid to take any medication. As I lay in bed, I wondered if I would be able to get to the toilet. I told work that I wouldn't be able to go in the rest of the week, and thankfully Scott helped me the best he could.

When I started to shiver, I rubbed arnica on my back which helped my body relax and me feel better. Scott went downstairs to bring up his prescription of Vicodin in case I couldn't take the pain. I hadn't taken acetaminophen since 2012 but I knew I might need something if the pain got worse.

By early morning the pain *was* unbearable. A half tab of the Vicodin helped immensely. During the next few days, I took two more half tabs until the pain subsided enough to stop. This was probably the fifteenth time my back had gone out since 1991 and by far the worst. And I was just shaving my legs. Looking back, I realized I had lifted too many things during the weeks before.

Sunday, September 13: Matthew took Scott and me to see the chiropractor yesterday, Scott for a foot adjustment and me for the lower back, and then to the grocery store. With Scott walking slow and me even slower, I'm sure Matthew felt like his parents were falling apart.

When we got home from the store, Scott complained that his right foot was hurting…a lot. I was thinking, *What now? We just went to the chiropractor and I know she adjusted your feet.* Just as I was going to suggest he take his shoes and socks off so I could take a look, I noticed his shoes were on the wrong feet. Maybe the same problem happened to the person who fashioned the saying, "The shoe is on the other foot", or maybe it was just a lightbulb moment. I was relieved that we were able to solve the issue so quickly, yet disheartened to know that Scott couldn't figure this out on his own.

Feeling the need to take care of myself and my back right now, I am resolved to give notice at Catholic Charities. I just don't think I can work *and* take care of Scott—it's too overwhelming. Luckily, I started collecting Social Security benefits in January, so while money will be tight, I believe it is doable. And I feel so relieved!

Sunday, October 25: Around 8:00 last night, Jonathan called to say Charlie's water broke while they were eating at La Vera Pizza. They went to the hospital early this morning but the baby wasn't coming, so early afternoon Charlie said she was standing at the end of the bed rocking to help him come down. It seemed to work as she had a normal delivery a half hour later.

Our new baby grandson, Killian, weighed in at 6 lbs. 4 oz and is 19 1/2 inches long. He's perfect and beautiful and we are so excited to be grandparents for the first time.

Sunday, December 6: At the end of September, I started noticing a smell in the house whenever the air conditioner came on. I ignored it and tried not to use the air. But as it started getting colder, we needed to use the heater as Scott gets chilled easily.

On October 20, I called a HVAC company, which convinced me to get a new heater. Our 24-year-old heater was replaced on November 5, but that didn't solve the problem. Now we had two smells, the original and the new heater smell that was like a chemical odor. Over the next month the HVAC company tried different fixes trying to get the odors to go away. The odors were causing a burning pressure in my chest and Scott developed a cough. Frantic and scared, I was worried he'd come down with another pneumonia.

On the Tuesday before Thanksgiving, we moved into the Hilton Hotel for 10 nights. It was worrisome leaving Bob Kat alone, but I didn't know what else to do. We went to the house twice a day to feed and check on our girl. Scott never went inside the house as it remained 45 degrees during the day *and* he was still coughing.

For Thanksgiving, Bill and Marilyn invited us for a turkey dinner at the Quail Inn. I'm not sure we were good company, but we were happy to be with friends who tried their best to make us feel better. We were thankful and surprised when Bill insisted on paying. It gave Scott and me a feeling of not being completely alone in this unsettling situation.

On Tuesday December 1, the HVAC company installed new duct work. Bob Kat came back to the hotel with us, but she wouldn't eat or sleep. The outside noises had her watching the hotel room door. She could hear people walking around all hours of the day and night keeping her on high alert. Wednesday night she crawled under the covers with me, but sometime during the early morning I found her cowering under the bed.

Early Thursday morning, we loaded up the car with kitty stuff. We weren't sure if pets were allowed and didn't want anyone seeing her. So as the sun rose behind Fountaingrove's Round Barn, Scott carried the cat carrier by a few maintenance men working outside. The way they were watching us made us feel like thieves in the night. When we got to the house, I took Bob Kat inside to set up her food, water, and litter box while Scott waited in the car.

We moved back home the following day. As I unpacked kitchen essentials, I could smell smoke from a neighbor's fireplace coming in through the microwave vent. Apparently, the appliance company that installed our new microwave in January neglected to hook up the vent. Our neighbor and handyman, Greg Hurst, came over today to fix it.

The master bathroom has also been smelling disgusting on and off. After Greg left today, I went into the master bathroom to use the toilet. OMG—it smelled like a sewer. I was starting to feel like I was in a sci-fi movie and the house was alive trying every which way to get us to move out and never come back.

Greg was kind enough to come back over. He explained that a dried P-trap will result in a sewer odor from a sink or tub that hasn't been used in a while.

"What? Are you kidding me?" I was laughing and crying at the same time. We went around to the two showers, bathtub, and sinks to run the water. Guess what? The smell is gone. Who would have thunk! The funny part for me was that every time Greg said P-trap, I thought he was saying *Pee* Trap. I was giggling a lot, but mostly from relief that it was a simple fix.

The worst, though, is that because the original smell triggered respiratory problems for both of us, Scott had an X-ray on December 3. Since that didn't show anything, the heart transplant doctor ordered a CT Scan. They found a spot on his lower left lung and a biopsy is scheduled for December 10.

Now that we are back home, Scott doesn't seem as disoriented as he had been. Hopefully, the smells are behind us and the biopsy proves to be benign.

Note to Caregivers:

As I was writing this chapter, I could feel the enormity of our situation once again. Just when you think the worst has happened, something else turns up. I wish I could say that I made all this up, but a novel this is not. *(Although the spot on his left lung went away on its own, fortunately.)*

No matter what you are going through with your loved one, just know that there is someone watching over both of you. It may not seem like it, but life's challenges are a part of your journey. Feel your guides and angels sending you healing light to help get you through. They are so proud of you and what you've accomplished. And remember...you may not be able to change the outcome, but you can always change your reaction and attitude about any situation. So as you go about your day, when something feels out of your control, stop, feel, and know that you are never alone. Meditate on that!

19

How Do You Say Goodbye?

Wednesday, December 23, 2015: The house still smells. For the past three weeks, we have been living in our house without using the new heater. Instead we purchased three small heaters to keep us warm. Grasping at straws, a biologist from an indoor air quality company came out to perform an inspection last Thursday. We moved out for a night, leaving Bob Kat at home. The report showed four compounds during an eight-hour period with the heater at 72 degrees. We are still waiting for the final results, but the air quality report confirms that it is a toxic chemical. The really sad part is that Scott can't help me—not with figuring this out or making decisions. And I am running out of options.

Christmas Eve around 10:00 p.m. as we were watching TV, I saw something shadowy moving down the hallway towards me. It was Bob Kat and she was walking funny, limping on her back-left paw. I picked her up to calm her and see if I could figure out what was wrong. When I put her down on the floor, she limped over to her bowl for her treats. "Scott," I said, "we need to take her to the vet right now."

Since our vet was closed for the holiday, we took her to a local veterinary hospital. The vet believes Bob Kat has arthritis and put her on pain medication. This made her lethargic, so on Saturday we took her to a different vet hospital. There weren't any new findings so we waited until Monday to get her into our vet.

After a thorough exam, the doctor gave us the bad news. He could feel a big lump or tumor in her belly area. X-rays and blood work were done while we waited. Bob Kat spent the night to see if antibiotics and other treatments would make a difference. I was starting to wonder if our sick house had caused not just our respiratory issues but Bob Kat's tumor.

After leaving the vets, we went home to pack to move into the Sandman Motel. Even though the packing was up to me, I was thankful that Scott was able to carry most everything to the car and into the room. It may sound weird, but I felt safe in that compacted motel room with Scott. *(Note: It was in this room I came to realize that Scott wasn't able to set up his weekly meds anymore: a new task for me that included ordering, keeping referrals up-to-date, and making sure he took his meds correctly.)*

We met with the vet on Tuesday to discuss Bob Kat's options. Scott and I decided before the appointment that if he recommended surgery and could not guarantee a positive outcome, we would put her to sleep. She was already taking medication for a hyperthyroid condition, and she was 13. We did *not* want to put Bob Kat through any heroic measures to lengthen her life, especially if she needed ongoing treatments. The options the vet suggested were not promising. The next day, with heavy hearts, we put Bob Kat to sleep. We were both with her when she took her last breath, talking to her, expressing our love to help her on her journey to cross over the Rainbow Bridge. We said goodbye to our sweet baby girl.

January 2016: The month of January had us in and out of motels. The HVAC company agreed to remove the new heater and negotiated a settlement. Installing a Bryant heater stopped the chemical smell, but the original smell was still there whenever the heater came on. All during this time, Greg continued to look for the source of the odor. Going to and from the house and the motel made Scott anxious, but he seemed to understand that I was trying to protect both of us from getting sick and never complained.

Living in a motel was getting expensive, so on February 5 we moved into a two-bedroom apartment close to the house. Every day I would go to the house to do laundry or meet someone who may or may not have a solution.

Tuesday, February 16: Greg called. "I don't want to get your hopes up, but I think I found where the smell is coming from." When he tore out the linoleum in the laundry room there was a disgusting odor and he wanted us to come over to check it out. We did. Yes, this was the smell. Hallelujah!

Removing the same linoleum in the downstairs bathroom, he found mold and mildew in the shower walls. Remodeling would take care of the problem, and we could move back home.

But wait! Scott's Alzheimer's symptoms were increasing. He was having a hard time going up and down stairs. Frequently, our Alzheimer's Caregivers' support group discussed the importance of moving before it was too late. I felt that we were in the perfect position to sell the house and continue to live in the apartment while looking for a new place.

By March 25, the remodeled house went on the market; on April 13 it went into escrow. Now I had a house full of furniture, dishes, etc. to get rid of or move into the apartment. My work was cut out for me.

Moving had its own set of obstacles and I am happy to say that many people helped us get through them. Marilyn helped me go through bedrooms deciding what to keep and what to let go. She was the perfect person to help me clear out photos that were already on my computer— and she carried packed boxes downstairs.

Penny Grillo, a beautiful and engaging woman who lived right above us in the apartment complex, helped pack and move boxes over to the storage unit above the apartment carport. She also helped me with an all-day garage sale. What a lifesaver!

We kept only the furniture that would fit in the apartment. The rest was sold or given away. Both the Salvation Army and the Catholic Charities' thrift shop picked up furniture and odds and ends.

I kept wondering why I wasn't upset about moving out of our house of 25 years. In my heart I must have realized that Bob Kat would always be with me in spirit, Jonathan and Matthew were now grown men with their own lives, and Scott needed a safer place to live. We had been living in the apartment for three and a half months and it already felt like home. I didn't worry about Scott going up and down stairs as everything was flat. I guess the fiasco with the smell was God's way of pushing me out and toward a new place.

On the day the movers drove everything to the apartment, I took one more walk through every room trying to feel the memories, the laughter, and all the love that lived and breathed in this home. There were no tears, no regrets, just a realization that our lives were moving on. Feeling a lightness I hadn't felt in a while, I locked the front door for the last time, and got into the car where Scott was waiting.

Our lives started to settle down after the house was sold. Now our weekends were spent looking for a new place. To say I was being particular would be putting it mildly. Not only was I looking for a safe house for Scott, but I wanted someplace I would feel happy living in alone. I wasn't dwelling on Scott's passing, but that reality was ahead, and I was getting older too. What would benefit Scott in a home would benefit me in the long run.

While searching for a smaller house or condo with no stairs, minimal landscaping, and the right price, we continued to attend the Alzheimer's Early Stage support groups. Every Tuesday we met with our individual group. The facilitators were loving and compassionate women who truly cared about our individual plights.

Scott thrived in his meetings with other people with dementia. It was here he felt normal and could share his concerns and fears. The caregivers' group constantly heard laughter from their room and we were thankful that our loved ones were able to find an outlet for their frustrations.

We caregivers, though, were a serious bunch. There was a lot to share about our own difficulties in dealing with a person who was literally losing his/her mind. Scared and sad, grieving for what once was, this was our time to express our concerns from the past week. It was a godsend!

The groups became inseparable. For the next two years, we would get together outside of these weekly meetings for lunches and many other enjoyable outings. We sang our hearts out once a month at a group sing-along. Whenever we got together as a group, our lives seemed a little lighter, a little brighter. Since we knew what each other was going through, we never worried about our spouse being misunderstood or looked at with ridicule or exasperation. We had each other's backs and kept each other sane.

At the same time, Scott's friend Bob Evans scheduled golf dates at either the Sonoma County Fairgrounds Golf Course or Northwood Golf Course in Monte Rio. Scott's brother Gil also made it a point to take him out for breakfast or lunch. And I can't forget Scott's friend RPJ, who made it a point to stay in Scott's life while also helping me with odd jobs that we couldn't do ourselves. Not only did these outings give Scott something to look forward to, but they gave me a break.

Sunday, June 12: We celebrated Scott's 65th birthday a day early at Mary's Pizza Shack. After an early dinner, all of us—Janice, Olga Lee, Marilyn, Bill, RPJ, Charlie, Killian, Scott and I (Jon and Matthew weren't able to join us)—drove across town to see a house we were thinking of putting an offer on. Scott was ecstatic when Gil and Cynthia showed up, too.

This place had everything we wanted: no steps into the house, beautifully maintained, two bathrooms with one walk-in shower, plus gorgeous brickwork and landscaping in the backyard. A beautiful house except for one drawback—it was only 892 square feet. Even though we decided not to put an offer down, just being with family and friends made our day.

Meanwhile, we are diligently looking and have a possibility over in the Coffey Park area today. We are not worried as I'll know when the perfect house appears; there will be no obstacles and it will go right through.

Note to Caregivers:

I won't sugar coat it—selling our home of 25 years wasn't an easy decision. Yet, I know that in every stage of my life, I was making adjustments in order to be in the best living situation. Is it time for you to make that move?

Walk around your home and look for obstacles. With paper and pen in hand, note anything that could cause a fall or that needs fixing. Once you've got your list, sit down to determine what is fixable. Can you add handicap grab bars to your shower? Is that tub more of a handicap than a way to relax? Can you install a ramp so the stairs are no longer dangerous? Can you remove rugs that might cause a fall?

If you find that most of the obstacles on your list are hazardous and not fixable, you may need to consider moving. There are placement services and eldercare advisors that can help you locate a new home and help you with the moving process. Sonoma County has a Senior Resource Guide that includes housing placement services, repair and weatherization, legal aid, utility and rent deposit, emergency and transitional housing, low income and subsidized housing, and mobile homes. A quick check on the Internet for your county resources will help you find these services, including how to contact your local senior center.

20

Your Mom's in
the Shower

Monday, July 25, 2016: Last night Scott had fallen asleep in his chair. When he woke up, he asked, "Where's the Queen?" He meant Bob Kat. After reminding him that she had passed away last year, I felt awful. It is difficult in the moment to know what is appropriate to say so as not to cause pain or more confusion. Thankfully, Scott remembered and didn't seem upset.

Tuesday, September 20: Scott and Bob were planning to play golf but Bob hadn't called him back to confirm a time. In the early afternoon, Scott came out of the bathroom asking if he could take his wallet.

"What for? I asked.

"For golf with Bob," he informed me.

I asked him if he was confused as Bob hadn't called yet. Then said, "And when he does call back, it will be to let you know what time for tomorrow."

Later, I realized that asking Scott whether he was confused was a big no-no. I'm still learning how to respond when his reality is skewed. A kinder response would have been, "Bob hasn't called back yet, but

I believe he wants to play golf tomorrow. And yes, you should take your wallet."

Monday, October 10: Finding a new place hasn't been easy. Fortunately these past months, Scott and I have been spending a lot of time at Jon and Charlie's house or meeting them for lunch and dinners. I'm glad they want to spend time with us, and seeing Killian is an added benefit. We've also been invited to house parties with their friends, who treated Scott with the utmost respect. Weeks have turned into months without any property that meets our needs. But I'll know our new place as soon as I walk in that front door. Soon, I hope.

During the night, Scott got up to gargle with ACT mouthwash as his mouth was dry. After reading a note reminding him to fast for lab work, he woke me up. He was worried that he messed up the fasting. Having only gotten one hour of sleep, I was not happy. After explaining that he didn't mess up the fasting since he didn't eat anything or swallow the mouthwash, I realized how annoyed I sounded. As I tried getting back to sleep, I could hear him crying in bed.

Part of the lab work was to give a urine sample. The lab tech told Scott to fill the cup as much as possible, but he couldn't urinate. Since there was a bottle of water in the car, out we went so he could drink it. That worked as he was able to complete the sample. Between the first time he attempted it and the next, only about a half hour had gone by. Forgetting to remind him to fill the cup up, when he came out of the restroom it was only a fourth filled. Thankfully, the lab tech said it was good enough.

Later while fixing breakfast, I realized that I hadn't seen Scott for about seven minutes. I found him in the bedroom trying to put his jacket on a hanger. He had the jacket laid out face down on the bed but couldn't figure it out from there. After helping him with a task that I don't even need to think about, I let him know it was okay to ask me for help.

Thursday, October 20: Last Saturday, Janice met Scott and me for the Walk to End Alzheimer's. There were over 50 booths with companies that catered to seniors. Almost all of them were giving away healthy snacks and munchies. Scott and I had already eaten but that didn't keep us from sampling. It was a beautiful balmy day and I was able to get some gorgeous photos of people playing with giant bubble wands blowing out all the colors of the rainbow. Scott couldn't walk very far or fast, but Janice stayed with us as only a considerate and loving friend would.

Around 5:00 tonight, I asked Scott to go outside to check the weather. When I came out of the bathroom, I noticed that Scott wasn't in the apartment. I was frantic as I went outside to look for him. I could hear him but couldn't see him. He was knocking on the next-door neighbors' sliding glass door. Back inside our apartment, Scott walked into the bedroom and cried. I held him until he calmed down, then suggested we go next door to explain. Since the neighbor didn't know he had Alzheimer's, I described how Alzheimer's affects the memory. "So if you see him outside looking confused, please help him come back home."

Tomorrow RPJ is taking Scott to lunch. Concerned that RPJ wouldn't know he needs to stay with Scott at all times, I sent him this email: *We'll see you tomorrow around 11:15 or so. Just want you to know that Scott is getting worse. He tried to go into someone else's apartment today and was very upset about it. When you are with him, please don't let him out of your sight. If he needs the restroom, maybe you should go with him. I'll give him some cash, but he'll need help ordering and paying for his meal.*

Tuesday, November 22: As I walked out of the bathroom to go back to bed, Scott opened his bedroom door. As he stood there staring at me, I watched and waited for him to speak. Finally he said, "Why were you yelling *Scott*?"

"I wasn't…you were probably dreaming, so you can go back to bed."

There are so many things that Scott can't seem to remember anymore. One day he asked me if Engelbert Humperdinck was singing on the CD in the car. I wasn't sure, so we ejected it and it was. Now every day since, he asks me who's singing on this same CD.

The last few times Scott made egg salad sandwiches, he asked me how many eggs he needed. I told him he usually ate just one as he doesn't like it when egg salad squirts out of the bread. When I looked over to see what he was doing, he had peeled two eggs and was working on the third.

Sunday, December 11: When Scott woke up this morning, he didn't know where I was. He told me that he wondered whether I had gone to the store or to see Jonathan, but he never thought to open my bedroom door where I was asleep.

Later, while I was in the bathroom, Scott called Jonathan from his cell phone. That was strange in itself because he never calls anyone. He told Jon that I was asleep in the bedroom since I was so tired. It was 12:30 in the afternoon. I walked out to the living room and stopped eight feet away from Scott. He looked right at me as he continued to talk. When Jon asked Scott to give me the phone, he declared, "Your mom's in the shower but I can have her call you back later." Walking over to Scott, I said, "I'm right here. Is that Jonathan?" and he handed me the phone.

While watching NCIS tonight, I was wondering the age of actress Linda Hunt, who plays Heddy. My iPhone showed she was 67. I asked Scott to guess her age—and no, we were not betting.

"Is she 87."

"No," I answered.

"90 something?" Again I said no, then he asked, "Over 100?"

I hinted that she is just a little bit older than we are. He thought about it for a few minutes. "I think I'm in the three digits."

I wanted to go over to hug him as he was so serious and looked so adorable. Instead I said, "That would make you over 100 and you are not *that* old."

He was back to 90 something and wanted to continue guessing. When he suggested 63, I decided to give him a rest. "You are now 65 and the actress who plays Heddy is 67."

Note to Caregivers:

Living with someone who has dementia or any limiting illness can become overwhelming causing you to feel powerless at times.

You can do nothing but whine and complain to whoever will listen—OR you can get involved. Take a class at your local junior college, volunteer at your favorite non-profit, join a yoga or Tai Chi class, spend time with your grandkids, tutor, learn to play an instrument, join a walking group, find a support group—just don't sit at home and feel sorry for yourself. That being said, many caregivers find it therapeutic to talk to a health care professional or spiritual counselor for support and guidance.

If your spouse needs 24/7 care, hire a caregiver so you can get time to do something that makes you feel whole again. If you can't afford a caregiver, ask a friend or family member to help out. I know it's hard asking, but most people want to help. My downfall was trying to get enough sleep so that the witch in me didn't come out. And as a caregiver this problem is difficult to solve, especially if your loved one gets up during the night. Can you afford to pay for a night time caregiver? If not, can a family member take your loved one out during the day so you can relax at home?

By stepping out of your comfort zone and actively getting involved, you will begin to feel a sense of hope and that hope will be expressed outward to your loved one and all you meet. And who doesn't want to be around a hopeful person!

Patience Is a Virtue

Thursday, January 12, 2017: Scott started a class today called PLIE, Preventing Loss of Independence through Exercise. This clinical trial will test a novel exercise program for older veterans with dementia. Although Scott is not a veteran, he was able to join because he is in the Tuesday Alzheimer's Early Stage support group. The goal is to see whether these exercises will help to slow down the disease process. No matter what, it is a great way for Scott to get some exercise and be with other people in his situation.

Scott already knows five other men in the class through our Alzheimer's connections and I am looking forward to meeting other caregivers. I think for him to be in a class without his wife tagging along will help him feel more independent.

Wednesday, January 18: Our power went out at 8:00 p.m. The few candles we had weren't enough light in the apartment and the flashlight on my phone was draining the battery quickly. Over to Target we went to find a flashlight. When we got home, I lit some candles for the bathroom and kitchen then handed Scott a flashlight showing him how to turn it on and off.

Being in the dark threw Scott for a loop. He followed me around wherever I went, which was annoying. But then he would turn his flashlight off and I would need to help him turn it back on. Once in bed, he laid the flashlight on the nightstand with the light facing down. With as much patience as I could muster, I showed him how to place the flashlight with the light shining up. He just couldn't get the concept, though. I think in his mind, he thought he was doing exactly what was being asked, even if he couldn't see the light. A silly pun helps now and then!

Friday, February 3: I blew it. Last night after my shower, I asked Scott if he had taken his meds and he told me he had. I wanted to make sure that he took his Gengraf (brand-name for cyclosporine) at 10:15 p.m. so we could take care of his labs this morning. We left the house at 9:45 a.m. to drive over to Kaiser, Scott had his labs, and we went to the pharmacy to get some cough drops. Everything was going exactly as planned and I had a feeling of accomplishment.

Back home, I began making breakfast. As I was setting the TV tray up with his lunch meds, I noticed yesterday's pill box on the coffee table. *Scott must have put it there last night after he took the last ones for the evening*, I thought. There were meds still in it—the night-time meds that include the Gengraf.

I started yelling. I know I was wrong, but I was so furious at both Scott *and* me. Scott for having this horrible disease and me for not checking to make sure that he had taken those meds. When will I learn?

Last night I sent Scott outside to dump the trash while I was doing dishes. I was almost done washing them when I realized he hadn't come back in yet. I got my shoes on and went looking. He was heading in and I asked him if everything was okay. He said that he got to the door and couldn't remember if he dumped the trash can along with the paper bag. I explained that I only gave him a trash bag. He was so relieved.

Sunday, February 5: I lost it again this morning. I haven't had a good night's sleep for five nights, so I am at my wit's end. We have ants in the kitchen…again. I've cleaned everything, sprayed outside, and put out ant stakes. I told Scott that we can't leave dirty dishes in the sink and he seems to have remembered.

Before I got up, Scott couldn't find the kitchen towels hanging over the dining room chairs to keep away from the ant stakes. He went looking, but not in the drawer where the clean towels are, but above in the second-to-top shelf inside a bowl that you can't see through and pulled out three tea towels used for bread when entertaining. He left these towels right where all the ants have been accumulating. To make matters worse, the countertop is black laminate and the ants blend right in. When I got up to set the timer for his next set of meds, there sat the tea towels covered in ants—and that's when I lost it.

Scott laid down for a nap around 2:30 and me a bit later. I slept soundly until 7:00 p.m. when I needed to go to the toilet. After waking Scott up, we decided on salads for dinner. I instructed Scott to put the forks and knives on the trays. Taking napkins and silverware, he walked over to the trays while I continued putting together the salad fixings. Scott stood there looking at a second napkin on his tray, confused. I walked over to see if I could help him, but other than the extra napkin, he put the fork and knives exactly where they needed to be. I told him everything was good and that he could put the extra napkin away.

While I was washing dishes, I asked Scott to leave the hard-boiled egg slicer out after he dried it to air out. He asked me three different times where to put the egg slicer and each time I repeated, *Just leave it out so it will air out.* And I am happy to say I didn't get upset. *(Note: As I read this while completing our book, I wish I could just grab him, hug him, and love him. I miss him so!)*

Thursday, February 9: When I woke up at 1:50 a.m. to use the toilet, the bathroom door was closed. As I laid in bed waiting for Scott to come out, he finally emerged fully dressed with his shoes on. Perplexed, I explained that it was the middle of the night and he should go back to bed.

The light was on in the living room. When I went to turn it off his pill organizer was not on the TV tray where I left it. When I walked into the kitchen, the empty pill box was sitting on the counter. He had already taken tomorrow's pills. I guess I can't leave his meds out anymore during the night, so I am hiding them in my bedroom.

Since Scott was getting worse, I decided to call Dr. Walker from the Kaiser heart transplant department to ask about Scott's meds. My burning question was, *When do you stop meds for a person who has had a heart transplant and now has Alzheimer's?* She thought I meant stopping his meds now. Stunned by her response, I said, "No, no, I mean way into the future."

She said that a person 10 years out with a heart transplant who stops their meds goes through the same symptoms as someone before receiving a heart transplant: shortness of breath, lethargy, etc. My intent was to find out if he would go quickly, as I want the end to be a blessing, not a drawn-out nightmare.

We went to Trader Joe's tonight after dark. While Scott put the cart away, I waited in the car. As I looked in the rearview mirror, I saw him walk over to a car parked two spots down. He was just getting ready to open the passenger side door *and* there was a woman sitting in the driver's seat. Horrified, I honked the horn, rolled down the window, and called his name. If I had taken the time to get out of the car, he would have opened her door before I could get his attention. Thank goodness he heard me.

Wednesday, February 15: Someone hit my Honda Accord while it was parked so we've had a loaner car for a few days. Before picking the car up from the body shop, we went to the chiropractor. Scott went in first but when he came out he was only wearing a white T-shirt and I knew he came in with a blue shirt over it. After he retrieved his shirt, I was put into the same room where I noticed a pair of sunglasses laying on the table. I took them out to Scott and they were his. I didn't think to check if he had forgotten anything else.

When we finished the paperwork at the body shop and got into my car, I noticed Scott's water bottle wasn't with him. Back to the shop I went where it was waiting right where he left it.

When we got home, Scott couldn't find his phone. It wasn't in the house or the car, so I called the body shop. It wasn't in the loaner or on their counter. Meanwhile, we found that Scott's wallet was also missing.

At this point I was pretty sure he left both of them at the chiropractor's office and sure enough that's where they were. Scott was pretty upset and tired, so I left him at the apartment and went by myself to pick them up. After dinner, I asked Scott if he remembered that his phone and wallet had been missing and that I had found them at the chiropractor's office. He did not.

Saturday, April 8: Last month Dr. Canby gave Scott the Montreal Cognitive Assessment (MOCA) test. In about 20 minutes, it assesses memory, orientation, math skills, and the ability to concentrate. Six months ago, he got 16 out of 30, but this time it was 10 out of 30. Even though I knew his short-term memory was quickly getting worse, this score was very hard to hear. He is now in the middle stages of the disease. My love for Scott is helping me become more aware of how to respond to his disability. I am definitely a caregiver in training as I learn to be more patient and compassionate.

Scott went into the bedroom and after a while came back out with his jacket and hat on. I asked him if he was cold, as I had the slider to the patio open. When he said no, I asked why he put on his jacket and hat.

"I figured we were going out somewhere very soon," he responded seriously. At almost 8:00 p.m., I explained that we were in for the night.

Friday, April 14: Recently I said something to a new friend Diane Benjamin that may have sounded as if I don't love Scott. But I *do* love him and I do *not* know what my world would be like if he weren't in it with me. Twenty-five years of marriage has taught me many things. The biggest one is that I can handle what is thrown my way. I know very deeply that God would not send me a hardship that I couldn't handle, yet I still question whether or not I will be able to handle what's ahead.

Diane's husband, John, is in the PLIE exercise class with Scott. While we waited for the class to end, Diane and I talked about our difficulties in being caregivers. I mentioned that the last time Scott went to see Dr. Canby, he said he wanted to live a very long time. When he said that I wondered if he realized how hard the future will be for him. I told Diane that I don't want him living a very long time, but I didn't clarify what I meant by that. So next time I see her I will tell her that I would, of course, want him to live a long life as long as he can function as he is right now. What I don't wish on Scott is *not* being able to recognize his family and friends, to wear diapers, and not be able to feed himself. At that point, he will need to go into a nursing home as I won't be able to physically take care of him anymore. So no, I do not wish this on him at all.

I said a little prayer tonight for my angels and guides to help me manifest the perfect place for Scott and me to live: a bright and airy kitchen, comfortable walk in shower with handicap grab bars, an indoor laundry room, newer air conditioning and heater, at least two bedrooms with 1-1/2 bathrooms, 1200 square feet or more, move-in ready or *turnkey* as realtors say, front and back yards nicely landscaped with easy access, patio with no steps, quiet neighborhood with wide streets and beautiful trees, newer appliances, garage with easy steps or no steps, walkable neighborhood, very clean and up-to-date, and no odors. Please, no odors!

Monday, April 24: I forgot to put the fan on while taking a shower and called out to Scott so he could turn it on. No response, so I called him again. When he finally opened the bathroom door, he asked, "Where are you?" I was so sad that he couldn't see that I was standing in the tub taking a shower *and* it's a clear shower door.

Today we went to see Dr. Thorburn for referrals to a dermatologist and chiropractor. When we got there, I remembered that I should have reminded Scott to bring his wallet. When I asked whether he brought it, he blurted out, "No, I thought you did."

Before I freaked out, I asked the check-in person what she needed, hoping we wouldn't have to drive back home. She was able to use a photo of Scott on file. When we got home, I photocopied Scott's non-driver photo I.D. and Kaiser's I.D. card in color and put them in my wallet for future visits. Every caregiver should do this!

When the nurse came out to get Scott, I stood up too. She asked me to wait while she took his vitals and settled him in the room. I said, "No, he has Alzheimer's and I need to be with him." She seemed bent out of shape but let me in. There was no way I was going to leave him alone with someone he didn't know.

After the appointment, I asked the front desk to type the diagnosis, ALZHEIMER'S, in big bold letters at the top of his chart. I hope this helps our future appointments.

Wednesday, April 26: During the night, I got up for a glass of milk. The freezer door was open a bit, the ice cream was melting, and the refrigerator was making strange noises. Scott had gone into the kitchen right before he went to bed, so I think the freezer had been open for at least three hours. Ugh! Another thing to check before I go to bed.

Walking back to the bedroom, I saw a light on in Scott's room. Scott was sitting on the bed trying to put on a clean T-shirt, but not over his head. He had already gotten his two feet through the bottom opening of the T-shirt first, then each foot was placed in one of the arm holes. This would have been a superb feat if he were kidding around. But he wasn't and this just broke my heart.

We found a house! The realtor showed us a lovely two-bedroom, two-bathroom, single-level place that had everything we were looking for. Before making an offer, I wrote a letter imploring the owner to consider our situation. Explaining Scott's disability and how long we had been looking for a single story home without any stairs, I expressed how perfectly this unit would fit our needs. It's close to our sons and the HOA fees are less. The lower price means we can afford to remodel the master bathroom and order a new stove and refrigerator. The surrounding area includes a park that includes kiddie slides and swings, walking trail, pool, tennis courts, and bocce ball court. Our offer was accepted before anyone else looked at it. I knew it was our home the moment we pulled up to the driveway, even before we walked in the door. I am so excited.

Note to Caregivers, Friends, Family, Nurses, and Doctors:

"Patience is a virtue", they say. What the heck does that mean? *Virtue* has these synonyms: character, ethics, generosity, goodness, hope, kindness, love, patience, respectability, trustworthiness, to name a few. Sounds to me like virtue is a way of life we should all embrace, whether we are caregivers or not.

But how can caregivers be patient if we never get a break? You've been reading my frustrations at the medical community entrusted to care for Scott and frustrations with myself when I can't seem to keep it all together. There isn't any way a person who is thrown into 24/7 caregiving can be expected to be 100% on all the time. I'm the perfect example!

If you know someone who is a caregiver, call and ask what *you* can do, like taking them out to eat, offering to go grocery shopping, offering to stay with their loved one, or taking their loved one out so they can get some time at home alone. Think about what you would want from someone if you were in their shoes. Don't wait for them to ask!

Nurses and doctors can stock waiting areas and exam rooms with brochures from organizations that help caregivers find support. When a patient arrives with a caregiver, ask the caregiver if there is anything they need help with. Train your staff to be mindful if they notice an overstressed caregiver who needs support.

There are always people who will tell a caregiver, "You can handle it. It can't be *that* bad." Lucky for us, Scott's PCP knew our dilemma. While he was, of course, first concerned about Scott's welfare, he also asked about me. He let me know that my caregiving role was important and he took the time to answer all of my questions, always addressing my fears with kindness, respectability, and hope. Now that's virtue!

22

It Broke My Heart

Monday, May 8, 2017: Scott's confusion shows up more often now at the grocery store and the cashiers get annoyed when he does something strange. From now on I will tell the cashier that my spouse has Alzheimer's and we need help with bagging. I did this at Trader Joe's and was given great service. This way the cashier and bagger know that we aren't taking our time, that he really can't help, and bagging is one of those things he cannot do anymore. Otherwise, I am trying to keep an eye on Scott, pay *and* bag all at the same time. And then they get annoyed with me.

It's hard to remember to check on Scott when he is doing a task. He dries the dishes okay, but when it comes to taking a shower, not so good. Just now, I didn't hear anything for a bit, so went in to check. He was sitting on the bed. I asked tentatively, "What are you doing, honey?"

Looking sad, he said, "I don't know." He had put his dirty underwear in the hamper, but he had taken out two clean pairs and put one on. I had him take the clean pair off and give me the other one, then walked him to the bathroom to help him get into the shower. He was fine once he knew what to do. No wonder there are always so many clean pairs of underwear, socks, and T-shirts in the hamper. I need to figure out how to help him, but most times he won't let me.

We hired a contractor to remodel both bathrooms in our new place. We've made a lot of trips to Home Depot getting the perfect tile for the walk-in shower for the master bathroom. Taking one of the drawers from the guest bathroom to Home Depot helped me to choose the right color for a cabinet that will replace the tiny shower in that bathroom. Otherwise, the shower space will be useless.

Saturday, May 20: We visited Jonathan, Charlie, and Killian today. Killian is such a joy and I love running around after him. He lets me grab and kiss him, then runs away again. Using a walkie talkie, Killian was pretend-talking to Grandma on the phone. I loved it!

Scott went in to take a shower at least 45 minutes ago. I wanted to shower, too, so I went to see what was up. He was still sitting on the bed looking confused, with only one sock on and the other sock was nowhere in sight. Opening the dresser drawer, I found his socks all messed up and two pair of underwear in with his T-shirts. It's amazing how I keep forgetting how debilitating this disease is until moments like this.

My heart breaks a little more each day for what he can't do anymore. I can see in his eyes how he feels so much less of a person. And although I try very hard to be patient, sometimes my patience gets so thin that I'm not sure how much more I can take. My voice must sound frustrated when I respond. Sometimes I just finish what I am waiting for him to do.

Thursday, June 8: Scott came into the bathroom to use the toilet as I was getting into the shower this morning. As I dried myself off, Scott stood up from the toilet but didn't pull his underwear up all the way. I asked why but he wouldn't respond.

When he pulled his T-shirt up above his waist, I could see he was wearing two pairs of underwear. The first one was twisted with the second one and it was totally weird. After he sat on the bed, together we pulled down the first pair and the second, and then I showed him how to put it back on. It's difficult to watch my sweet man struggle like this.

Later Scott took a nap. He got up around 5:00 p.m., went to the bathroom, then back to bed. Not wanting to wait much longer, I ordered chicken parmigiana and a salad from Mary's Pizza Shack for dinner. By the time I was done eating, Scott got up.

After he ate, I had him get in the shower. When I checked on him, he was washing his body with shampoo. In that moment, I realized why his hair always looked greasy even after he said he had washed it. When I texted Jon about it, he mentioned a 3-in-1 body wash that can be used as a shampoo as well. Then I texted Jon, '*Yeah, but will he know to use it to wash his hair?*'

Being the smart ass that Jon can sometimes be, he responded with, '*I don't know. Just tell him to wash everything with it.*' We bantered back and forth so I could sound off about how horrible this disease is. We ended on a positive text from me: *Looking forward to seeing my sweet Killian on Sunday. Oh, you and Charlie, too. LOL*

Sunday, June 11: Last night at Jon and Charlie's, Scott and I had a lot of fun with Killian playing Ring Around the Rosie and throwing a ball back and forth. When we were leaving, he waved goodbye for the first time. Killian seemed to warm up to Scott more, too.

At 11:20 p.m., I suggested Scott go to bed. He left the living room for a bit, so I assumed he was getting undressed. But he came back fully clothed, then sat down in his chair. When I asked, he confessed that yes, he was confused. After guiding him to the bedroom, I helped him take off his clothes. He climbed into bed and pulled up the blankets just under his neck. I held his hand and did my best to comfort and help him relax. Each time something new develops, my heart breaks a little bit more.

This afternoon, Bill, Janice, Olga Lee, and two friends from the Alzheimer's support group, Gloria and Geoffrey Brecher, came over to celebrate Scott's 66th birthday. About ten minutes after Bill arrived, he asked if I had seen his glasses. "I've looked everywhere and can bet that I had them on when I got here!" As he looked at me in hopes I had the solution, I decided he was too serious to take him up on that bet.

As Bill and I searched, I noticed Scott's glasses on his nightstand. Yet Bill's glasses were nowhere to be found. Bill went out to his car to make sure he didn't leave them on the console. As I put candles on Scott's birthday cake, Bill wondered out loud, "Wouldn't it be funny if Scott were wearing my glasses?"

Sure enough, Scott was wearing Bill's glasses. Scott was embarrassed, but everyone made light of it. We were laughing at the situation, not at Scott. Later tonight, I talked to Scott about wearing Bill's glasses and he remarked, "That's Alzheimer's for you." We agreed that we need to laugh when these little snags happen and not take them too seriously. After all, we all do crazy things now and then.

Tuesday, June 13: Today is Scott's actual birthday and we celebrated at the Alzheimer's support group with cupcakes. After the meeting, Gloria took me aside to tell me that on Sunday, Scott told her that we wouldn't be going to the support group anymore. He asked Gloria to tell Wally that he would miss him. Now that I'm thinking about it, I wonder if he is confusing the Wally at the PLIE class with the Wally in the Tuesday support group. Now that makes sense!

Later, Matthew came over to the apartment for the first time to wish his dad a happy birthday. Soon after Matthew left for a running meet, Jon, Charlie, and Killian arrived for leftover pizza and my angel hair pasta with spaghetti sauce and meatballs. What do you know, Jonathan liked my pasta with meatballs. He thinks my meals are bland, yet every time he eats something I've made, he loves it. Go figure.

Sunday, June 18: It has been so hot that I've kept us indoors as much as possible for the last couple days. I waited until 7:30 last night to go to the grocery store. After Scott put the bags into the car, he insisted on taking the cart back. Since the cart drop off was close by, I felt Scott could handle this on his own. Besides, I needed to get the air conditioner going.

But then I noticed that Scott had walked by the cart stand and gone back inside the store. Quickly turning off the car, I followed him, petrified that he would get lost. As I got close to the entrance, Scott came out with the cart then put it on the side. He looked relieved when he saw me. I took his hand and we walked back to the car as I tried my best not to show the fear I felt inside.

Monday, June 26: Since Scott can no longer wash his hair and body on his own, I stand next to the tub to help. Since I am usually soaked after his shower, the walk-in shower in our new place is looking pretty good! With a handicap grab bar on the side and back of the shower, he will have an easier time stepping in and holding onto the grab bars and I'll have an easier time rinsing him down with a hand-held showerhead.

We went to Skechers yesterday to find some shoes for Scott, who has been having discomfort with all his shoes. Adding insoles doesn't seem to help. At Skechers, I had to tell Scott to take off this shoe, try on this one, put your sock back on, take the right shoe off your left foot, now put it on your right foot. Sometimes I feel that all I do is tell him what to do. And I pray that I can continue to be as patient as possible.

Today, Scott's foot issue has been solved! It seems that the ball of his right foot hurts when he walks. A local podiatrist, Dr. Hogan, and a Kaiser podiatrist suggested certain insoles and neither worked. Even double insoles were too thin, so I doubled up on the double insoles. That helped so much that Scott decided to go for a walk with me tonight.

Each time we walk I worry that Scott won't be able to find his way home, but I continue to let him try. Our routine is to walk together down one street, make a left, then at the next street I continue on for a longer faster walk, while he makes another left to walk straight back to the apartment, using his key to get in. So far he has found his way home and has been able to let himself in. Tonight I had the strongest urge to take my key as a precaution.

When I was a few blocks from home, I just happened to glance across Waltzer Road where a lone person was walking quickly towards San Miguel. It was Scott. Calling his name, I raised my voice telling him to wait for me. But as soon as he saw me, he started walking towards the curb to cross the street. Traffic was coming both ways and he wasn't looking for cars. Yelling *STOP* at the top of my voice, I watched as he got closer to the curb. I yelled *STOP* one more time, and he stopped.

I was horrified. "What happened, did you get lost?" I asked when I reached him. Well, of course he got lost and he looked scared.

With a look of relief, he related, "When I got to the parking lot, I couldn't figure out where to go."

Once we were home, I stood in the kitchen berating myself for letting him walk alone. Then Scott came in to say he was sorry.

"Sorry for what?" I asked feeling like the worst caregiver ever.

"For getting lost."

"There is nothing you need to be sorry about," I said, and gave him a big reassuring hug. Now I know that when he goes out he needs someone with him at all times.

Tuesday, July 4: When I woke up this morning, Scott appeared to be sleeping, so I went back to bed. Penny was coming over at 10:00 to help pack and move stuff to our new place. When I checked on Scott at 9:00, his eyes were open, but he was panting and said he felt really off and cold. I covered him up with blankets and took a quick shower. When I went back into his bedroom, he was too hot and still panting. I took the blankets off, turned on the fan, and went back to the bathroom to put makeup on.

When I finished, he was very agitated, moving around, touching his forehead, then his arm, squirming all over.

"Do you want me to take you to the emergency room?" I asked. He nodded. "Do you want me to call an ambulance?" He nodded again. The dispatcher kept me on the phone asking questions and comforting me while the paramedics were on their way. Holding Scott's hand and crying had me wondering if this was how it all ends.

At the ER, all the tests came up negative. The ER doctor couldn't figure out what was wrong and I was worried that they would send him home without a diagnosis. Whatever was happening was serious. Another doctor came in looking flummoxed and sat down in front of me. In a very serious and concerned voice, she said, "Explain to me exactly what your husband looked like when he was lying in bed."

I was afraid to say it out loud with Scott laying there watching, but I did because he trusts me completely.

"His body looked like it was in rigor mortis." She looked at me, thanked me, and walked out. Later, I found out that as soon as I said the words *rigor mortis*, she knew exactly what was wrong. After checking Scott's phosphorus level, she found that it was dangerously low.

This new diagnosis is called hypophosphatemia. Thank God, she knew what to ask and I knew how to describe his appearance. Scott spent six hours on an intravenous phosphate drip before he was discharged. He will now need to drink liquid sodium phosphate until his level gets back up to normal. Another condition to monitor!

Saturday, July 8: After handing Scott his sweats and noting he was putting them on correctly, I went into the kitchen. When he came out of the bedroom, the sweats were inside out and backwards. Back to the bedroom we went to help him dress again. When I thought he was good to go, I went to the kitchen again, where I heard him call out, "Do you want me to come out to you?" He was standing in the bedroom doorway in his underwear.

Now you would think that I would have learned to stay with him while he dressed, especially the second time. And it may appear that I was being obstinate, but the sad truth is how many times it took for me to recognize a new challenge for Scott.

Monday, July 10: Yesterday was busy getting moving stuff done with Penny's help; she took lots of boxes, picture frames, and mirrors over to our new place.

Scott was home alone in the apartment while I was at our new place ironing drapes. When I was done, I picked up burgers for dinner. After we were done eating, the two of us lay down together, talked a little, then fell asleep. Afterwards, we went for a short walk—Scott's first walk in a few weeks. When Scott settled into a TV show, I took a longer, faster walk by myself.

Then it was time for Scott's shower. I tried to let him do what he could, like put the towel on the towel bar and his T-shirt on, but when he started to turn his T-shirt inside out, I intervened. To say he was annoyed at me would be putting it mildly. He didn't say anything, but I saw it in his face. Annoyed myself, I left the bathroom to let him figure it out on his own. When Scott was finished dressing, he came into the living room. Looking quite pleased with himself, he announced, "I'm done!"

The bedtime ritual now is to help him get into bed then set up the compact disc player with a favorite CD. Unexpectedly, Scott took my hand and said, "I promise not to wake you up tomorrow morning," remembering that he woke me this morning.

I've noticed that I have more patience with him now, which is a good thing, as losing one's memory must be scary and unsettling. For me, I'm adjusting.

Friday, July 14: After a long and involved situation involving drapes versus grommet curtains, the grommets won out. The drapes were returned and grommet curtains ordered at JCP. As Scott and I walked around the store looking at different curtain patterns, the teal grommets with the diamond and leaf patterns struck my fancy. When I asked Scott which design he wanted for his room, he picked a plain teal. *It must be a guy thing*, I thought.

Yesterday, Matthew treated Scott to the movies and sandwiches so I could go over to the new place to iron the grommet curtains. When the installer came back today I was amazed at the difference the teal grommets made in the rooms instead of the boring beige drapes. So happy!

But I digress. When I got back to the apartment, Matthew and Scott seemed to have had a fun time together and I spent a few moments with Matthew. That evening, a pensive Scott asked, "Who was that young man that took me to the movies today?" It broke my heart that Scott didn't remember his son. When I told him, it broke Scott's heart that he didn't remember.

Later that night while Scott was in bed with the lights out, he called my name. When I came in, he asked if it was Matthew that took him to the movies today, then informed me that he felt very safe with him. He also wanted me to know that he tries to be aware of his surroundings when we are out, that he looks around a little when we are in the store to get his bearings. He knows that I will always be making sure he can see me, but he's told himself that if he loses sight of me, to just stop and wait as he knows I'll be right back. We talked a bit about this and it makes me feel better to know what to do if I lose him in the store—backtrack.

Wednesday, July 19: On Monday, the movers arrived at 8:00 a.m. After we gave instructions and exchanged cell phone numbers, Scott and I left for Chloe's Restaurant to get breakfast. When we were done, we met Marilyn in town so Scott could spend the day with her.

When the movers hooked up the washer and dryer at our new home, the cold water hook up had a small leak and the dryer vent was completely clogged up. The realtor quickly remedied the situation. The washer and dryer are working perfectly in a clean garage. Yeah!

My first shower in our newly remodeled bathroom was heavenly. I closed my eyes as the dirt and sweat washed off my body, sending little streams of soap down the drain. And Scott's first shower Tuesday morning was easier for both of us. For Scott, stepping into a shower stall with handicap grab bars allowed him to stand up straight; for me, having a handheld shower head to rinse his hair and body worked like a charm. The only issue now will be getting his cooperation as he wants to do it all by himself.

Note to Caregivers:

When we first started attending the Alzheimer's support groups, we were dealing with the smell in the house, living in and out of motels, selling our house, moving the rest of our accumulated stuff to the apartment, then looking for a new place to buy. All this upheaval had taken a toll on Scott, not to mention me. In my heart of hearts, I felt sure that I would know when the right place showed up. I trusted in the magic or mystery or whatever you want to call the intuition that is given to us for important times in our lives.

As a caregiver, I've been concerned with Scott's limitations and wanted to eliminate anything that could cause a fall or more confusion. The apartment on the bottom floor with virtually no steps, made it easy for Scott. The way we found it and the feeling I had when I walked into it the first time, told me to take it.

Scott doesn't understand all that has happened but just goes along trusting me to make the right decisions. That trust from him helps me to remember to trust in my God. As long as I listen to my gut or inner wisdom, life in the moment seems to flow. This has worked for me all my life. What I'm trying to say is that if you are trying to find a new, more suitable place, continue to look and watch for signs. You *WILL* know if a move is the right choice, and if you are open to the possibility, you *WILL* know your new home when it is the right one.

23

What Ifs

Monday, July 24, 2017: For weeks, Penny, Marilyn, Matthew, and RPJ have been helping me unpack boxes and put pictures up. Even though Scott couldn't help, having friends and Matthew's help has made it bearable, and I've gotten it done quicker.

It's starting to feel like home. Picture frames, mirrors, and photos line the walls. The dining room table and card table are covered in knick knacks but off to the side to make sure Scott won't trip. I sorted our CDs by artist before placing them in the cabinet, so I can quickly find CDs when Scott asks for one of his. This took a few days, but well worth the extra time.

Each day I make progress, but my back pays the price. I have been careful with lifting and know my limit, so will stop and ice my back when needed—calling it quits when I know I've pushed it to the max.

Tonight I took Scott for an MRI that was ordered after his last ER visit. Per the doctor, I gave Scott a lorazepam (generic for Ativan) before we left the house. As we walked on the sidewalk to the front of Kaiser, Scott stopped cold and told me he didn't want to fall in the hole. I think between the lorazepam and Alzheimer's, he was hallucinating. Taking his hand, I said, "Honey, there aren't any holes, it's just the medication making you feel weird." He trusted me and we arrived in the waiting room without incident.

While waiting, he seemed agitated, looking around and under the chairs. "There's a critter running around and I'm trying to find it," he said. When he almost fell in the dressing room, I showed him how to hold onto the handicap grab bar as he sat down to undress. When he started moving his hands around weirdly, he couldn't tell me why, but it seemed like he thought he was playing with something.

When the technician came to get Scott for the MRI, I explained that he was hallucinating from the medication and to make sure he didn't fall. I wondered how I was going to get Scott safely to the car. Thankfully, when the technician returned with Scott he found a wheelchair and pushed Scott to the car. At home later, I pondered why I didn't think of this solution.

Tonight while I was in the bathroom shaving my legs, Scott came in to say goodnight. "I'll come in to say goodnight after my shower," I reassured. A few minutes later, he came back in to say goodnight, and once more while I was drying myself off. After the last time, I asked him in a comical way, "Do you realize this is the third time you've come in to say goodnight?" He looked at me with a silly expression and we both started laughing. Moments like these are precious.

Saturday, July 29: Early this morning, I heard doors opening and closing. As I opened my eyes, there was Scott in my bedroom staring at me. Getting out of bed, I noticed my bedroom door was closed. As usual, I asked him why he closed the door then realized that he doesn't know the answer to that. He just did.

In the hallway, the bedroom *and* bathroom doors were closed. He was cold, so we got his sweats and socks on, then got him back in bed under some blankets. As I was getting into my own bed, I noticed my bathroom door was closed as well.

When I got up a bit later, Scott was still in bed. I got him up and gave him a bowl of cereal for breakfast. Then he started coughing. After he drank some water, he was still agitated so I gave him a cough drop. As I was getting ready to step into the shower, he came in to say he couldn't stop coughing. Even though Scott never drinks tea, I decided to fix him a cup of a lemon blend. I think this helped calm him down and get rid of the tickle in his throat.

We were meeting Gloria and Geoffrey for lunch at Jeffrey's Hillside Café. Since there wasn't enough time for Scott to take a shower first, I improvised. After I had him change shirts, wash under his arms, and put deodorant on, I combed his hair and we left.

Saturday, August 12: Our day began with a satisfying stop at Chloe's for a decaf latte for me and a peanut butter cookie for Scott. These little treats make Scott happy, which makes me happy. Then onto Kohl's to get some bath mats and Home Depot for a few more household items.

As we drove home, I decided to stop for groceries. It was senior discount day at Oliver's, so the express line was longer than usual. When we got up to the cashier, I handed Scott an empty folded paper bag to hold. While I handled the credit card, the cashier stopped to look at Scott.

"Sir? Are those your apples?" she asked as Scott loaded the empty paper bag with apples the man behind us was buying. Explaining to Scott that they weren't our apples, I helped him take them out of the bag. I explained to the cashier that my husband has Alzheimer's. She seemed to understand, and for that I was grateful.

On the way to the Union Hotel tonight to celebrate Matthew's birthday, I handed a birthday card to Scott, suggesting he might like to give it to him. He looked perplexed and didn't answer. I asked if he knew who Matthew was.

"No, I don't," he confessed. After I explained that Matthew was his son, Scott asked, "Who's the mother?"

Not sure how to answer this question, I blurted out, "You were married before me to Linda and she was Matthew's mom." That seemed to satisfy his curiosity.

During dinner, Scott seemed confused by Matthew's presence, but he did join in the conversation when he felt he could respond. Matthew came to the house afterwards, but I could tell that Scott still wasn't connecting that he was his son.

Saturday, August 19: My former colleagues and I met at Tomatina's for lunch yesterday for my birthday. We don't exchange gifts, but bring a birthday card for the birthday person. Mary was waiting patiently when I walked up, and handed me a card. The envelope wasn't sealed, and the card wasn't signed. Thinking she just forgot to fill it in, I handed it back asking her to sign it. Handing it right back to me, she said it was mine to use for someone else if I'd like. As lunch went on, it became apparent that Mary was having severe memory issues. This was interesting because at our last get together a few months ago I hadn't noticed anything odd.

When Eileen, Toni, Joyce, and I talked about local places like Coddingtown Mall, Kohl's, and the Town of Windsor, Mary would ask, "Where's that?" or "I've never heard of Windsor before," and "I'm not sure I would know how to get to Coddingtown." We looked at each other, wondering silently whether she has Alzheimer's or another dementia. Mary lives alone and has a boyfriend who lives in San Francisco, but we're not sure how often she sees him or whether he can tell that something is terribly wrong. We didn't know what to do and we are a bit scared for her.

Thursday, August 24: Tuesday night we took a scenic drive over to Calistoga for dinner at Scott's favorite Mexican restaurant. He loves their enchiladas, but Scott didn't remember the restaurant. And he certainly did *not* like the enchiladas. These little losses of memory are so sad for me. For him, he just doesn't remember.

Today was Scott's first day at Catholic Charities for the Adult Day Care Program at the Shaw Center. He seemed fine when I left him with the volunteers. When I picked him up he cried, "I was scared when you left." It felt like Jonathan's first day of kindergarten, except back then I was the one who fell apart.

Tomorrow is my 65th birthday and we are going to Howard's Café in Occidental with Gloria and Geoffrey for breakfast. Tonight, Janice and Olga Lee came over to celebrate a day early as Olga Lee is having carpal tunnel surgery tomorrow. Tomorrow night we will celebrate with our sons and regular group of friends. I can't wait!

This email was sent to RPJ for a favor: *'I just dropped Scott off at Catholic Charities for his first day of adult day care. He knows four people from the ALZ support group, so I think he will fit right in. I'm wondering if your barbershop quartet would be willing to volunteer an hour to sing to the people with dementia. There are about 20 people, which includes the volunteers. If you are interested, call the Program Director as she would love to have you sing.'* RPJ said yes which meant the world to me.

Friday, September 1: When I picked Scott up from the Shaw Center yesterday, he seemed to have had a great time, even dancing with the director and a volunteer. He told the ladies that they were going to get him in trouble for telling me that he danced.

Today I got an email from the Program Coordinator: *Julie, I wanted to let you know that Scott was really concerned yesterday about dancing with us because he thought you would be upset. Do you mind letting him know that it is okay if he wants to dance with us?*

When I asked Scott why he thought I'd be upset about him dancing, he seemed flustered. Was he remembering when we first got married and I was a jealous woman with serious PMS?

"Did you want to dance?" I asked.

"Not really," he said timidly.

"It's okay if you don't want to dance, sweetie. I'll let them know not to push it, okay?"

My email reply said: *Scott may not have wanted to dance and please honor his wishes if he says no. Also, please tell Scott that I will not be upset if he wants to dance.*

When we drove by MacDonald's today, Scott kept looking at it like he'd never seen one before. Curious, I asked what he was looking at. "I haven't seen a drive-thru in a long time," he said.

We played the card game War. Scott could read the numbers but had a hard time figuring out which card was higher or lower. To stimulate his brain, I bought a children's puzzle book, but even with my prompting he couldn't understand how to complete these simple brainteasers. I think we'll skip these games. They only remind him how little he can do anymore.

Wednesday, September 13: Last Thursday when I picked Scott up from the Shaw Center he didn't want to leave. Tonight I let him know he was going again tomorrow, which made helping him with a shower and shave much easier.

While Scott is at the Shaw Center, I'll meet Penny at Chloe's for coffee, walk with Gloria, and do some errands. These are things I need for me—to be with people who will respond and nurture me. Otherwise, I'm with Scott, but he's not with me. I'll ask him a question and he either doesn't hear me or doesn't have the capability to respond. Sometimes I have to ask him three times before he acknowledges me.

Scott had already taken off one shoe as he was getting ready for bed, so I walked away to do something else. When I came back, he was retying the shoe he had just taken off. This means that I need to stay with him while he undresses to make sure he doesn't redress himself. It is so hard to see Scott lose the ability to take care of himself—and it takes so much time out of my day to do all that needs to be done. It's probably why I haven't finished putting pictures of the kids up on the wall in the hallway. I'd rather be out with friends when he goes to Catholic Charities.

A Home Health Care (HHC) grant through Redwood Caregiver Resource Center will give me a caregiver three hours a week. This way I will have extra time for myself. After signing up for a six-week course called The Savvy Caregiver provided by the Alzheimer's Association, I realized that the HHC grant wouldn't start until the following week. This past Monday, Marilyn came over to stay with Scott so I could attend. So thankful to have friends like her.

Sunday, September 17: On Thursday, Dr. Canby told us that the MRI taken in July shows that Scott has had some transient ischemic attacks (TIA)—aka mini strokes—over the years. This means that besides Alzheimer's, Scott has vascular dementia. His most recent MOCA test score was a low six, which means he is now between Stages 5 and 6—moderate to severe cognitive decline.

Last night, Scott swallowed his mouthwash instead of swishing it in his mouth and spitting it out. After he went to bed, I hid it under the sink. Tonight he had the hand soap unscrewed. I believe he was getting ready to swallow it, thinking it was mouthwash. I'll need to be more attentive when he goes in to brush his teeth.

Tomorrow a caregiver will come to the house for the first time. I'm nervous but also looking forward to someone else taking care of Scott and giving him a shower. I am hopeful that all will go well as I really need this help.

Thursday, September 28: At the chiropractor last Friday, I was telling her that Scott had an MRI showing he's had TIA's over the years. She was glad that I had told her as she will *not* be adjusting his neck anymore. Apparently, adjusting the neck for someone who has had TIA's could cause serious problems.

When I picked Scott up from Catholic Charities today, he was sitting with one of the volunteers looking out the window. He looked so frail and fragile. The volunteer told me he's such a gentleman and I agreed. Now don't get me wrong, he wasn't always this mellow and sweet, but with the heart transplant, aspergillus pneumonia, and Alzheimer's he has turned into a very loving, kind, and gentle soul.

Our caregiver, Victor, is wonderful. Not only does he give Scott a shower and shave, he sweeps both patios, takes Scott for walks, and putts around the living room with Scott's putter and golf balls. I'm loving this extra help.

Friday, October 6: Scott mentioned that two men tried to take his wide brim hat at the Shaw Center today. We laughed at the thought that there could be a brawl if someone takes something that doesn't belong to them. Time to put his name on his personal items.

I called Laurie White, Scott's Alzheimer's support group facilitator, on Tuesday to talk about Scott's participation or lack thereof. It is obvious to me that he is now in the middle to late stages of the disease and it must be obvious to her. We agreed that this eight-week session would be his last. We've been in these groups for almost two years now. I will be able to stay with my group for one more session and then will need to switch to the Alzheimer's

Transition Group for caregivers whose spouses are in the later stages of the disease.

Earlier this year, Diane (a fellow caregiver and special friend) and I took over coordinating the monthly sing-along for people with Alzheimer's and their caregivers. Together with Shawna, the accompanist, we create a song list and I type up the lyrics. The Alzheimer's Association photocopies the song list and now Luther Burbank Center for the Arts (LBC) has agreed to host the monthly sing-alongs waiving the room fee as well as covering our accompanist fees. This is great news. The sing-along is uplifting for us all and we hope that the Alzheimer's Association will take the program on as its own. Diane and I are planning ahead for the yearly holiday luncheon and figured out how to consolidate expenses in order to lower the cost per person. It'll work!

Monday, October 9, 2017, Day 1 of Tubbs Fire: Last night as we were leaving Jonathan and Charlie's house, my car barely started. Jon checked it and felt confident that the car would make it home but urged me to call AAA in the morning for a new battery.

At 1:00 a.m. this morning, Matthew called to tell me to evacuate as there was a fire raging in the hills behind our place. I got dressed thinking, *Close by? Seriously?* I couldn't fathom what to do. It took me 15 minutes to realize I needed to wake Scott and get him dressed. As I started putting things in the trunk of the car, I realized that the car battery was ready to die.

Half asleep, I started thinking about all the friends and neighbors that needed to be notified and started making calls. I left voice mail messages for Gloria and Janice and texted our neighbor Shawne. After she and I connected, we split the names of other neighbors to call and wake up.

Our power was out, so Janice and her sister Karen came over to help us open the garage door. We couldn't, so we loaded our stuff into Janice's car and went back to their place while they packed.

All five of us arrived at the United Methodist Church around 4:00 a.m. As we connected with Gloria and Geoffrey we were wondering what to do next. Scott and Geoffrey were calm and seemed to trust both

Gloria and me to take good care of them. I had left voice mail messages on both Jon and Charlie's iPhones, but neither one had responded until around 7:00 a.m.

While waiting at the church figuring out where all of us were going to go, I called AAA to have the tow truck driver meet us at home to replace the car battery. Gloria and Geoffrey took us back to the house. The tow truck driver refused to replace the battery because phones were down and he couldn't scan my credit card. Instead he jump started my car. Not thinking clearly due to the stress of the fire and trying to take care of Scott, I turned off the ignition. To make a long story shorter, neighbors were able to jump start the car again. When we finally made it to Jon's house, he bought and installed a new battery.

Tuesday, October 10, Day 2 of Tubbs Fire: The Coffey Park area—about a half mile from our old house and across the street from the apartment complex we lived in for 18 months—was devastated by the Tubbs Fire. Our new place is on the borderline where people are being evacuated, but so far today our area hasn't been mandated. It is very scary, though, as the fires are all around us. Scott and I are staying with Jon and Charlie since our power is out and the smoke is worrisome.

This evening our grandson Killian gave his mom a kiss, then walked over to give me and then Grandpa Scott one, too. It's amazing how little children, like animals, seem to know when we need to be comforted and loved.

Wednesday, October 11, Day 3 of the Tubbs Fire: The air quality at our place is horrendous and the power has been out for two days. We're so thankful Jon and Charlie have opened their home to us. So far Scott has been a trooper and has had only minor issues. Jonathan, an officer in the Army National Guard, has been deployed here in Santa Rosa to help coordinate services with other agencies.

Tonight while we were watching the news on Channel 4, Jon said to me, "You know, if you were my dad, I'd be wanting to wring your neck by now." Those weren't the exact words he used, but I think that was his way of giving me a compliment. If it weren't for Matthew alerting me to the fire and Jon and Charlie giving us a place to stay, I'd be a basket case.

Thursday, October 12, Day 4 of the Tubbs Fire: We are sleeping in a queen-size bed at Jon and Charlie's. When Scott gets up to use the bathroom, he'll walk right by the open bathroom door then try to open the closed bedroom and closet doors. It will be nice when we are able to go back home to give him some normalcy. Except I'm realizing that there is no normal for Scott anymore.

Friday, October 13, Day 5 of the Tubbs Fire: We are home again. We have heat and hot water and I made a hot breakfast and am washing clothes. I loved my first shower. Today is the smokiest day of all, so we are wearing masks wherever we go. Wish we had better masks, though.

Scott is a bit more confused today. I could tell when we went grocery shopping and he tried to put a bag of groceries into the car parked next to us. Tonight the winds are supposed to be 40 to 50 miles per hour. We certainly don't want these fires to get out of control again. Saying prayers!!!

Saturday, October 14, Day 6 of the Tubbs and Nuns Fires: When the phone rang at 5:15 this morning, it was Jonathan telling me to evacuate—again. The winds had picked up and the Nuns fire was heading towards us. We still had stuff in the car, but this time I had pre-packed even more. Jon called back to tell me not to leave until I heard back from him as the police needed to evacuate those closer to the fire first. After getting us both dressed, I packed even more items, then watched the news to wait for Jon's call. At 7:30, Jon called to implore that we leave now, and thankfully there was hardly any traffic.

As I headed west on Highway 12, I glanced in my rearview mirror. The hillside behind us was an ominous bright red ball of fire. It was the scariest and most awesome thing I had ever seen. We are back at Jonathan and Charlie's just praying and trying to remain optimistic. I am so proud of Jonathan for his role with the Army National Guard and of Charlie for helping horse owners find places for their horses to stay. Matthew went over to the Finley Center to get N95 masks for Scott and me. So thankful for our children.

Sunday, October 15, Day 7 of the Tubbs and Nuns Fires: We came home again today. Matthew got our garage door open and working again now that the power is back on.

As the day progressed, I realized we needed some company, so I invited Gloria and Geoffrey for dinner. Our neighbor Shawne called to see if we were home, so I invited her and her roommate, too.

We had bean tostadas, ice cream sandwiches, and chocolate chip cookies...oh, did I mention wine? We all had so much to share about the fire, about each other, and just being together. None of us wanted to be alone.

Monday, October 16, Day 8 of the Tubbs, Oakmont, and Nuns Fires: Today was a quiet day. The air quality was the worst since the fires started, so we stayed indoors. We have the right masks, but I didn't want to go outdoors with embers flying in the air. Tomorrow we'll go get more food to refill the refrigerator and meet friends from our Alzheimer's support group for lunch. We all need to start feeling normal again. It appears that the worst is over, but I am afraid to go to sleep for fear we'll have to leave again in the middle of the night. It's a catch 22 as I really need to sleep, but the *what ifs* are getting to me. I think my biggest fear is that I won't wake up if the phone rings or there is an emergency alert. But no matter, today was a good day, the weather is cooperating, and we have lots of support coming in from other areas.

Luther Burbank Center for the Arts (LBC) had major smoke damage. The towering outdoor wood sculptures that were on loan to LBC and created by one the caregivers in our support group burned to the ground. Since we can't have the sing-along there this month, the Alzheimer's Association will let us meet in their offices this Friday, October 20. I am sure we will sing our hearts out with gratitude for surviving these terrifying days.

Tuesday, October 17, Day 9 of the Tubbs, Oakmont, and Nuns Fires: We met other caregivers and loved ones at Mary's Pizza Shack in Rohnert Park to try to have a normal day. But a normal day is not swapping our horrendous experiences or trying to keep our lives normal for our spouses who have Alzheimer's. We did have a wonderful lunch and it felt good getting together.

The windows are closed, but the sulfurous smoke odor is getting horrible inside. Tomorrow I will try to find an air purifier.

Thursday, October 19: Yesterday morning after I got us both dressed, we picked up two Honeywell Air Purifiers from Home Depot. They were easy to set up and have been running all day on turbo.

Lots of people called yesterday: Redwood Caregivers checking in, Marilyn to invite us for dinner, Diane regarding the sing-along, Olga Lee wondering if we had found air purifiers, and Gloria to invite us for dinner Friday night. Feeling loved!

Marilyn fed us spaghetti and meatballs, salad, and garlic bread for dinner. Scott was quiet as usual. Bill talked about a few women he worked with, then pondered who he would date if he had to choose between two older women that I won't mention (not work related, though). It wasn't racy but apparently it bothered Scott as he asked me afterwards if Bill and Marilyn were married. I believe he felt that because of the way Bill was talking, they were not a couple. Scott and Bill have been best friends for 28 years and he loves Bill like a brother. Bill feels comfortable talking about off-the-wall things to us, but Scott doesn't remember that these off-the-wall conversations are not to be taken seriously.

It was the middle of the night and Scott was sitting on the toilet calling my name. As I walked into the bathroom, he started to cry. He didn't know what was wrong. His pants were around his ankles, but his underwear was still on. I asked him if he went potty in his underwear and he said no, so I helped him stand up to pull his underwear down. Seeing his poor body shaking and knowing his brain wasn't functioning was so sad to watch.

Note to Caregivers:

No matter how much a person prepares for a fire in advance, sometimes you can't save your house. If there is a lesson here, it's that you can't plan for every single scenario that can happen in your life. Just do your best and ask for help when you need it.

The same is true for a caregiver. Planning ahead is great, but the *What ifs* can really get you down. What if my spouse becomes incontinent? What if we go through all our money and there's nothing left for me? What if he/she has to go into a nursing home? What if I die first? What if I can't do this anymore?

Before I became Scott's caregiver, many people would approach me after I gave a Medicare presentation wanting to know how to get help for themselves and their spouses. They were caregivers and they were stressed. In each person's story, one of the biggest issues that came up was how the caregiver's friends, doctors, and/or family members made them feel: guilty for not doing enough; inadequate in the way they were caregiving; selfish for wanting outside help; and uncaring because they were worried about finances for themselves in the future.

After listening, I would suggest certain agencies that could give them the help that they needed. My suggestions helped, but my listening really made them feel better. The fact that someone else cared lifted their spirits. It felt good to see the worry in their faces change to gratitude and hope.

Caregiving is one of the most demanding jobs and the *What ifs* can be overwhelming. So try not to dwell on the *What ifs*, but think about what you need in this moment. Afterall, tomorrow *will* take care of itself.

24

Lobster Mac and Cheese

Tuesday, November 14, 2017: Feeling run down, last Monday I was a royal grouch. The caregiver Victor came over that day to give Scott a shower; he also vacuumed and swept the patios and that made my day. By Tuesday morning, I felt a cold coming on. Exhausted and wishing I didn't have to take care of Scott, I thought, *It just doesn't seem fair.* Sometimes I just have to complain so I can get this *poor me* attitude out of my system.

Even though I am on the mend, my patience is nil. When Scott tries to help by drying the dishes over and over again, it tests my patience. I've been wondering why I am so annoyed lately, and think it's because I want to believe that Scott is normal and that he can still do normal things. When he tries to help, I am reminded over and over of how little he can actually do. And that makes me so sad. I keep feeling the loss of my husband, the man that I married, the man who could do things for himself *and* did loving things for me. I miss that man!

Saturday, November 18: Four couples from the Alzheimer's support group went to a concert to hear RPJ sing with the Redwood Chordsmen and the Barbershop Quartet: Scott and me, Geoffrey and Gloria Brecher,

John and Diane Benjamin, Dave and Joan Crady. Geoffrey, John, Dave, and Scott all have Alzheimer's or some other form of dementia.

Afterwards the Benjamins and Cradys followed us to our new place for a tour. After showing off the new shower and teal grommet curtains, the Cradys followed us over to the Brechers' house for pizza and salad. (The Benjamins weren't able to join us.)

As we pulled up, Joan waved me over to her car. "I've been trying to get your attention. There's a big pile of wood chips not far from your cul-de-sac that may have smoke coming out of the top." She was concerned that it could be a fire. After helping Scott and Dave get situated in Gloria's house, Joan and I drove back to investigate.

Since we didn't know whether the wood chippings were combustible, we called the fire department who immediately drove over. The young fireman patiently reassured us that while decomposing wood was hot, it would not start a fire.

As we drove back to the Brechers' place, I asked Joan, "Do you realize we left Gloria alone with three men with Alzheimer's?" Grasping our faux pas, Joan's face dropped in remorse. There was nothing we could do about it now, so we decided to just let it be.

While the ladies stood in the kitchen talking, Gloria mentioned in a joking manner, "I was putting the pizza in the oven when I realized that you left me alone with three men with Alzheimer's." Looking totally mortified and feeling terribly guilty, Joan and I apologized the best we could. We weren't thinking of the guys we left behind, but of a potential fire, especially after the horrendous fires we had just been through.

"After you left, I didn't know what to do," Gloria continued. "They were all sitting quietly in the living room and no one was talking, so I decided to play some music." At least the soothing melody helped Gloria cope, and the three of us learned a valuable lesson for future outings.

Wednesday, November 22: At Trader Joe's last night, I guided Scott as he pushed the shopping cart up to the young female cashier. While I was giving bags to the grocery bagger, Scott started pulling the cart towards me just as the cashier was pulling the cart towards herself. She told Scott that she would take care of it and I took him by the hand. That's when the male bagger and female cashier glanced at each other and snickered.

It really hit me hard so I chided them: "I don't appreciate you laughing at my husband. He has Alzheimer's." Of course they didn't know what to say and now felt like they had mud on their faces, but it really made me angry. The young woman tried to fix it by asking me what we were doing for Thanksgiving and the young man was now bending over backwards while he finished bagging our groceries.

The doorbell rang while I was in the bathroom this morning. Scott knocked on the closed bathroom door, so I told him to go back to the living room and I would be right there. When I opened the bathroom door, an alarmingly big man with greasy hair was standing in the hallway staring at me in an intimidating way. Not expecting anyone but Victor from the HHC agency, I asked who he was and why he was standing in my hallway. The way he looked at me made me feel like he had been hoping to catch me undressed, and I was furious.

He said he was from the HHC agency, but I insisted on some form of identification. After he produced his name tag, I called the agency to find out why no one had told us that someone new was going to show up. An apology did not make me feel any better.

After showing this stranger Scott's clean clothes, the shower in the master bathroom, and explaining his limitations, I left to get some much-needed errands done. Once I was parked safely at the store, I called the agency back so I could go into more detail about how vulnerable it felt finding this stranger standing in the hallway to my bathroom. Any normal person going into someone's home for the first time would have gone into the living room to wait. It was *not* Scott's fault.

Scott did get a shower, but he wasn't shaved. Yet this stranger insisted he had helped him shave. When I glanced at the TV there was a weird sexual TV show playing. Chuckling, this dunderhead said, "Your husband is enjoying the women." *Nice try, buddy!* The next day,

I called the service telling them emphatically that I did *NOT* want this man back again...ever.

Thursday, November 30: Last Saturday I took a nap and fell into a deep sleep. As I awoke from an intense dream, I remembered yelling at Scott saying, "I can't do this anymore. It's too hard." I wanted him to be normal again, and I was quite surprised at the angry feelings that were revealed in this dream.

On Monday and Wednesday, Scott's new caregiver, Anthony, arrived promptly. Not only is he personable and clean cut, but he took Scott on an outing. Anthony showered Scott and dressed him in clean clothes and the white socks that were on his bed.

Earlier, I had put heavy maroon socks on Scott's feet to keep them warm. When I got home, one of the socks was missing. I looked everywhere: in his dirty clothes hamper, in my hamper, on top of the dryer, under the bed, you name it. Couldn't find it anywhere, so I quit looking knowing it would show up eventually.

That evening as I was helping Scott take off his left shoe and sock, there was the maroon sock underneath the white one. I asked him if his shoe had felt tight. *No*, he said. When he realized how weird that was, we looked at each other and laughed.

Friday, December 8: Around 2:00 this morning, I went to the bathroom then checked on Scott. His bedroom door was closed, which was unusual. I opened the door to find him standing in the dark holding a pair of soiled underwear with his sweats laying on the bed. Stunned, I asked Scott to stand still as I checked out the bathroom. There was poop in and around the rim of the toilet, but luckily none on the floor or the hallway or bedroom carpet. I quickly got him into the shower to wash him down. As sure as I am that he felt better after a warm shower, I'm quite confident he won't remember this incident.

Later that afternoon, we both took naps and then I started to get ready to go to Gloria and Geoffrey's for dinner. Once dressed, I went to see if Scott was awake. He was and then told me how enormously sad he was to wake up knowing he was still the way he was—a person with Alzheimer's.

Thursday, December 14: After I put Scott to bed last night, he told me he loved me and thanked me for taking such good care of him. I hope he knows how much I appreciated those words.

During the night, I found Scott by the door that goes out to the garage. It was unlocked. What if he opens the front door without my knowledge? What can alert me? After I talked to Marilyn about this new development, she brought over the perfect bells that now hang on the doorknob.

After dropping Scott off at Catholic Charities, I went over to Walmart to buy some Christmas gifts for Killian. Then onto Target. When I got home I had two more free hours before I had to pick up Scott—until I noticed that the Walmart receipt showed two charges for one toy. Heading back to Walmart, I was going 50 mph up Fountaingrove Parkway, a 35 mph zone, when I passed a motorcycle cop with his radar gun aimed right at my car. *Uh oh*, I thought. When I stopped, the officer came over to the passenger side door and said, "I pulled you over because you were going 50 mph, *but* I'm not going to give you a ticket, just a warning." Taking my registration and driver's license, he went to write up a formal warning.

When the officer came back to the car, I started crying, telling him about my husband who has Alzheimer's, and that I had had a rough night. He told me about his father who died from dementia and how his mom took care of him until the end. Together with his brother and sister, they worked out a schedule for each sibling to be with his dad so their mom could get a break. He was sincere and compassionate and reassured me that there's a lot of support out there. I mentioned that we get a lot of support and have made many friends from the Alzheimer's Association and Catholic Charities. I'm so grateful he didn't give me a ticket.

On to Walmart to get a refund for the toy I didn't buy and then to Catholic Charities' Shaw Center to hear RPJ and the rest of the quartet sing for the adult daycare program.

The quartet sang upbeat Christmas songs and I was happy to have made it on time. I sat next to a very happy Scott. He enjoyed the caroling and accolades received for being RPJ's friend.

Back at home we were greeted by a big package from Williams Sonoma, addressed to someone else. Completely exasperated now, I wondered what to do with a perishable item that was packed in dry ice that didn't belong to me. After speaking 20 minutes to a young woman at Williams Sonoma, she told me to discard it, use it, or give it away. The box contained four separate portions of a Lobster Mac and Cheese casserole. A quick text to Gloria and we had a dinner date for the next night.

Sunday, December 17: Scott was getting ready for bed when he asked me to come into the bathroom to help him. He had already flushed the toilet but wasn't sure what to do with the used toilet paper he held in his hands. I suggested he put it in the toilet, and we washed his hands. Since he doesn't understand how to wash the inside and top of his hands anymore, I help him with this ritual. As I was getting him into bed, his underwear wasn't up at his waist. After I helped him fix his underwear and sweats, he climbed into bed.

In the past few weeks, Scott's needs have increased drastically. He now needs help getting into bed and I even have to help pull the blankets up to his chin. He doesn't get out of bed in the morning until he sees me up and moving, which is actually helpful, because I can sleep in if I have a bad night.

Sunday, December 24: This has been a busy month with lots of Alzheimer's-related parties. On the 16th, Scott and I joined Gloria and Geoffrey at the Walk to End Alzheimer's at Sonoma State University. We had fun checking out the booths and I was able to get Scott to take the elevator to the second floor to walk around the balcony. He was able to walk it twice and I was so proud of him.

Catholic Charities had a Holiday Party and Cookie Exchange on the 20th. There was a plethora of cookies, from gingerbread and brown-eyed susans to my favorite, chocolate kiss cookies. A big bag came home with us.

The Christmas Sing-along and Holiday Luncheon was a hit as Diane and I welcomed 40 caregivers and their loved ones. The caroling and sumptuous buffet put everyone in the holiday spirit—a wonderful way to lighten our day, if only for a moment. Ron and Lupe, a couple in our Tuesday Alzheimer's support groups, created holiday boxes of succulents from their garden as a gift to each couple and individual attendee to take home. When it was all over, Diane and I were exhausted but very pleased with how well it turned out.

Yesterday when Scott woke up from his nap, he seemed really off. He couldn't seem to figure out where to sit. Instead of sitting in his recliner, he sat in a regular kitchen chair. He did weird things and was shaking more than ever.

Needing to vent, I texted Jonathan. He asked what I would like him to do. Texting back, I said, *Nothing, I just needed to tell someone.* He invited us over, and we played hide-and-seek with Killian. It reminded me of the times Bob Kat and I used to hide from each other at our old house. So many changes in the last two years and I haven't had time to mourn any of them.

It's 4:00 in the morning and I am still awake. Hearing Scott walking around, I scooted out of bed to check on him. He was in the living room, standing in the dark.

"Honey, what are you doing out here?"

"I'm getting dressed," Scott offered as he stood there fully clothed. Taking his hand, I walked him to the bedroom where he climbed into bed and I tucked him in.

Around 7:00 a.m., I heard him again. Looking everywhere but not finding him, I called his name. For the first time ever, he was in my bathroom peeing. It's so hard watching him not be able to do the things that I take for granted.

Scott came into the bathroom while I was fixing my makeup and hair and he was panting. This is a new thing when he needs to poop or pee. I helped him pull down his pants then guided him to the toilet. I took out a clean wash cloth, wet it, then wiped him. That's when I realized I needed some type of wipes. Thinking I need to be proactive with incontinence issues, I texted Charlie about the wipes she uses for Killian. She texted me a picture of what she orders and offered to let me try some. I agreed and texted back that this was all new to me.

Later, when Scott and I had just come out of the grocery store, Charlie replied, *It's new to us too. Don't worry. We can get thru it together.* Reading this out by the car after assisting Scott into the passenger seat choked me up and the tears flowed. I realized that this was hard on them too, watching their dad go downhill…and quickly.

Thanks sweetie. I'm so scared sometimes, I admitted.

Sometimes I wonder what I would do if Jon were to get like that and I get so sad, she texted back. *I'm here for you! We both are.*

Tomorrow Christmas dinner is at our place. We'll have ham, turkey breasts, gravy, dressing, potato casserole, deviled eggs, salad with ranch and bleu cheese dressings, Artisan bread, chocolate and pumpkin cream pies, and ice cream. Everyone contributes something. As always, it should be lots of fun. No one knows this yet, but this year I am starting a new tradition after Christmas dinner—caroling. It should be fun for all, especially for Killian to hear all of us old folks sing our hearts out.

Note to Caregivers:

Whether it's dementia or some other illness, bodily changes happen. Instead of dwelling on these new and difficult losses, I'd like to review the memorable moments in this chapter:

- Scott and I were both able to attend the ALZ sing-alongs.
- I gave two Trader Joe's employees a lesson in compassion and respect for people with dementia.
- The motorcycle cop showed compassion and didn't give me a ticket.
- We accidently received a free dinner of lobster mac and cheese sharing this delicious meal with good friends.
- We enjoyed fun-filled holiday parties with the many friends we've met through the ALZ Association.
- Our friends and family began a new tradition of singing holiday carols after Christmas dinner, which went over fabulously. Killian was in awe watching everyone sing, especially his dad.

These are moments I will treasure forever because these moments in time were spent with Scott (except for the motorcycle cop). Now…your assignment, if you accept, is to remember and create your own special moments that you will treasure for always!

25

Why Won't You Answer Me?

ednesday, January 10, 2018: Last Wednesday, I sent an email to Dr. Canby that I was concerned about the speed of this disease. When we connected on the phone, she was concerned that Scott may have a urinary tract infection (UTI) or had a mini stroke (TIA). I told her that Scott had an appointment for minor surgery with the dermatologist Friday, and asked whether this was a good idea. After reading the dermatologist's report, Dr. Canby said to cancel this appointment until we knew if something else was going on. Relieved, I cancelled it.

At Kaiser the next morning for lab work and a urine sample, Scott couldn't pee. We brought the sterile container home and after some ham and cheese omelets, I gave Scott a shower and shave—and then I became totally depressed. When he finally peed in the cup, back to Kaiser I went by myself.

Gengraf (brand-name for cyclosporine) is an immunosuppressant drug used to prevent organ rejection after a heart transplant. Lab work is done once a month to measure the amount of Gengraf in the blood, so the doctor can adjust the dosage as needed. Last Wednesday's lab work showed that his Gengraf level was a low 40, when a month ago it was a normal 79. The transplant team increased the evening dosage from one to two capsules, so I was pretty sure the sample we took today would be higher than the normal level. It was and needed to be adjusted back down.

On Sunday, Scott had finished eating dessert and we were watching the TV show, *This is Us*. Seeing movement out of the corner of my eye, I turned my head to look at Scott. With a deliberate motion, Scott placed the empty ice cream bowl on top of the mug filled with milk. Concentrating, he brought the cleanly licked spoon up to his mouth, sucking on nothing. Totally shaken, I walked over to his tray, picked up the ice cream bowl, and gently took the spoon out of his mouth. "Honey, why don't you drink your milk," I suggested with a calm I didn't feel. His lack of comprehension about his actions chilled me to the bone. I went in the kitchen to cry.

Today when we met with Dr. Thorburn to review the latest lab work, I was prepared to talk about Scott's future. After he asked Scott a few questions and received nonsensical answers to all of them, Dr. Thorburn understood that Scott couldn't comprehend our conversation, we could speak in front of him.

"What will happen from here and how do I prepare?" I asked.

He suggested looking back at the last six months to determine how quickly this disease will advance in the next six months. He said Scott could pass away in his sleep or end up in the ER due to a fall or other ailment. At that point, he would be sent to a nursing home or go home on hospice services.

My tender heart says he doesn't have a lot of time left. I pray that God will be gentle with him and allow him to slip away quickly and compassionately.

Friday, January 19: It was dinner night out with Bill and Marilyn to one of our favorite restaurants, Mary's Pizza Shack. The four of us had pepperoni and mushroom pizza and their Mary's salad. As I sat there with our good friends, I sipped a glass of Rodney Strong merlot enjoying its smooth, velvety finish. I relished each sip. Everything was *magnifique*.

As we talked Marilyn tapped my hand. Scott was trying to eat his salad with a knife. Gently taking the knife, I handed him a fork. Then in a low voice Marilyn said, "Scott picked up his water glass twice then put it down looking confused—maybe he needs a straw." Once I placed a straw in his glass, he drank deeply as if everything was normal. So excited to be out with friends, I was forgetting to keep an eye on my guy.

I was in bed reading when I heard a weird sound. It was so soft that I decided it must be a squirrel skulking around on the roof. Then I heard the sound again and saw movement in the master bathroom. Scott had peed on the floor. Even though I knew this moment was coming, it was still distressing. After wiping up the floor, I had Scott undress so he could take a shower. Tomorrow is the first time I will buy Depends.

Thursday, January 25: Yesterday, Scott had his second peeing accident. Thank God he was wearing a Depend. I had him sit down on the toilet to finish. I kept asking whether he was peeing or pooping, but he wouldn't answer. I asked him again. Still no answer. Frustrated and a bit annoyed, I asked, "Why won't you answer me?"

"I think I'm just peeing," he finally affirmed.

This whole caregiving situation seems so awful for both the caregiver and the person needing the care. It's all up to me, even though I haven't been trained in handling all the activities of daily living, and we can't afford 24-hour care. A referral to hospice from Dr. Thorburn should help me figure this all out.

A nurse from Memorial Hospice came over today to explain the timing for hospice services. We talked at length about what Scott can and cannot do on his own. To qualify for hospice services, the doctor must certify that Scott is terminally ill with a life expectancy of six months or less. Other signs must be present, such as weight loss, insufficient hydration and nutrition, difficulty swallowing, increased shortness of breath, incontinence, recurrent infections, and rapid disease progression, to name a few.

Then she asked if we had any questions. Now mind you, Scott sat listening to the nurse this entire time without any response whatsoever. Before she stood up to leave, Scott said, "Can I ask you a question?"

"Of course," she responded kindly.

"I just want to know if I can still play golf once in a while." Scott hasn't played golf all year, but he doesn't remember this. And although she was startled, the nurse reacted perfectly. With compassion, she told Scott that because his balance is off, playing golf would *not* be a good idea right now.

"Julie can take you out to hit balls, but you would have to be very careful."

When Scott asked the nurse about playing golf, I wanted to gently caress his face and kiss him—he looked so adorable and I miss our intimacy.

Saturday, January 27: When I walked into Scott's bedroom in the middle of the night, my feet felt something wet on the carpet. Not wanting to wake him, I checked his bathroom finding a soiled Depend on the teal bathroom rug. I was so angry that I pulled the blankets off his naked sleeping body and told him to get out of bed and get into the bathroom. After he wiped his penis area, I brought him back to the bedroom where together we put on another Depend. After covering him up, I went out to the garage to get spray for the carpet, then kneeled on the bedroom floor to rub the urine away.

"I didn't sign up for this crap!" I wailed. I felt better just saying that out loud. I was just so angry—not at Scott, but at this disease and these demeaning and horrific bodily issues. Scott never heard what I said, because he fell right back to sleep.

On Friday, I went to the sing-along by myself after dropping Scott off at the Shaw Center. It was nice not having to worry about him *and* I was doing something I love. Where Scott receives enormous pleasure listening to an artist sing, my alto voice needs to belt it out. When we sang, *How Do I live Without You*, I pulled out tissues to dab at my eyes, noting for next time that uplifting songs are more appropriate for caregivers who are losing their loved ones to this disease.

Tuesday, February 6: Jonathan and Charlie are expecting another baby in August. At a gender reveal party on Saturday, everyone stood outside waiting for Jon to dump the load to reveal the gender color confetti already placed in the bucket of his huge tractor. I firmly believed it would be another boy, yet secretly hoped for a granddaughter. When he lowered the boom pink confetti spewed out. I was overjoyed. So happy that I'll have both a grandson *and* granddaughter. Scott didn't understand what was going on, but he told me later that he had fun playing with Killian's twin cousins, Jayleigh and Leighana.

On Monday night, Scott had just eaten yogurt and a cookie. Standing up, he walked towards the kitchen for more milk. When I asked if he needed help, he emphatically said no. Even though I knew he wouldn't be able to do it, I decided to let him try.

Suggesting he put the light on, I saw his eyes dart all around the small kitchen for the light switch. I gave him directions and he finally found it. As I heard him fumbling with cupboards, I blurted out that he wanted more milk. After opening a cupboard by the light switch, he gazed inside for a moment. When he went to turn the light off, I asked again if I could help.

With a dejected look and a sigh, he muttered, "Yes, cuz I guess I can't find the milk."

Friday, February 23: Sometimes when I am alone with my thoughts, I wish my caregiving days were over. If Scott knew all that I do for him on a daily basis, he would feel an enormous amount of empathy and gratitude. Because he can't acknowledge or discern his feelings, my thoughts help me through the tiredness and sadness that weighs me down. The loss of this beautiful man and the life we once had is unbearable to consider, yet this day-to-day caregiving is the pits. I am tired of feeling tired all the time.

Searching for joy in each day is becoming harder too. Right now I feel alone, helpless, frustrated, and defeated. No wonder that after getting Scott to the bathroom, dressed for the day, and fed breakfast, I am already exhausted. On shower days, it takes a good hour from beginning to end, and he ends up annoyed as I assist. Then I have to take care of me—and most days I just want to crawl back to bed and forget about my needs.

Today while Scott was at the Shaw Center I had almost five blessed hours to myself. After finishing errands, I treated myself to a home-cooked omelet with sautéed sweet onion, crimini mushrooms, turkey, and cheddar cheese on top. It was *so* good. After putting away clean clothes, I laid down for a nap until 2:30 p.m. then back to pick Scott up by 3:00.

While Scott napped, my scenic walk around our neighborhood searching for cats needing some petting was relaxing and invigorating. After dinner, we watched the movie *Wonder*. Heartbreaking and heartwarming at the same time, the movie made me realize that even though Scott is the one with Alzheimer's, it is not just about him. It is about every single person that is affected by him. *Wonder* confirmed that it is also about me, the caregiver, and how I react to Scott each and every day. Messing up by being human and wanting to just be me without Scott at times is a natural feeling. I know that Scott enjoys his time at the Shaw Center as he always comes home renewed. Maybe that is all that each of us needs at times, a way to breathe new life into our days.

Note to Caregivers:

On a good day, it took 45 minutes to give Scott a shower from beginning to end. Think about all of the steps it takes a person with an intact brain to complete the six activities of daily living (ADL): bathing, dressing, eating, transferring, toileting, and continence. Now pretend your brain isn't functioning as you undress, step into the shower, wash your hair and body, rinse, dry yourself off, redress, shave, brush your teeth, and use the toilet. Within each basic task are many movements that need to be completed before you go onto the next one. People with advanced dementia cannot remember to do most of these basic tasks on their own. They need help, constant vigilance, and a caregiver.

I'm not a perfect caregiver; I got upset and said things I wouldn't have said if I had gotten enough sleep or had enough help. I loved Scott so much and was not upset with him…what was affecting me was the disease that was taking away all his abilities.

If you are or were a caregiver, I applaud you and all that you do/did for your loved one. Every single caregiver, including paid caregivers, deserves accolades for the love, compassion, and caregiving that is done every day. You did it because you cared, because you loved enough to stay. And although you may not have been perfect, the fact that you gave of yourself in order to make sure your loved one had his or her needs met, you deserve acknowledgment for what you did. So pat yourself on the back and know that you are appreciated. You are one of God's angels on earth.

26

There Is so Much
Love in This Room!

Saturday, February 24, 2018: Last night after giving Scott a shower and helping him get dressed, I pulled his sweats up over his hips really high to see if I could get a laugh. As I giggled, he looked at me with a chuckle. I ran out to grab my phone to take a picture to text to Jonathan.

This couldn't have taken more than 10 seconds, but when I got back into the bedroom, Scott had already pulled his sweats down around his ankles. In a teasing manner, I told him what he had done and he laughed, too. After pulling his sweats back up over his T-shirt high above his bellybutton, I asked Scott to wave to the camera. My text to Jonathan challenged, *Scott says, Hi! What's wrong with this picture?*

Jonathan texted back, *LOL.*

I remember thinking, *That's all you've got? My son the jokester and all you can come up with is LOL?* I expected more of a response, but okay, Scott and I were having fun.

This morning, after helping Scott get up, we washed his hands at the kitchen sink. After squirting soap on my hands, I covered his with mine to wash them thoroughly. Once our hands were rinsed and dried, I could tell he was upset. As I put my arms around him and said how proud I was of him, he began crying lightly. We hugged a bit. With a frog in my throat, I suggested, "When you leave your body look for your mom and dad as they will be able to help you cross over. They will be so proud of you and how you handled these illnesses." Hugging a bit more comforted both of us.

Tonight we drove over to Gloria and Geoffrey's house for dinner. I went all out on the salad fixings and packed them in a thermal insulated bag. When we got out of the car, Scott had his water bottle and I had everything else. Climbing the three steps, I looked back to make sure Scott was holding onto the hand railing. Geoffrey held the front door open as I rushed past him to put the food on the dining room table. As I headed back out, I watched in a panic I never hope to feel again as Scott turned his head to the right and let go of the railing, tumbling down the first two steps.

I stood frozen as I watched Scott hit his head and land in an awkward position. Some blood was coming out of his ear. It was the worst fall I have ever witnessed. I remember saying over and over again, "Oh s*it, oh s*it, oh s*it." And I'm not one to cuss. The three of us got Scott to a sitting position, but when we tried to stand him up, he was in horrible pain on his left side. I had Gloria get a chair from inside the house and a blanket to cover him. Once he was sitting down Gloria called 911 and handed me the phone to answer the dispatcher's questions.

Two male paramedics rushed over to examine Scott and transport him to Kaiser. I followed closely behind. At Kaiser's ER, the long process of tests began. One of the paramedic's came into the room to ask how we were holding up. He seemed sincerely concerned and I thanked him profusely for his compassion. He said we were such a nice couple that he wanted to make sure we were in good hands. His concern for how scared we both were helped calm us down.

When Scott groaned in pain and favored his left side even after an X-ray showed no broken bones, the doctor ordered a full body scan. Again, nothing showed up. While at the hospital, I called family and friends to give them the unfortunate news about Scott's fall promising to update them as I could.

As I was leaving around 11:00 p.m., I asked the nurse to make sure the next shift was told how to give Scott his meds. He promised me that he would instruct everyone and not to worry.

Sunday, February 25: The ER doctor called after midnight asking about Scott's day before the fall. The lab work indicated he may have had an infection. A rectal temperature showed a fever of 100.9. That was weird as last night his oral temperature was 98.5. I know he is in good hands and hope there will be more answers in the morning. Right now I need to get some sleep.

This morning Scott was admitted to Room 411. When I got to Scott's hospital room, a nurse and an aide were with him. The chairs looked like they would wreak havoc on my back, so a man named Alex found one that worked. I gave him a big hug in thanks.

The attending physician, Dr. Ying, was concerned with Scott's pain when standing up. The weird thing was that when he first fell, it was his left leg he favored. On Sunday, when they had him stand up, it was his right leg causing the pain.

When Dr. Ying took another look at the scans, he found that Scott had broken his *right* pelvis. It's a hairline fracture, but it definitely would cause that amount of pain. I'm wondering now if due to Scott's memory loss, he didn't know the difference between left and right anymore. If a similar situation happens to your loved one, make sure the doctor checks both sides of the scan.

After Dr. Ying left the room, I noticed that two fingers on Scott's left hand were swollen black and blue. After I mentioned this to the nurse, an X-ray was ordered that confirmed one broken finger. The only treatment for a broken finger is a wrap; the only treatment for the right pelvis is to keep pressure off the leg.

The nurse Georgia was very sweet and attentive. She was concerned this morning because she couldn't get Scott to eat his breakfast before I arrived *and* he was agitated. Scott was panting, but he wouldn't respond to me. Explaining where he was and why, I asked him if he needed to pee.

"Honey, there's a catheter inserted in your penis so you can pee in bed. You don't have to get up." When he finally understood, he was able to urinate and stopped panting. I helped Georgia give him his meds, demonstrating the simple words I use to guide him: *put it in your mouth...drink...head back...swallow*—waiting until he completes each instruction before giving him the next dose. This was our routine at home and it certainly took some figuring out on my part.

Since he hadn't eaten breakfast, Georgia produced a cheese omelet, but he needed assistance as he couldn't hold the fork. He ate every bite and when Georgia came back into the room, she commented that he looked much better since I had gotten there.

Later that afternoon, Georgia came in to thank me. "I've learned a lot about taking care of someone with Alzheimer's. And I just have to say that there is so much love in this room." As we hugged, tears streamed down my face. Georgia's acknowledgment of Scott's and my love was an uplifting surprise.

Monday, February 26: The days seem to be running together, but I do know that Scott was moved to Room 415 today and the palliative care team came to talk. Two doctors took me into a private room to explain Scott's discharge. They seemed genuinely concerned about the next step in his medical care, but when they started talking to me about *my* contribution in Scott's care and how to help *me* move forward, I was taken aback. No one in the medical field has ever asked me if I needed any type of help. When I grasped the idea that these two doctors wanted to know how to make this transition easier on me, I didn't know how to respond.

They told me that Scott needs to be moved to a skilled nursing facility (SNF) where he could improve with physical therapy. Then one doctor asked me if there was something I have been wanting to do, a place that I'd like to visit for some *me* time. The answer to this question was easy: Mendocino and Fort Bragg. Asked if I had a friend to go with me, I admitted that I would want to go by myself so I could just *be*. Their suggestion that I plan a trip when he was transferred to the SNF was commendable, but it didn't feel like the right time. *(Note: I never made this trip while Scott was alive, as I didn't want to be away from him.)*

I was impressed with the compassion and patience of the two physical therapists. Communicating with someone who has Alzheimer's is difficult, yet Scott was able to grasp their instructions. As they teach him how to stand without putting weight on his right leg, he is improving. But Dr. Ying wants to keep him one more night since they haven't figured out the bug yet.

I went to look at some skilled nursing facilities to see which one would be best for Scott. The first and only place I toured was Sunnybrook

SNF. The receptionist gave me a tour explaining how rehab works and what to expect. Sunnybrook is a smaller facility (55 beds), has its own PT room, did *not* smell like urine in the hallways, and is only five minutes from home. This was to be Scott's new abode.

Tuesday, February 27: A nurse from hospice came by this morning to assess Scott's condition and review his chart. After meeting for an hour or so, all my presentations on Medicare seemed to pay off. Hospice could *not* become involved until physical therapy stopped working or Scott hit a plateau. Between talking to the nurse, handling Scott's needs and making sure he was out of pain, my hands were full. When the nurse was getting ready to leave, she smiled and said, "There is so much love in this room. You and your husband have such a special bond and it is evident from both of you." The tears in her eyes made my eyes water, too. I thanked her and said it was nice to know that she could see how much we love each other.

How wonderful it was to be complimented by two totally different individuals, and in the same week. It made me realize that how a couple expresses their love in public can be a testament to others that true love really does exist. We were doing something right!

Friday, March 2: Scott keeps improving but because the blood work is inconclusive, they don't want to transfer him to the SNF yet.

On Wednesday, Gloria and Geoff invited me over for dinner, but I didn't want to leave Scott alone. After he fell asleep around 11:30 a.m., I drove over to Spring Lake for a walk and took some great photos of an egret that posed for me. After I had lunch and returned to the hospital room, Scott continued to sleep. That's when I decided that I didn't need to stay with Scott while he was sleeping, I *could* be with friends. After all, the hospital staff would call me if Scott needed me or his status changed. Texting Gloria I asked if the invitation stood. Having dinner with good friends gave me a few moments of 'normal'.

Tuesday, March 6: Last Saturday, Scott was moved to Sunnybrook. I arrived an hour later to help get him acclimated. The next morning,

Scott was sitting in a wheelchair in front of the nurses' station. He looked dejected and tears were running down his face, but he lit up when he saw me.

Today when I arrived, a speech therapist was watching Scott eat to see how he does with different foods. She decided, and I agreed, that any meat needs to be ground up to make it easier for him to chew. He is having problems trying to urinate and is constipated, but there's nothing I can do to help except calm him down. Walking to and sitting on the toilet is painful, but the pain should subside after four to six weeks.

Already I've met wonderful people and Scott's mood has changed drastically. As he adjusts to the new surroundings, I feel comfortable leaving him in the capable hands of the Certified Nursing Assistants (CNAs).

While I was eating lunch at home, Matthew called. He was having problems with his roommate and asked if he could stay with me while he finds a new place to live. Of course I told him yes. Isn't synchronicity amazing?

Matthew has visited his dad the last few days and it sounds like they have been good visits for both. When he left Scott yesterday, Matthew went out to his car and cried. Knowing he may be close to the end is heartbreaking in itself, but watching the new struggles Scott is having to endure without understanding them makes it even more difficult.

Saturday, March 10: The other day Scott's roommate Dick was talking to his wife and son. Dick is in his 80's and their son is visiting from out of the area. Dick and his wife live in an independent and assisted living community that provides meals. After his wife described how good the eggs and sausage tasted at breakfast, their son mentioned how delicious his spinach and cheddar cheese omelet was. Dick told them he had oatmeal with milk, honey, and a banana. Then it was back to his wife who praised the chocolate cake she ate for dessert the night before, while the son boasted about the chocolate mousse.

With a straight face, Dick blurted out, "They gave *me* a stool softener."

Their banter sounded so much like a TV sitcom that I burst

out laughing. When all three turned to look at me, I felt guilty for eavesdropping. As soon as they realized how their conversation sounded, though, laughter filled the room. And that made Scott laugh, too.

Last night, the nurse called me at home, concerned about Scott's breathing and non-responsiveness. I went over to Sunnybrook to see what might be wrong. We couldn't wake him up but I told her not to worry, he didn't appear to be distressed, just very tired. Interesting that I was calming her down, not the other way around.

Penny had me over for pasta, salad and garlic bread tonight with two other women. It was a nice break from reality. We played a card game called Scattergories, where you roll a die with letters and then answer questions with one or more words using the letter that lands on top. It was a lot of fun, but as a first-time player I came in last. I don't think the other two ladies were adding up their scores correctly (heh, heh)... or maybe I really am a sore loser.

I'm excited that Jon, Charlie, and Killian are visiting Scott tomorrow. We haven't seen them since the gender reveal party. Janice and Olga Lee are visiting, too, and I realize how much I've missed seeing everyone.

RPJ emailed me about his visit with Scott: *I stayed with Scott for a little over an hour. He recognized me, but I had difficulty hearing and understanding what he was saying. He kept chewing on the bandage around his fingers. He did eat some lunch and drank lemon tea and milk, so he got some nutrition. He did say, 'Thanks friend', at one point so I think he appreciated my visit. I shall go again next week.*

Friday, March 16: At dinner Wednesday night, Scott sneezed, so I asked if he'd like a tissue. As I held the box out to him, he appeared to be oblivious about his nose running. When I put the box closer to his face, he pulled one out.

As I worked on a Crossword puzzle, my eye caught him chewing a piece of the tissue while folding the rest in half. "Scott, you can't eat the tissue!" Spitting it out, he looked chagrined and said he was sorry.

Later, as I was tucking him in for the night, he looked at me with love and in a very serious voice said, "You take care of yourself."

Marilyn met me at Sunnybrook Thursday morning, as I wanted another person's eyes and ears when I met with the Kaiser staff. Because the physical and occupational therapies make Scott lethargic, Dr. Jaffe wants to discharge him to home on Monday. I explained that I had applied for Medi-Cal on March 8 and based on Medi-Cal rules, Scott would qualify. One person mentioned that unless Sunnybrook had a Medi-Cal (Medicaid) bed, he wouldn't be able stay at Sunnybrook. Pointing to Scott's bed, I declared, "It's right there." The doctor and staff promised to review Scott's situation and get back to me on a Medi-Cal bed. What they didn't know yet was that I knew Scott's rights.

At this point, no one is expecting Scott to survive much longer—even me. I asked the doctor whether it was time to take him off the Noxafil (brand-name for posaconazole) medication for aspergillus. She suggested we watch his recovery a bit longer before taking him off all of his meds, not just the Noxafil. That sounded so final that Chloe, a Kaiser social worker, came over to give me a hug. As she held me, I sobbed hard as the finality of our situation took me by surprise. I turned around to find Scott watching me. "That's so sad!" he responded and I knew he thought I was crying about somebody else.

When I got home, Kathy, the Ombudsman for Long Term Care, returned my Monday voice mail message. Per Kathy and the CANHR (California Advocates for Nursing Home Reform) website's fact sheet on Medi-Cal, Sunnybrook cannot make Scott leave the facility while a Medi-Cal application is pending. Thank goodness, as I know I cannot take care of him anymore.

Occasionally, Scott seems more with it, but when I see him struggling to eat ground-up food I realize he could go anytime. It feels like I am back at UCSF wondering if he is going to live or die. Sometimes I wonder if other people realize how stressful to always wonder, *Is it today? Is it today? IS IT TODAY?* This not knowing is a slow torture.

When Scott came back after a half hour of physical therapy with Ben and was helped into bed, he looked at me and mouthed *I love you.* Happy to hear these cherished words, I responded with *I love you, too.*

(Note: Scott was put on a mechanical soft diet that consisted of pureed foods, making them easy to chew and swallow. Changing as many meds as

possible to liquid form was another positive choice. If liquid form wasn't available, the tablets were ground up and put into pudding or yogurt to make swallowing easier.)

Saturday, March 17: I woke up yesterday feeling very alone and vulnerable, thinking about all the people we met through our Alzheimer's support group. We met almost every week for two years to talk about our issues, and got together for lunches and group activities. These people became our family and now this part of my life is coming to a close. Will they feel awkward being around me now that Scott is in a nursing home? Will I feel uncomfortable around them? When Gloria called me later that day, we promised to always be friends and be there for each other to the end.

When I arrived today at Sunnybrook, Scott was shivering in his wheelchair in front of the nurses' station. The Occupational Therapist (OT) asked Scott if he was cold. After bringing Scott a blanket, I took him back to his room and gave him another blanket and a heavy flannel shirt on top of that. Standing behind the wheelchair, I rubbed my hands up and down his arms to warm him. It took 15 minutes for him to stop shivering.

As I rubbed, a lot of memories flooded my brain: Scott with Bob Kat, dinner together at a favorite restaurant, how his face lit up when I laughed. All these memorable times I took for granted. I was too young to realize how fleeting life can be. Looking out the window at the magnificent blue sky with intermittent stormy clouds, the words *this too shall pass* came to mind. Am I ready to say goodbye? How will I feel when that final moment comes? Will I cry, feel relieved, surrender to an achy pain that won't go away? Or will I be able to move on quickly to find who I am without this man that I've been married to and loved for 26 years?

Scott sat up and was alert as he ate dinner but it was difficult to understand him. He just wasn't making sense. When it was time for the CNA to put him to bed, I realized that the physical part of caregiving is no longer my responsibility. I can leave him because he is in good hands. I don't have to wait while they change his brief (the more respectful term for 'diaper' used in the SNF). I can go home and not feel guilty.

Note to Caregivers:

When two nurses professed to me, *There is so much love in this room*, it brought me comfort, joy, and thankfulness that Scott's and my love was apparent to others. Would our love have grown this strong without Scott's illnesses? I can only surmise. What I do know, though, is my commitment and love for Scott has grown deeper with each disease. My spirituality has also given me a basis to work with: stay positive, look for joy, treat other people with the concern and kindness I would like them to show towards me, find humor wherever I can, laugh at my mistakes, and pray to my God when in doubt.

I think that this is the best wisdom for caregivers. Make your spouse laugh in the moment that you are ready to wring your hands; think of something funny you both enjoyed in the past; find joy in your life. When I visit Scott, I pull out my phone to find cute photos and videos of cats *and* our grandson Killian. Watching kitty antics or Killian being Killian brightens both of our lives. These are our joy finders in a jiffy. Before Scott fell, we watched sitcoms that made us laugh. I don't think Scott understood the dialogue, but when he heard my belly laugh, he laughed too. Find your joy!

27

I'm Still Working on Her

Monday, March 19, 2018: Scott couldn't remember my name today. The lump in my throat won't go away.

A different hospice nurse met me in Scott's room to complete paperwork and sign forms. Scott had just had a shower and looked refreshed. Once Scott was back in bed, the nurse ordered Norco to be given at least 45 minutes before the staff takes him anywhere.

The nurse asked Scott these questions. What's your name? Can you tell me the year? What city and state do you live in? What's your wife's name? Is your wife in the room? He looked at me and said yes. He could only answer his name and the state he lived in.

After the nurse reviewed his chart, she took me outside to talk. Hospice doesn't cover Scott's meds, so I will need to find out if they will be covered by Kaiser. When I got home I read Scott's benefit booklet. Apparently, Medicare Part D will cover any meds *not* related to hospice care. What a relief.

Matthew was already home and we talked about all these changes happening to his dad. It was good to have someone to talk to. Then Marilyn texted, *How is Scott today? Still in the same room? Bill is off tomorrow and we will stop by sometime. How are you?* This brought tears to my eyes.

I texted back with, *Yes, he's in the same room, and when the hospice nurse asked me about funeral arrangements, I almost lost it.* The hospice nurse's *laissez faire* attitude had hit me like a ton of bricks.

Thursday, March 22: At lunchtime, Scott was already in the activity room, surprisingly alert and able to feed himself. Afterwards I went over to Target to buy Scott two long sleeve shirts, two sweatshirts, and three sweatpants. A bargain at $6.00 each!

Taking a walk before I went back for dinner gave me some respite. When I returned, Scott was almost awake, but after the CNA changed him and got him into the wheelchair he was wiped out. I persisted in feeding him until he completely woke up and started feeding himself. When he was done I gave him a piece of his favorite See's candy. Amazingly, he was able to chew and swallow this tasty treat without a problem.

Later I noticed Scott chewing on something. The CNA had already taken his food tray so I asked him to spit it out into the napkin. It was the band aid that had been on his broken finger. I showed it to today's CNA and asked her to let others know that he can't tell if something is edible or not. The next day while he was eating his lunch, he put a towel in his mouth.

As Scott was being wheeled away to get a shower, I asked the CNA to shave off his mustache. There isn't any way he can keep it clean anymore.

Tuesday, March 27: Last Friday RPJ stopped by to visit Scott. It was good seeing Scott's face light up when his good friend walked in the door.

On Saturday, the CNA helped Scott get onto the toilet, changed his brief, and laid him back in bed. Scott wouldn't answer questions from either of us, so we were left on our own to figure out his needs.

At dinnertime, in walked Matthew. Five minutes later, Jonathan, Charlie, and Killian surprised us all. OMG, from Scott's reaction, you would have thought the Pope had arrived. When Charlie asked Scott a question, he responded with a six-word sentence. This is more than I get from him on any given day.

Killian, now 2-1/2, was playing with a toy truck that made loud noises as it ran around the chairs and under Scott's wheelchair. It was keeping Scott's attention and he had a look of pure joy on his face. At one point, Killian was getting cranky so Jon put him on his lap so we could play pattycake. He finally got the gist of it with his hands patting mine, then faster, then *'pick it, pick it, pick it'* then *'throw it away'*. Later that night Jon texted me a video of Killian trying to play pattycake with Charlie. Seeing my grandson playing a game that I was teaching him was the best ending to a stressful day. And Scott was in seventh heaven.

Today when I arrived, Scott's head was down and he looked dejected. I pulled up a chair next to him blinking back my tears as I rubbed his back. At a loss for words, I knew he was feeling the heaviness of his new reality.

Lunch was a gross-looking chili. I knew I wouldn't have eaten it, so I asked for a grilled cheese sandwich. After I cut it up and began hand feeding Scott a bite, he grabbed a piece and began feeding himself. Of course that's when the hospice nurse came into the room. She didn't see the Scott I saw when I first arrived, but the Scott he became after I got him to eat. And he responded to her questions.

Scott told the nurse that he was sad that his friends weren't visiting. So I explained that RPJ visited on Friday, Matthew, Jon, Charlie, and Killian visited on Saturday, and Bill and Marilyn on Sunday. With a look of surprise, his demeanor changed completely. When I reminded him that he didn't remember the visits because of Alzheimer's, he got it for the moment.

While the hospice nurse was talking to Scott, the hospice social worker called to see if he could stop by. Since we haven't met him yet, I was baffled when he started by asking "How *are* you?" in a condescending tone. That tone and the *poor you* approach *put my back up*. Scott has only been on hospice for a week, and I am starting to think this hospice is not a good fit.

(Note: When Scott was first diagnosed, he told anyone and everyone that he had Alzheimer's. He wasn't ashamed and we often talked about it between ourselves. So continuing to talk about Alzheimer's in front of Scott at this point didn't seem odd to me where it may seem cruel to others. Each situation is different, though, so if your loved one is having a hard time adjusting to the diagnosis and doesn't want to tell people, please

honor his or her request by not talking about it in front of them. This is not to say that you shouldn't tell concerned family and friends, just make sure that when you do your loved one isn't in the room.)

Sunday, April 1: Scott hasn't had a shower for almost a week. From the head CNA at Sunnybrook I learned it was now the hospice aide's responsibility to give him a shower. When the CNA called hospice to find out why the aide hadn't given him a shower, the excuse was that Scott had clean band aids on his fingers. As far as I was concerned, that was not a valid reason. Why couldn't he have put a glove over Scott's left hand? On Thursday, I emailed Dr. Jaffe about my disappointment with hospice and their staff.

Today is Easter Sunday. Matthew and I went out to brunch with Gloria and Geoffrey, then visited Scott. A female resident at Scott's table was talking non-stop, first saying her husband died without notice, then wanting to find her car and get the heck out of here, the food sucked and her husband was out playing golf. Scott would respond with something totally off the wall and unintelligible, but the two of them seemed to make it work. Scott hadn't talked so much since he's been here, and he seemed to distract the woman from whatever was happening in her mind. The Occupational Therapist (OT) Desiree noticed their banter and said they must put these two together from now on.

Tuesday, April 3: Yesterday was an extremely emotional day. When I arrived, Scott was in the Activity Room sitting with two older men. One was staring into space and the other was eating his food with extra heavy adaptive utensils for residents who have hand tremors. I tapped Scott on the shoulder then pulled up a chair. When he started crying, I couldn't figure out how to help him. Fifteen minutes later, I had someone call his nurse.

Back in his room, we tried to figure out what was wrong. I mean, I know what's wrong. This whole darn thing! I'd be crying too if it were me. The nurse gave him a Norco and five minutes later he was smiling and eating. He ate most of the tuna sandwich, all the cottage cheese, fruit, and a cookie, drinking his milk and a MightyShake. Roberto Huerta, one of the CNAs, came in around 2:30 p.m. apologizing for Scott not getting a shower on the weekend. He told me that he would take really good care of him at dinner and give him extra milk. I left feeling better.

Today was busy. First Scott's cousin Doug called to say he was driving up from San Jose to visit. Then Sunnybrook called to say that Scott was going to be moved to another room with four beds. Even though I knew this would happen, I wasn't happy about it. Also, the nurse from hospice was coming in for me to sign forms ending hospice services.

The fun part of today was going to lunch with my Tuesday Alzheimer's support group, although I felt a deep sense of loss for all of us as I reflected on how everyone will have to go through the changes that Scott is currently experiencing.

Doug and I arrived at Sunnybrook at the same time. I tried to prepare Doug that Scott would not look like he did the last time he saw him, which was at least four years ago. When Doug saw Scott sitting alone with his lunch tray, tears welled up in his eyes. Quickly composing himself, he reminisced with Scott for an hour and a half, then became emotional again as he was leaving.

After Doug left, Scott was moved into the four-bed room. I covered him up with four blankets. Even I was cold in that room! After Dr. Jaffe examined Scott she suggested we try OT again. Now that his hip isn't painful anymore, we are hoping with a little help he'll be able to stand up on his own again.

After Dr. Jaffe left, Scott fell asleep exhausted from the long day. Then the nurse from hospice arrived with the paperwork to terminate their services. I was so relieved. *(Note: I had heard some talk that Scott may have recovered well enough to disqualify him for hospice services. This gave me the perfect justification to discontinue their care, and I knew that I would be able to choose a different hospice when the time came.)*

Wednesday, April 4: When I arrived, Scott was already in the Activity Room sitting with his old roommate, Dick, and his wife waiting for lunch to be served. At one point, Scott said, "My mom took really good care of me."

I waited a few seconds, then said, "What about your wife?"

After a brief pause, Scott said, "I'm still working on her!" We all busted up laughing. Then Scott looked at me and said, "*What?* It made you all laugh!"

After a busy afternoon with the ALZ Transition Group, running errands, and a walk with Gloria, I had the strongest desire to check in on Scott to see how he was doing in the new room. He was sitting in his wheelchair off by himself and he was shaking. It wasn't a shaking that meant he was cold, though. Moving his wheelchair over to his bed, I had him drink some water. The shaking stopped and I could tell he was starting to feel better. To cheer him up, I texted Jonathan in hopes we could FaceTime. Killian was sitting on Mom's lap as she read *If You Give a Mouse a Cookie* by Felicia Bond. He was adorable as he showed us his bottle, the book, and all his stuffed animals. Then Jonathan went into another room so he could talk with Scott privately. This definitely lifted Scott's spirits.

It took a while before someone came in to put Scott to bed. Because the CNAs were having a hard time getting him out of the wheelchair, I suggested they have him stand up with the walker. *Wow!* That worked incredibly well. He was able to get into bed more easily *and* quicker doing it this way. With a hug and kiss goodbye, I left feeling thankful that I followed my intuition.

Saturday, April 7: Yesterday, Scott ate most of the homemade PB&J sandwich and the dessert that came with the meal. At this point, any added calories are helpful. A dietician said Scott had lost another seven pounds since the beginning of March. We talked about a plan to get him to eat more: serve only sandwiches; if I'm not there, have someone nudge him to eat; and don't leave him alone. After the dietician left, I kept pushing the food. At one point, he gave me a mischievous smile and said, "Yes, mother!"

At the nurses' station I told Roberto how Scott was able to use the walker getting into bed. Roberto got another CNA to check it out. Holding onto the walker, Scott stood up, pivoted, then sat on the bed.

Roberto was ecstatic that Scott was able to do this almost all on his own and will inform everyone of Scott's new accomplishment.

At lunchtime today, Scott was sitting with the residents who can't feed themselves. He had tears in his eyes. I wrapped my arms around him and asked the CNAs if they could move him to another table. I told them, "I think it depresses him when he is sitting with the older residents who can't talk."

Because Matthew visited earlier, I asked Scott if he had a good visit. Scott quipped, "He never stopped."

"Talking?" I asked.

"Yes, he never stopped."

A bit later, I told Scott that the man at the next table wanted to go back to his room and had been waiting quite a while. With a little smirk on his face, Scott said, "Damn those women!"

Later, I pushed him outside. The brisk, 64-degree air felt good to me but was too cold for him, so we went to his room to get a jacket and tried it again. Even after bundling him up with a blanket from my car, he shivered, so back inside we went. He wasn't ready for a nap, so we kissed goodbye and I left him sitting in front of the nurses' station to watch TV with the other residents.

Monday, April 9: Listening to the loud TV noises coming from Scott's roommates' beds, plus all the noises men make, was getting me depressed. Only a curtain separates one roommate's bed from Scott's. Every time this man cleared his throat, Scott woke up. After Scott finally fell into a deep sleep, I left.

Roberto called later that night to tell me he had tried to give Scott a shower. Scott kept hitting the razor away so Roberto had to stop shaving for fear he would accidentally cut Scott. Just the fact that Roberto called to update me meant a lot.

That night I tossed and turned, upset by how little control I have over Scott's care and wondering whether he'll be able to walk again. In the morning, I called Kaiser's social worker to see if we could start hospice again and stop his meds. She understood what I was feeling and even repeated it back to me: that I can't stand seeing him like this; that I wonder if he would want me to stop his meds; and that it feels like the most humane thing to do. She strongly suggested calling his brother Gil and our sons to make sure that everyone is informed. She will call Sunnybrook's social worker Jennifer to discuss all of this. I tried Gloria first, and started to cry when she didn't answer. Jonathan, Matthew, Gil, Janice, and Olga Lee didn't answer either. My last call was to Marilyn and I was finally able to tell someone.

On Tuesday I brought Scott an egg salad sandwich, banana, cottage cheese, and strawberries. After lunch, Dr. Jaffe stopped me in the hallway, suggesting we wait on hospice to give OT more time. Since Scott had done so well at lunchtime, engaging friends who stopped by for a visit, I was in full agreement. Scott was improving and that made me feel better.

After lunch, Ben the PT guy had Scott stand up from the wheelchair while holding onto the walker. *HE DID IT!* He walked down the hall like he had been doing this forever. Walking backwards in front of Scott, I took a video of him looking all full of himself with everyone clapping. Ben was right behind in case he faltered. I asked Scott to say hi to the boys, which he did as he kept walking to the end of the hall then back to the nurses' station. When Marilyn arrived, she was thrilled to see him standing *and* walking. Next Ben had Scott walk outside around the entire building with me behind pushing the wheelchair. Marilyn brought up the rear.

When I got home, the Kaiser social worker called to ask if I felt she had pushed hospice on me. I told her no, since I was the one who called her about it. The only thing I wish I hadn't done was call everyone right away. But I sent a text with a copy of the video to Gil, Jonathan, Matthew, and Gloria, saying, *This is a game changer.*

At dinnertime, we FaceTimed with Killian. If you thought nothing could top Scott's walking, you would be wrong. Killian was the highlight of his day. When Killian saw us, he said, "Grandma," with the unconditional love that only a two-year-old can express. That was so special. When we said goodbye Killian kissed the phone twice.

Walking at Spring Lake that evening was balm to my soul. The setting sun caused orange hues to reflect off the lake. As I walked by Canada geese it was obvious I was intruding on their space. The melodious sounds of the countless birds chirping all at once were a choir of angels to my ears. From the top of the hill, the sunset was breathtaking, and the now blue hues reflecting off the calm ripples in the lake below along with the majestic trees was indescribable. Maybe a gift from God to remind me that life really is a miracle.

Wednesday, April 11: Today was Bingo with a volunteer, Shirley Hightower, who just happens to be Marilyn's best friend. Scott and I had oodles of fun playing with the other residents. Scott couldn't read the numbers, so I played for him winning Bingo once. As usual, I had to keep reminding myself that winning was for the residents.

I really wanted to stay for the sing-along, but Desiree took Scott for OT, so I left to get some errands done. While I was out, I picked up a chocolate banana smoothie to surprise Scott, then went home to fix my dinner.

When I returned with the smoothie, Scott was shivering in the dining room. Down to his room I went to get his jacket and hang up his clean clothes from home. I introduced myself to his roommates Joe and Ron. They both seemed nice and I will make more of an effort to acknowledge them. Ken, the third roommate, is usually in the dining room.

Over dinner, one of the other men at the table said to me, "You seem like a nice person."

I responded with, "I try to be."

Scott whispered in my ear, "Is he trying to put the moves on you?"

I laughed and said, "No, he's just being nice." Before today, I would have sworn that Scott didn't have a jealous bone in his body.

Thursday, April 12: Do you know what it feels like to watch your loved one be sad every day and there's nothing you can do about it? It must be similar to watching a loved one endure mental illness or ongoing grief. Every day I watch Scott struggle with this horrible disease, my heart breaks a bit more.

Scott's friend Bob Evans met me at Sunnybrook today. He was holding a nine-iron with Scott's name on it, which he put in my trunk. Then we took Scott to the Activity Room for lunch. While I concentrated on making sure Scott ate, Bob was full on entertaining everyone within hearing distance. One of the CNAs noted that Scott was happier today. That gave me a good feeling, until the nurse came over to give Scott his meds. She whispered, "Scott was upset this morning—he asked me to move him to a room where he could have some privacy to cry." There goes my heart again, breaking apart.

Scott wouldn't let the nurse give him his meds this morning. He pocketed the Sandimmune (brand-name for cyclosporine) capsule in his mouth, so she decided to wait until I arrived because she knew he would be more apt to swallow them then.

Sunday, April 15: At lunchtime Friday, we sat with Jeanne, who has lived at Sunnybrook for three years. She's 69 years old and seems to have taken a shine to Scott.

Once the CNA put Scott down for a nap, I headed over to the Honda dealership to replace the left spring in the trunk which took less than 45 minutes. The service technician was good enough to charge me only for the parts. While I waited, all of a sudden I felt exhausted. After I got home and ate a sandwich, I fell right to sleep. When I woke up around 6:30 p.m., I didn't have the energy to visit Scott again.

RPJ called for an update on Scott. I shared my concern about possibly having to decide to stop Scott's meds down the road, and that I didn't want to have to make that decision. RPJ told me that no one should make me feel guilty if I do need to make that decision, and that I could call him anytime I needed a shoulder.

After lunch on Saturday, we went outside so I could trim Scott's fingernails and clean under his nails. He hasn't had a shower since Tuesday, so I spoke to Roberto. They will change his shower time to mornings when Scott has more energy.

After wheeling Scott back to his room, I sat with him for a while to see if he would tire and want a nap. Just as I was getting ready to leave, in walked Matthew. What a relief! I could leave knowing Scott had company. Matthew stayed a few hours, and then Bill and Marilyn showed up. At that point, Scott was ready for a catnap.

The CNAs say that Scott receives more visitors than anyone else. Unfortunately, he can't remember these visits. Although he can't articulate his feelings to me, I believe each time he wakes up he thinks I've abandoned him. This must be why he is so sad in between visits.

Scott was in the Activity Room today when I arrived. When he saw me, he started to cry. "Do you know that I love you?" he asked.

"Yes, of course I do. Do you know that I visit you every day?"

"No," he admitted.

"Yesterday Matthew visited for a few hours and Bill and Marilyn came by." He stopped crying and smiled.

It was nice to see the tables set with linen tablecloths and napkins. But I was upset that his hair looked greasy, so I went to the nurses' station to ask about his shower. A bit later, a CNA told me that Scott would be given a shower around 2:00 p.m. Another CNA mentioned that she saw someone take Scott into the shower yesterday. If that's true, why does his hair look so greasy? And whoever gave the supposed shower didn't shave him completely either. Maybe it's Scott making it difficult, but why don't they tell me?

The food did not look appetizing: peas, a potato casserole, chopped up ham, a roll, water, orange juice, and for dessert, a white cake with strawberries and whipped cream (okay, that looked pretty good). I helped Ken and Jeanne get their napkins on and assisted Ken (the resident who uses thick utensils) a few times with eating his food.

Scott tried to talk but I couldn't figure out what he wanted to tell me. Then all of a sudden, he had to either urinate or have a bowel movement. One of the CNAs wheeled him to his room while I trailed behind them carrying the leftover cottage cheese and dessert. I made a second trip back for the rest of the water and orange juice. Once Scott finished on the toilet, he was put into bed for a nap with two heavy blankets on top of him.

It's chilly and 60 degrees today. Janice and I met at Tomatina's for lunch, and when she paid for my meal that made my day. It started raining pretty hard when we walked out of the restaurant, so we stopped at just one store in Montgomery Village before heading our separate ways.

A few weeks ago, I decided to do Scott's laundry since most of his clothes ended up in other residents' closets. I've got one load of laundry in the washing machine and another load in the dryer. As I lay down on my bed to read a new Stuart Woods novel, I could feel the stress of the day fly away.

Tuesday, April 17: Today I was able to park in the parking lot when I arrived around noon. That was a boon! Usually I have to park across the street, since there aren't enough parking spaces in Sunnybrook's lot. Crossing the busy street is a bit scary.

Later, I brought Scott some root beer. He usually loves it, but today he took one sip and set it down with a grimace. Oh well, I tried. I coaxed him into eating half of an egg salad sandwich and vanilla pudding by promising a nap right afterwards. At one point, he said, "I am so tired of all of this." All I could do was agree with him as I can't say that I know how he feels.

When we got to his room, I told him I needed to get home to eat dinner. No one was around to put him to bed, so I wrapped a few blankets around him to keep him warm. He looked forlorn and said, "I don't know why, but I feel scared."

Trying my best to reassure him, I said, "Honey, you don't need to be scared. Everyone knows you now and they take very good care of you." The hardest part is that I wish I could take him home, so I have to remind myself how hard it was before he fell.

Wednesday, April 18: At dinner tonight, Scott was sitting in between Jeanne and an older resident named Margaret. Apparently, they had played a game and Margaret won three tickets. She gave Scott a ticket so he could get potato chips or candy.

"Scott doesn't like potato chips, Margaret, but he does like chocolate," I suggested. Angie Gatt, the Activity Director, opened up a bag of Ruffles for Margaret, who then proceeded to put a few chips in Scott's hand. As Scott looked at the chips with a confused look on his face, Margaret nudged him and said, "Go ahead…you can eat them." I gave Angie a look that let her know I had my eye on Scott to make sure he didn't choke.

Jeanne and Margaret were a captive audience as I gave them a brief synopsis about Scott's heart transplant, the aspergillus pneumonia, and all the meds he takes. When Margaret learned that Scott has Alzheimer's, it seemed to answer her question as to why she could never understand him when he tried to communicate.

"Are you his guardian?" Margaret asked.

"No, I'm his wife." She told me how sweet that I always come in to help him.

Scrolling through my Facebook page, I found some photos of Killian. The ooh's and ah's from the ladies made Scott laugh. Then I texted Jon to see if we could FaceTime with Killian. Jeanne and Margaret were in seventh heaven as they watched Killian and listened to his baby talk. Killian threw everyone kisses as we hung up, and I secretly hoped that Scott was able to hold onto these precious moments a bit longer.

Friday, April 20: Scott's cousin visited again today. I was so glad he did, because Scott was in rare form, talking and telling his off-the-wall jokes. Doug seemed to really enjoy this visit and I was glad he saw Scott feeling better.

The speech therapist sat with Scott at lunch to see how he did with pureed foods. He tried all three portions but we couldn't tell what they were. The color of each glob of food didn't match what other people were eating. When she asked Scott to try some chicken, Scott pointed to one portion and said, "So that's chicken? I think it's moving."

After lunch, we went outside to enjoy the sunshine. Scott dozed off, so I took him back to his room to take a nap. When the CNA came in to put him to bed, she excitedly exclaimed how thrilled she was to see Scott walk earlier in the day. While attempting to guide Scott to stand up with one hand on the walker and one on the wheelchair, Scott explained how to assist him into bed. Once he was lying down, he reassured the CNA by saying, "You'll learn how to do it better after a few times." It was comical to me, but I wondered if the CNA was bothered that this man, who can't dress or shower himself, wears briefs, and can't clean himself on his own, was telling her how to do her job. Guess he's feeling his oats.

Note to Caregivers:

When Scott first came home from the hospital after his bout with aspergillus pneumonia, I felt resentment. Taking care of Scott after working all day was exhausting. Most times he was depressed because no one visited and he felt so alone. I was his sounding board. After one particularly brutal commute and two presentations, I was upset when Scott told me he had gone for a walk and then had lunch with RPJ. Man did that hit a sore spot!

A bit miffed, I retorted, "I went to work then spent my lunch picking up your meds." I was resentful that he was out enjoying the warm, sunny day while I worked and used my lunchtime to run an errand for *him*. What I needed from Scott in that moment was an acknowledgement and a great big *Thank You* for my part in his recovery. I didn't get that. He just kept talking about his eventful day.

When you start feeling overwhelmed and resentment sets in, you can:

Take a Break: A break can do wonders for your outlook. Taking a walk out in nature will definitely lift your spirits. So will going to lunch with a friend. If your loved one can get out of the house, plan a short field trip or a drive in the country.

Find Support: Many local and online organizations offer support groups. You'll be amazed how comforting it feels to talk to others in a similar situation. Who knows? You may meet a forever friend.

Take Care of Yourself: The most common remark I heard as a caregiver was, *Be sure to take time for yourself!* I get it, we get it, we have to take care of ourselves. But think about it. If the person we are caring for is with us 24-hours a day and they need 24/7 care, exactly *how* are we supposed to take care of ourselves?

Assess your situation. Focus on what *you* are able to provide, then get help for what you can't do yourself. Accept help when offered from family and friends. Set realistic goals and know your limits; in other words, say *NO* to requests that are draining. Eat a healthy diet and drink plenty of water. Make sure you get enough sleep, and if it is a problem, see your doctor or try over-the-counter remedies—but remember that even over-the-counter remedies can have side effects with other meds as well.

I am happy to say that my feelings of resentment never lasted very long and an evening walk usually changed my outlook. And Scott was always telling me how thankful he was that I was in his life and how much he appreciated all that I did for him. May you find all the support you need!

28

That's the Best
You've Got?

Monday, April 23, 2018: I'm disheartened when I see Scott take his frustration out on the staff. At lunchtime yesterday, everything went well in the beginning. When I asked him to eat, though, he gave me a look and said in a menacing tone, "*I KNOW!*" With some coaxing, he ate half a tuna sandwich plus some of the regular meal.

After lunch we sat outside in the shade while a slight breeze blew softly around us. Scott mentioned *again* about leaving this place and I explained *again* that it wouldn't be safe for him.

When I arrived at dinnertime, Scott was sitting on his bed with the dinner tray in front of him. His arms were crossed defiantly and he was *not* in a good mood. While I was hanging up his clean clothes, he started to cry. I calmed him and suggested we go to the dining room to eat.

In the hallway looking for someone to take his food to the dining room, I overheard the CNA tell the nurse that Scott refused to eat. When the nurse saw me, she seemed relieved. It all worked out fine, but I really worry about him. He can't remember why he is where he is and doesn't understand why he can't go home. Repeating the story about how he fell and ended up at Sunnybrook helps get him through that moment.

Once everyone else had left the dining room, I did a word search puzzle while Scott ate a tuna fish sandwich. Then he wrapped plastic around a glass of orange juice and fretted, "I miss my dad."

Scott was already in the dining room eating his lunch when I arrived today. He was eating without any prompting. Lunch was chicken fettuccine Alfredo, which at home he wouldn't have liked. I buttered half a roll and put it in his hand to eat. He tried the chicken, but didn't seem to like that. He told me he liked the veggies until he found out they were green beans. I chortled, "Too late...you already said you liked them. Think of it as broccoli or brussels sprouts."

"Now you're talking!" he quipped and ate half the beans.

Jeanne and Ken were sitting at the table next to us when Ken asked me who I was. After I stated my name, he seemed satisfied. Jeanne said she was going to the mall on Thursday with Angie to get some clothes. She's told me this for weeks now, but never goes. Scott wondered out loud why there was an opening in the wall. Once I understood what he couldn't grasp, I explained that it was a window to let the sunlight in the room. Jeanne told us *again* that she was going to the mall on Thursday. The older man sitting at our table kept clearing his throat, then proceeded to spit out phlegm in his food. "That's disgusting!" cried Jeanne. "He should eat in his room." I half-smiled and looked away. Nothing seems to bother me anymore.

Wednesday, April 25: Scott was shivering again when I arrived for dinner. Luckily, his heavy sweatshirt was draped behind him on the wheelchair. After a bit of maneuvering, I was able to pull it over his head, but getting his arms into the sleeves took tremendous effort.

As we went back to Scott's room, his nurse for the evening said she needed to give Scott his meds. My back was bothering me, so I wrapped him up with blankets and left. As I walked by the nurse, she asked if I was going home. When I said yes she looked a bit miffed. Feeling guilty, I briefly thought about turning around, but didn't have the energy to stay. It had been a long day and I wanted to go for a walk before it got dark. Sometimes it just needs to be about me.

Monday, April 30: Last Saturday afternoon, Roberto called to say Scott was sad and wanted to talk. Scott said he really missed me. I said I missed him too and assured him that I would be there in about an hour and that Matthew was coming, too.

Scott was in a silly mood and teased Matthew. Sometimes I just don't know what gets into him except that I think his younger playful self is emerging. After Matthew left and Scott was done eating, I rolled him in front of the dining room TV to watch *Animal Planet*. Jeanne was reading a book, but put it away to watch the show with us. The room felt comfortable and intimate with just the three of us in it. There were a lot of *oohs and aahs* as we watched exotic bats, a baby snow leopard, and baby gazelles.

Scott's sister Carol from San Jose came to visit. At first Scott didn't recognize her, but he knew her voice. To keep him engaged, we played a card game with the other residents. Scott didn't even try to read the cards facing up on the table. When he seemed tired, we left so Carol could get settled at my place.

We met Matthew, Jonathan, Charlie, and Killian at Tomatina's for dinner and all ate well. Killian got a child's cheese pizza that was almost as big as our personal pizza. Having everyone come back to visit Scott ended up being a wonderful idea. Not only was Scott surprised, but all the residents watching TV in front of the nurses' station were entertained by Killian's antics. He went right up to Grandpa for a hug, then played chase with me and Charlie. Coming back from the restroom, I snuck up behind Killian, grabbed him, and kissed his sweet baby cheeks. He loved it. He ran away, came back, and faced the other way, so I could grab and kiss him again. I loved it!

Scott was getting sad as we walked away. Out of the corner of my eye I could see him start to stand up. Carol and I ran over to keep him from getting out of his wheelchair. He looked at me and asked, "What do I need to do so I can come home?" It took everything I had not to cry right there. As I tried to explain that there isn't anything he could do, that I can't take care of him anymore, one of the CNA's walked over to ask if he'd like something to drink. That was our cue to sneak out.

I suppose a better response would have been, "I'm just leaving for a bit and will be back soon." This would have reassured him in the moment. I'm still learning.

Wednesday, May 2: On Tuesday, I met all our friends from the ALZ support group in Occidental for breakfast. Carol, Diane and I took the scenic route through lush vineyards, unique wineries, and the quaint town of Graton. The tables were being set up for 20 as we greeted everyone for brunch.

Carol fit right in and it was surprising how many used to live in the San Jose area. Many stories and memories were shared. Without Scott, I could relax and not worry about helping him eat. The salmon omelet was the best breakfast ever.

When Carol and I got back to my place, she decided to stay home while I went to visit Scott. He was done eating lunch so we sat in the activity room to talk. At one point, Scott said, "My mom's mad at me today." When I asked him why, he couldn't remember. Maybe he was remembering how he felt as a child when his mom or dad were upset with him. I wish he would remember more of the good times.

At dinnertime, Scott was still in his room. He was too tired to sit up or stand. Roberto called for assistance and now *two* CNAs were struggling to have Scott stand up. Exasperated, I said, "Scott, I want you to stand up quickly then sit down in the wheelchair." That worked! With a CNA on either side of Scott, he stood, pivoted, and sat down. Roberto agreed to put the footrests on Scott's wheelchair, so he wouldn't have to walk his feet to the dining room. "Walk your feet" is a phrase I termed because when the footrests aren't on the wheelchair, Scott needs to shuffle his feet so they don't drag on the floor. He seems to understand it.

Scott and I were sitting together in the dining room. Alicia, one of the CNA's, was sitting at the same table doing paperwork.

Scott gave a little smirk, then asked Alicia, "Why aren't you helping me?"

Alicia said, "What would you like me to do, Scott?"

"That's the best you've got?" he asked. That made us both chuckle. I'm not sure if Scott understood what he said or why, but he did like the fact that he made us laugh.

Thursday, May 3: Bob and Scott were bantering back and forth as they sat in the dining room today, waiting for lunch to be served. Bob said he has to put hairspray on his hair every morning to keep it down.

Scott responded, "See what I have to work with?"

Alicia took Scott to his room to use the toilet, but someone else brought him back to the dining room. As the CNA walked away, Scott said, "I don't like these people." Uh oh! I asked him if anyone was being mean, but he said no, he just doesn't feel comfortable with anyone. I tried to explain that they are just trying to help and asked him if he understood that I can't do these things for him anymore. With tears in his eyes, he said yes. I told him that he should cry because things are very difficult for him. Instead, he ate the rest of his sandwich. When he was done, I wheeled him to the front of the nurses' station so he could watch TV with Ken. When I told him I wasn't feeling well and needed to go home to rest, he looked concerned as he hugged me goodbye.

Wednesday, May 9: I am so, so sad. I've had a cold since last Thursday and haven't been able to see Scott for six days. Today when we met, we hugged for a moment. I could tell that he knew I had been away for a while. He kept rubbing the cloth napkin that is secured by clasps around his neck. He hardly spoke to me, and when he did, he didn't make sense.

Gloria visited Scott both Friday and Saturday while I was sick. Gloria said she didn't think Scott recognized her until she mentioned Geoff. Scott did ask about his wife and Gloria told him that Julie had errands to do. That must have triggered something in his brain because a bit later he mentioned me by name.

After Gloria and Geoff visited on Saturday, she sent me a text message that said, *Scott told Geoff, You need to keep your eye on those two*, meaning Gloria and me. I texted Gloria back, *I love it! He can be such a card sometimes. That will go in the book. Oh, my nose is runny, my face hurts, and I look a mess. Hoping for a good night's sleep.*

Thursday, May 10: Alicia noticed I wasn't there on Friday and Saturday, but said she saw a woman with Scott both days. I explained that I had been sick with a cold so Gloria and Matthew visited for me. She also said Scott was asking for me a lot on Saturday. Jeanne said she wished she had known because she also heard Scott asking for me. Jeanne asked if she could tell him, *Julie's on her way and will be here soon,* so he doesn't stress out so much. I thanked her for caring and agreed that saying a phrase like that would help Scott in the moment.

I showed Alicia and Jeanne the video of Scott and Geoffrey that Gloria took while I was out sick. Oohing and aahing, they thought it was the cutest thing. And then I showed them a photo of Killian with a buzz haircut. After I showed Scott the same photo of Killian three times, it was as if he was seeing it again for the very first time.

Friday, May 11: At lunchtime, Scott was so tired he looked like a zombie, but eating a small burrito and tuna sandwich perked him up.

To get Scott ready for a nap, the CNA changed Scott's brief while he was standing. It's much easier this way. In bed, he started to cry. Out of the blue, he took the CNA's hand as she jumped out of her skin. "I'm not going to hurt you," Scott said. "I just want to thank you for all that you do. And will you tell your coworkers I said thank you to them too?"

She recovered her composure and said yes.

"You probably don't hear this enough from people," he said. He seemed quite lucid in that moment, like he realized exactly what was going on. We both had tears in our eyes as I rubbed his arms to help him through the sadness.

By dinner, his mood had changed. He was mad and upset. As Scott sat on the side of the bed glaring at Sandy the CNA, she attempted to coax him into the wheelchair. Another CNA said, "Oh, we're *so* glad you're here." Noticing me as he turned to see who had walked into the room, he immediately let Sandy help him stand up then sit down in the wheelchair.

In the dining room, Jeanne was in her wheelchair just inside the door at a dead stop. No one could leave or enter. She then bellowed, "There's no one in this room but a bunch of old people!"

Shocked, I countered with, "Jeanne, we're right behind you and we're all old people." A surprised Jeanne changed her tune quickly.

Since Scott was depressed, I texted Jonathan to see if he could FaceTime. Seeing Killian made Scott smile. When Matthew arrived, he was a new man.

After Scott was done eating, I brought out a hand wipe for his hands. Matthew watched dad wring the towelette, fold it into fourths, open it again, and fold it again. Then Scott brought it up to his mouth. Matthew and I both jumped up to grab it from his hands before he bit into it. Realizing he was doing something not quite right, Scott tried to make it seem like he was just fooling around.

Sunday, May 13: In the dining room, we sat down at a table next to Ken. Matthew walked in and surprised Scott.

"Is this young man related to you?" Ken asked.

"Yes, he's our son," I answered politely.

Ken told Matthew, "You have a nice Grandma."

Matthew and I started to laugh. "No," I reiterated, "he's my son."

"But you look much too old to be his mom."

Matthew whispered, "I think he just thinks I'm much younger than I am." Aw...thank you, Matthew, for trying to make me feel better.

Ken then asked a female resident, "Are you okay?"

"I'm cold," she replied.

"If I had bigger wheels, I'd roll over there and sit close to you and warm you up." We all erupted into laughter. Sometimes, the best moments are moments like this.

After dinner, Matthew wheeled Scott outside around the building. We ended back in front of the nurses' station where an even bigger crowd was watching TV. The word must have gotten out that those who leave their rooms have more fun.

As we were getting ready to leave, Ken mumbled something to Matthew. On the way out, Matthew said that Ken told him how good I was. Sweet, but I think he was making up for telling me I was too old to be Matthew's mom. Nice try, Ken!

Wednesday, May 16: Bette is a tiny thing and Margaret is tall. Bette has a form of dementia so doesn't always make sense and Margaret is hard of hearing. Listening to them chat back and forth is comical.

At dinner, Bette complimented Margaret by saying, "You did good," referring to how much food Margaret ate.

Margaret responded with, "Yes, it was!" I guess she thought Bette said *The food was good.*

Matthew was with us tonight, so I took pictures of Scott and Matthew. When I asked Scott to smile, he spit a seed at me. Matthew and I were shocked.

"Why did you spit at your wife?" I asked a bit bewildered.

Immediately contrite, he apologized, but apparently he knew exactly what he was doing.

A few residents were watching *Friends* when we arrived in front of the nurses' station. As we were getting ready to leave, Scott apologized a few more times for spitting at me. After we held each other for a moment, I walked away feeling lost and alone. I could tell that Matthew felt a sadness, too, as we walked out the door together into the overcast evening sky to go our separate ways.

Monday, May 21: Tonight when Tina the CNA was trying to put the nightgown over Scott's head, he was livid.

"I don't like how you are treating me," he told her. She laughed nervously, and Scott said, "Oh, now you're *laughing* at me?"

Getting down to wheelchair level so Scott could see my face, I exclaimed that Tina was just trying to help him into bed and she wasn't laughing *at* him. Then I admitted to Tina that Scott wasn't normally like this. I explained that sometimes Alzheimer's causes the person not to understand what is happening. Asking Tina to be patient and Scott to understand the pressure the CNAs are under seemed to help the situation. Although Scott calmed down, I know he won't remember his outburst.

Wednesday, May 23: Today was very scary. When I walked into the dining room, Scott appeared to be sound asleep. Bob was sitting behind him. I tried to wake him up, but he wasn't responding and didn't seem to be breathing. Was he dead? Why was his body so rigid? I freaked out and so did Bob when he saw my face. One of the CNAs came over, looked at Scott and said, "No, no, he's okay. He won't look like that." When Scott finally started to move his eyelids, I began to breathe. A good 15 minutes later, Scott came round and ate some food. Phew!

Friday, May 25: This morning I joined the Alzheimer's support groups for the sing-along. It felt like homecoming and I'm getting used to the fact that Scott isn't there with me. Joan and Dave sat on my left with Gloria and Geoffrey on my right. Gloria was helping Geoffrey turn the page and I think this was new for him. We sang some great songs by Gordon Lightfoot, Peter, Paul & Mary, Paul Anka, Huey Lewis, John Denver, The Beatles, Fleetwood Mac, et al. It was good for our souls.

Next was lunch with the HICAP girls. It was so good to catch up with everyone!

When I arrived at Sunnybrook, Scott looked so forlorn sitting in front of the nurses' station facing the hallway, not the TV. After putting away his clean clothes, I pushed him down to the dining room where a man was about to play the piano and sing to the 11 residents.

The piano man placed his small dog on a resident's lap. Kristy, one of the residents, was sitting next to the dog and was so smitten, looking back at me with a look of pure ecstasy, then back at the dog. Margaret maneuvered her walker over to the dog by holding onto the handles of everyone's wheelchair along the way. When she sat back down in the high back chair, I noticed the little dog in her arms. How did she hold onto the dog *and* get back to her chair without falling?

For the May birthday party, there were confetti-type decorations on the tablecloths. Some were about the size of a quarter, some smaller, some larger. Scott picked one up enthralled, turning it over and around in his hand. Just as the residents showed up for some cake and ice cream, Scott put a confetti piece in his mouth. As he prepared to bite, I yelled out, "*SCOTT, NO!*" probably a bit too loud for his comfort.

Monday, May 28: Scott seems more tired lately, which has me worried. On Saturday, he was still in bed at noon, not quite sleeping, but not awake either. Roberto was his CNA for the day and he brought Scott's lunch tray. Roberto is one of the sweetest men I have ever met and takes such wonderful care of Scott. He told me that while changing Scott on the bed, he reached over him and said, "Scott, I need to raise your bed up higher."

Scott replied, "Don't you normally jump into bed with the guy before you get him naked?"

Roberto also talked about helping a 98-year-old woman get into bed. "There's room in the bed for you, too," she said. "No one will know as my dad won't be home for a couple of hours."

At lunchtime yesterday, I was talking off and on to Bette. At one point, she looked intently at Scott and said, "He looks so nice." Then she looked at me and said, "What happened to you?" I wasn't sure if I should laugh or cry!

After lunch, I wheeled Scott back to his room for a nap. Ken was in his bed moaning saying his butt felt like it was on fire. He kept calling over to me, "Nurse, I need your help."

"Ken, I'm not a nurse."

"You're not? You're so pretty. Help me."

"Ken, I can't help you."

"Give me a hug."

"Nice try, Ken, but I can't give you a hug." I put my arms around Scott from behind and said, "I can give Scott a hug since he's my husband."

"He is?" Ken responded with a mischievous smile.

Then Scott said, "Yeah buddy, and you keep your hands off her!" The idea of them trying to fight over me made me chuckle to myself.

Neither one can stand up unassisted! Ken eventually fell asleep so I guess his butt pain went away.

Scott was still in bed when I arrived for dinner yesterday. With Anna the CNA's help, we got him up and down to the dining room. When Matthew joined us a few minutes later, Ken proceeded to give Matthew one compliment after another. "You are a handsome man. Are you from Hollywood? Well, you are no Marlon Brando, but you could be a detective in a movie. You have a nice smile. Are you from Hollywood?" He kept repeating himself and Matthew was loving it.

When Scott finished his spinach quiche, corn bread, and chili, I spooned some chocolate mousse into his mouth. Scott wanted to take over, so I put the spoon in between his fingers and the bowl in front of him. As Scott held the spoon, he let it dangle in his right hand. We didn't know if he was going to spill the chocolate mousse all over himself or put it in his mouth. The problem is that he'll start out right, but then his brain goes somewhere else and he spills the food in his lap. This is tough when I'm trying to get him to eat and he gets mad at me because I am spoon feeding him. He'll grab the spoon and turn it upside down. He does this all the time.

Back to the chocolate mousse, though, that Scott was dangling between his plate and lap. Ken was concerned that Scott was going to spill the chocolate mousse. He was very uncomfortable. This was surprising to me as he has Parkinson's and uses thick silverware to keep his hands from shaking.

"Put it in your mouth, you're making me nervous," he said, and grimaced at me. "You need to help him or he's going to spill it all over himself. He's making me nervous."

Scott seemed to understand what Ken was saying. He finished one last bite and decided to tease Ken by *not* putting the spoon in his mouth. He was moving the spoon around acting like he was going to turn it over. Ken said in a low voice, "Put it in your mouth." Then more loudly, "Put it in your mouth!" With voices raised and in concert, Matthew and I called out, "*SCOTT/DAD, PUT IT IN YOUR MOUTH.*" We didn't want Ken to have a conniption fit.

Matthew wheeled Scott to the front of the nurses' station. Loud enough for the nurses to hear, I said to Scott, "Anna and Hannah are going to give you a shower tonight. They are going to wash and shave you, so you will feel much better." The first thing I noticed today at lunch was how clean he looked. That was great—after a week with no shower he was starting to smell.

Note to Caregivers:

When I first saw Scott looking comatose, it felt like my life force was being sucked out of my body. If he had been dead, what would my response have been? I know it is coming and it's inevitable, but how do I prepare myself for that final moment?

If he had been dead, I would have been so thankful that Bob was there. The people at Sunnybrook would have been wonderful, but knowing that someone close to Scott was there with me would have been helpful. I keep wondering what that last moment will be like for me. I'm not ready for him to go, but I would never want Scott to stay because of me.

This is the life of a caregiver. So many ups and downs. Any given moment could be our last with our loved one. And then there are so many times that we don't know how much more of the caregiving we can handle. At least at Sunnybrook, I feel like I have wonderful people taking over to give Scott the things I can't provide, especially the physical part of this ongoing journey. And for now, that's the best I've got!

29

You're Not a Part
of Me Anymore

Thursday, June 7, 2018: On Tuesday, I did something for me by going to a retreat for caregivers. Sponsored by the Redwood Caregiver Resource Center at The Bishop's Ranch in Healdsburg, it was free to all seniors. Being surrounded by the wonders of nature filled our hearts and souls with joy.

During the lecture, I raised my hand to share that my husband was in a nursing home with Alzheimer's, and that getting to know the residents and staff helps me cope. I shared some residents' comments that bring humor to a difficult day and keep me smiling.

After a scrumptious vegetarian lunch, I sauntered over to the chapel to meditate until it was time for a 15-minute massage. Lying on the table in the shade, I enjoyed the slight breeze and the chorus of joyful birds singing in the background. It was the best thing I've done for myself in years.

Monday, June 11: Yesterday Scott was sitting in front of the nurses' station with only a nightgown on. If he could see what he looked like, fidgeting with his hands and pulling the gown up to his brief, he would be humiliated. Roberto told me that Scott wouldn't let him put sweats on when he changed his brief earlier. Together we were able to nudge him to cooperate and then took him down to the dining room for dinner.

Ken's favorite drink is root beer. While we were sitting with him and Jeanne, Ken said, "I'm like root beer."

"How's that, Ken?" I asked.

"I taste good, too." You can't make this stuff up!

Immediately after dinner, the CNA put Scott to bed as he couldn't keep his eyes open. As I was covering him up with blankets, he became annoyed. "*JULIE!*" he said loudly. I was startled and dumbfounded. I said, "Hey, you know my name!" I'll have to get him annoyed more often.

Tonight after dinner, I was wheeling Scott to the nurses' station to plant him in front of the TV. "I've got to get out of here," he said.

"Where are you going to go, sweetie? They take good care of you here." He agreed and we continued on. At the nurses' station, I had to maneuver everyone around so I could put Scott next to Ken. Well, you would have thought Ken and Scott were forever friends.

"Hi Scott," Ken offered in a jovial manner.

With a big smile, Scott beamed, "Hi, how are you tonight?"

As Ken's face lit up, he confirmed what I already knew. "He really is a nice guy!"

"Told you, Ken," I responded with a big grin.

Scott started getting a cold or some sort of bug on Thursday. At each visit, I mention his ailment to the CNAs and nurses to make sure they keep an eye on him. But the next shift claims they weren't informed. Today, Dr. Jaffe came in at lunchtime to listen to his lungs. She seemed to think he was okay, but he's got a deep cough and that always worries me. An X-Ray looked normal, so Dr. Jaffe ordered Mucinex to help with the runny nose and cough.

Tuesday, June 12: Today I met people from my old support group for lunch at Rosso Pizzeria. I felt out of touch with most of them now that Scott is at Sunnybrook. Their spouses are still able to communicate and most were there.

Someone mentioned she was thinking of visiting Scott. Telling her he probably wouldn't recognize her, I left it at that. Another person suggested that I purchase a guest book so friends can sign their name when they visit, so I can remind Scott who came by. It's a good idea if your loved one is still aware of what is happening around him or her, but for Scott it would be futile.

Later it dawned on me why I told this friend in a subtle way not to visit. When I am with Scott, I am focused on his needs. If he's eating and all of a sudden needs to use the toilet, I make sure it happens. When he's tired, I make sure he is put back to bed. Most times I stay until he falls asleep. And until I arrive at Sunnybrook, it's hit or miss as to whether he'll be asleep, grouchy, or happy to see me.

So when someone who is not a close friend visits, the expectation is that I will be there, too. Since Scott isn't really able to interact with anyone, much less entertain well-meaning friends, this falls on me. It becomes more of a burden than a joy. Now I can understand why when someone's loved one is dying, they request that no one but family and very close friends sit vigil. You don't have the energy to entertain anyone else.

We celebrated June birthdays this afternoon. Scott's is tomorrow. Angie outdid herself setting up the tables with decorations and balloons. There were two cakes: German Chocolate and White Strawberry with vanilla ice cream. Scott was coughing and his nose was running so I was constantly helping him use tissues. Like a child, he doesn't know how to blow his nose anymore. I don't think Scott knew the party was for him and Jeanne.

(Note: Since Scott was constantly fidgeting with his hands, which is a new Alzheimer's symptom he's developed, I found a sshlumpie elephant blanket for his birthday. As the months went by, the CNAs made sure the sshlumpie was always in his hands while lying in bed or sitting in his wheelchair so he could rub the soft floppy body between his fingers. He loved it!)

Thursday, June 14: Today was a day I was dreading. When I walked into the room to help Scott get ready for dinner, Sandy was changing him. I could tell she was having a hard time, so I walked up and tried to help. Scott looked at me and said, "Who are you?" in a nasty voice.

I explained, "I'm your wife, Julie, and I'm trying to help Sandy get you ready for dinner." He followed my cues and did get up. Once he really looked at me and heard my voice, I think he recognized his wife.

Monday, June 18: It was difficult to watch the movie *Breathe* last night—a true story about Robin Cavendish who became a quadriplegic and responaut (someone who needs a respirator to breathe) at the young age of 28 from polio. I wondered how Robin's wife, Diana, was able to care for her husband from age 28 to age 64. Apparently they were able to afford excellent in-home care.

Visiting the Hallberg Butterfly Gardens (HBG) on an overcast day to take photos brought disappointment as butterflies need the sun. I used both my Canon EOS and my iPhone camera to compare the quality. The Canon's photos of the flora came out much sharper. Volunteering to create HBG's 'thank you' cards for donors fills my heart with joy; the photos of butterflies I've taken over the years are used on the front cover of each card. Afterwards, I stopped at Grateful Bagel for a lox and bagel sandwich, then went to see Scott, who thankfully seems to be feeling better. After getting him into bed after lunch, I came home for a nice hot shower that felt exhilarating after my hike in the dust at HBG.

When I arrived tonight Scott was sleeping in bed. After coaxing him awake, I had him drink a MightyShake. Roberto came in a bit frenzied as he had lost track of time and wanted to get Scott out of bed and ready for dinner. He couldn't find Scott's shoes, but we found Ken's shoes sitting on Scott's smaller wheelchair. Roberto found Ken, swapped shoes, and came back to get Scott up.

It's so difficult for Scott to sit up in bed, stand up, then sit back down in the wheelchair. He has a hard time understanding what the CNA is telling him to do. When I'm there, it seems to go more smoothly, or so they tell me. Most of the time he doesn't want to get up, though.

Scott ate most of his food, talking and even joking with me at times. It was good to see that, but then he couldn't figure out what was food and what wasn't. When I came home, I was wiped out. Maybe the big difference between us and Robin and Diana Cavendish is that Robin could still talk and express himself to Diana.

Tuesday, June 19: Today I decided to go to the Honda dealership to buy a white Honda Accord EX-L. I love it! This is my fourth Honda Accord since 1990.

While visiting Scott tonight, he kept chewing something in his mouth.
"Scott, what's in your mouth?"
"I was just going to ask you the same," he replied.
"You were going to ask *me* what was in *my* mouth?"
"Yes," he said with a big grin on his face.

Thursday, June 28: Last Sunday night at Sunnybrook, we had a private 65th birthday bash for Scott in the dining room. His actual birthday was June 13, but that date didn't work for most people. Showered, shaved, and wearing a royal blue shirt, Scott looked quite spiffy.

It was a great turnout with Matthew, Janice, Olga Lee, RPJ, Jonathan, Charlie, Killian, Alexis (Charlie's mom), Breanna (Charlie's sister), Leighana and Jayleigh (Breanna's four-year old twins), Gloria, Geoffrey, Gil, Cynthia, and residents Ken, Ron, and Jeanne. The Costco cake was chocolate with white frosting decorated with yellow, red, purple, and blue balloons. The cake along with fruit punch, trail mix, and assorted fruits of red grapes, melons, and strawberries provided plenty of leftovers for the employees. I'm not sure if Scott understood what all the hullaballoo was about, but I think he enjoyed watching everyone.

On Tuesday night Scott started breathing irregularly while in the dining room. By the time the nurse on duty arrived a minute later, everyone was frantic and I was scared. Back in his room, he ate some dinner and seemed to perk up a bit. I helped lay his head down then sat with him a while to see if he would go to sleep. His eyes still open, he just laid there staring straight ahead. Now I was nodding off, so I told him I needed to leave. He always asks where I am going, so now I tell him I am off to do errands and will be back soon. If I tell him I am going home he gets upset. A little white lie makes it easier for both of us.

Wednesday he was fine at both lunch and dinner, but today at lunchtime he started breathing irregularly again. We got him back to his room where Juli the CNA changed him and put him to bed. He had a hard time standing up and an even harder time turning for her while he was being changed. He was asleep as soon as his head hit the pillow. As usual the bed was lowered almost to the floor in case Scott or any resident falls out of bed. This prevents worse falls.

Tomorrow is the sing-along then lunch with Gloria. In the afternoon, Charlie is having an ultrasound for new baby Tatum. This may sound selfish, but I hope Scott will continue feeling better so I can enjoy these outings.

Saturday, July 14: Nothing much has changed, but no news is good news, right? Yet, the other day had me wondering when Erika, one of the CNA's, took Scott into the bathroom after lunch. When she opened the door to help him get into bed, he looked straight at her and said rather nastily, "Who are you?" After she explained, Scott said, "I don't need your help. None of you know what to do." Appalled at how he was speaking to her, I felt really bad that my sweet husband would talk that way.

Skip forward to today. I woke up, took a shower, then ate a sandwich while watching the beginning of a Stephen Colbert show to get some laughs before I headed over to Sunnybrook. When I arrived, Scott was sitting at a table with Jeanne, Ken, and Carol. I gave him a hug, greeted everyone, and they said *Hi* back. As usual I hooked my tote on the back of Scott's wheelchair, then took out a fruit cup for Scott and some peaches for me. I moved a high back chair between Scott and Jeanne and sat down. After putting my arms around Scott again, I asked about his day.

In a very mean voice he said, "Why are you here?"

After a moment's pause, I said, "I'm your wife, Julie, and I'm here to help you eat lunch."

"You don't need to come here anymore. You're not a part of me anymore," Scott said in a nasty tone that hurt me to the core.

Jeanne, looking just as shocked as I felt, said, "Scott, that's your wife, Julie, and she comes here to help you eat."

"I don't need you to baby me anymore," was Scott's snarky response.

As my heart was breaking, I started sobbing uncontrollably. "Why are you crying? *Why is she crying?*" asked Ken. He was very upset, as was Jeanne, as was I.

Picking up my purse and rushing down the hall with everyone watching, I hurried to the Social Services room. The light was out, so I turned around confused, not knowing what to do. Luckily, the social worker, Heather saw me and took me back to the room. With heavy sobs, I told her what happened. I knew that this might happen someday, but I wasn't ready for that someday to be today. Once I was composed, we walked back to the dining room. As I stood behind Scott, Heather asked if he would like his wife to eat with him. No answer. The second time she asked, he said flat out *NO!*

I had Heather pick up my tote as I picked up my pad and we walked the long hallway to the entrance. As we walked by the nurses' station, I heard Roberto calling me. Unable to respond, he gave me a big hug. He tried to soothe me by relating that Scott seemed really off this morning.

"Please make sure he eats lunch and then put him down for a nap," I implored him. "I'll be back at dinnertime to see if he remembers what he said to me."

I cried all the way to the car. I tried to call Gloria. No answer. I tried Jonathan. Again no answer. Janice and Olga Lee answered and I drove to their house to get some much-needed comfort. It was exactly what I needed as they listened and we discussed this horrible disease called Alzheimer's.

Later, Heather called to let me know that Scott was taking a nap. She said that Jeanne berated Scott for 15 minutes about why he needed me to come in to help him. A while later, Heather found Jeanne crying alone by herself. When she asked what was wrong, Jeanne said, "Julie's never coming back." Heather reassured Jeanne that I would indeed be coming back *and* would be there at dinnertime.

Back at Sunnybrook that night, I helped Scott eat in his room. My heart still hurt and I was skeptical about how he might treat me. I asked if he remembered what he had said at lunchtime. He did, but I'm not sure that he understood how hurtful his words were.

Tuesday, July 17: Matthew stopped by Sunnybrook on his way home from work on Monday. While Scott was in bed, Matthew decided to have some fun in Scott's wheelchair. First I texted Jonathan a picture of Matthew sitting in the wheelchair making a serious face. Jon texted back with a photo of him winking and pointing a finger. Then Matthew had me make a video with him rolling back and forth challenging Jon. Jon texted back with a video that Charlie took of him sitting on the toilet. Then Charlie took another one of Jon sitting on Killian's little three-wheel bicycle (and this is a 6 foot, 5 inch man). You can hear Killian laughing in the background. Matthew wheeled the chair down the hallway towards the nurses' station, but turned around before anyone saw him. It was a fun time, although the roommates thought we were crazy.

At lunch today, Scott was sitting with three men: George, Don, and Jack. After helping Scott put his bib on, I cut up his food. I was blown away when he actually thanked me for helping him and even planted a kiss on my lips. Was I surprised! Maybe he was trying to prove a point to the other three men.

Jack's feet didn't touch the ground while he sat in his wheelchair. Since he appeared to be a big man, that seemed odd. When I mentioned my observation to Jack, he boasted, "It's not my feet that are getting big under the table." Turning a deaf ear, I let the comment slide.

A young CNA came over to help Jack. He apologized for something he had said to her yesterday. Sounding contrite, he stated, "I wouldn't have blamed you if you had slapped me."

Looking at Jack, I blurted, "I'll slap you if I hear you say that to her again." One of the CNA's laughed out loud, but Jack knew I was serious. Now, I'm not a prude, but I am sick and tired of listening to men of any age with their sexual innuendos. I heard it all as a young woman and when I hear older men who should know better make sickening comments, I just want to scream *GROW UP!*

Sunday, July 22: Albert was Scott's CNA today—a nice man, but very hard to understand. After Albert helped Scott in the restroom, Scott was upset. "He's mean and I don't like him," he said. When I asked one of the roommates if he liked Albert, he said he did but that he *does* talk and move too fast.

Scott was awake and feeling better when Bill and Marilyn arrived. He was animated, where a moment before I couldn't get him to respond. Of course, right? He remembers both Bill and Marilyn and says a few things as if he knows exactly what's going on. After they left, he was unable to finish a sentence. I'm not complaining. It's just hard and tiring.

After dinner, I wheeled Scott back to his room to get into bed. When Sandy showed up to help Scott on the toilet, I zipped out for my own toilet break. Returning, I was shocked at how Scott spoke to Sandy. My guess is he doesn't understand what they are asking of him, so he tells them off. This isn't my sweet husband, the one who never said a mean thing to anyone…well hardly anyone. This is not who he was before this disease.

He pulled his sweats up over his brief that was hanging below his butt. He was mad and told her so. Together, we adjusted his brief, got him into bed, and covered him up with blankets. His outbursts and the amount of care that he needs confirm that I cannot take care of him anymore. I try not to feel guilty about leaving him in a nursing facility, but I still do.

Monday, July 23: Talking with Erika the head CNA, I mentioned that although I was happy with Albert, Scott says he is mean and doesn't like him. Albert's broken English (even I can hardly understand him) must make it extremely difficult for someone with Alzheimer's. Erika agreed to take Albert off Scott's watch.

Wondering whether Scott is ready for hospice services again, I decided to get a consultation from a different provider. When the nurse from Sutter Hospice arrived, we went outside to talk. I explained the reason for the consultation and my concerns about Scott. She stated that Scott is definitely at end-stage but needs to be at Stage 7.3 in order to qualify for hospice services. I just printed out a sixteen-page list of Stages 1 through 7 and he is definitely at Stage 7.0.

Talking with her, I realized that my feeding him and making sure he drinks water is helping to keep him alive. Am I prolonging the inevitable? Would Scott want me to do this? I don't think so. So many times he has cried and said he's so tired of living like this. I've decided to let Scott guide me about eating or drinking and let him control his food and liquid intake. Easier said than done.

After we finished talking, the hospice nurse spoke with a few Sunnybrook nurses. His chart shows he weighs 158 lbs. so there is a weight loss. Then we went to his room finding him in bed. Wouldn't you know he spoke effortlessly and courteously to the nurse, although when Erika came in, Scott turned nasty. The nurse witnessed Scott's callousness, and of course, while what he said to Erika made no sense, the tone was mean. When the hospice nurse said, "Goodbye Scott, it was good to meet you," he responded respectfully saying, "It was good to meet you, too." Sometimes I just don't get this disease—it's no wonder we caregivers want to pull our hair out at times.

Wednesday, August 1: We talked with a new resident while Scott ate lunch. She told us she was leaving Sunnybrook in a week. As Scott reached over to touch her arm, he joked, "We won't hold that against you."

Scott is out of it today and I feel the same way. Remembering I needed to tell him something important, and wanting to get us both out of our defeatist mood, I exclaimed, "Scott, it's our 27th wedding anniversary on Friday."

Scott looked up with a half-smile on his face and said, "*OH—MY—GOD!*"

Sunday, August 5: When I arrived for lunch last Thursday, Scott asked me if he had done something wrong. I took his hand and assured him that he hadn't. Then he asked, "How can you spend that kind of money..." then took a bite of his lunch without finishing the sentence.

When I was getting ready to leave, Scott questioned, "Are you mad at me?"

"Of course not, honey, I'm just leaving to get some errands done. I love you and will be back very soon."

A bit later, I saw an acquaintance who seemed to feel it was her responsibility to tell me what I needed to do with my life, insinuating that I should stop visiting Scott so much. I was totally outraged by her lack of empathy. When I go to see Scott, that *is* for me—it is what I need to get through all of this. When he is gone I don't want there to be any looking back, any regrets. I love him and will continue to be there for him even when he doesn't want me there anymore. What is it about people who think they know what's best for others?

When I told Bette today that last Friday was our 27th wedding anniversary, she said with a straight face, "And they said it wouldn't last!" Everyone within earshot laughed.

As I looked at Scott to see his reaction, I noticed that he didn't look well. I asked what was wrong, but when I realized he wouldn't know, I called Lindsay, a Restorative Nursing Assistant (RNA), over. Both Lindsay and the CNA wheeled him to his room and helped him into bed at lightning speed. As soon as they loaded him up with blankets, he was sound asleep. That was my cue to go home, ice my back, and take my own little nap.

Tuesday, August 7: When I got to Sunnybrook for dinner last night, Scott was already in the dining room watching the movie *P.S. I Love You* with the other residents. As I kneeled in front of him, the relief on his face was plain to see. Misty-eyed, he asked, "How did you know where to find me?"

"I always know where you are and will always find you."

He looked totally surprised at my answer. My eyes welled up with tears. I feel like I'm losing him more and more every day.

On a lighter note, there were a few cute remarks today. As I got Scott ready to take a nap, I said softly, "I'm going to put your head down. Ready?" Scott said, "I've been waiting for you all my life."

Bette's nurse asked if she liked the braised beef served for lunch. Bette looked down at the bowl, back at the nurse, then asked, "Do you want it?"

While we were waiting for dinner to be served, Jeanne asked me for the third time if I knew what was for dinner. Scott said, "Nothing, as of yet."

Bette said, "I was looking at Scott the other day and he looked so nice. But he was staring at me like, *What are you looking at, old lady*?"

Bette and Jeanne don't like each other and it was getting heated at the table. As Jeanne was leaving the room, Bette looked at me and said, "You can have Jeanne." Then she looked at Scott and said, "No, you can have Jeanne and I'll take your husband."

Note to Caregivers:

Looking back, I can see how I would respond today to remarks Scott made when he seemed almost lucid. When Scott asked, "How can you spend that kind of money…?" then forgot where he was going, I wish I had said, "Scott, You were starting to ask me something," and repeated what he had just said. At least I would have I tried to find out where this idea was coming from and maybe ease his mind. This wasn't the only time he couldn't finish a thought and maybe with a bit of coaxing, we could have had a conversation. Now I'll never know.

If your loved one begins a conversation and either forgets or changes his/her mind, do both of you a favor and see if the two of you can open up and talk about it. If it is you, the caregiver, who has some unfinished business, don't wait. You never know when it will be too late.

30

We Need to Talk

Sunday, **August 12, 2018:** No grandbaby yet.

Friday night Scott asked, "Are you afraid of me?" Anna had just changed his brief and we were trying to get him to stand up with the walker.

I looked at him and said, "No. Why would I be afraid of you?" Of course, he couldn't respond, but something in my face told him I was afraid. In reality I was afraid *for* him not of him, but how could I explain that?

Scott has a new roommate named Jack. When we met in the dining room a few times, he was pretty obnoxious. But tonight when I asked Jack if he needed anything, he was nothing but polite. He is hard of hearing, so I had to repeat my question three times.

If you had told me a year ago that Scott would be in a nursing home and I would visit twice a day, I would have said, "Are you crazy? I could never do that!" But here I am. And if you had told me years ago that I would become a good caregiver for my husband, I would have laughed in your face. I didn't think I had this much giving in me. Life can take us through some enormous changes and we can either go with the flow or fight it. Guess I decided to go with the flow.

I'm finding that when one of the residents is crying, my heart breaks and tears well. I have fallen in love with all these people who can't care for themselves.

The other day Frances, who can no longer speak or express herself, started to cry after I innocently said *Hi*. When Roberto saw her face, he comforted and consoled her, telling her how everyone loves her and that she is safe. Maybe the tears came to me then because it's so close to home. Watching Scott in tears always breaks my heart.

The other day Scott said, "I wish this was over."

"That means you won't be here anymore," I said, which was probably the wrong thing. It's not that I wish him to stay in the condition he is in, I just want him to know how permanent it will be when it's over.

Bette continues to bring laughter to our table. Yesterday Matthew joined us for dinner. Bette said to Matthew, "I'm sleepy."

"Me, too!" he responded. It was Matthew's 33rd birthday and he ran a 10K run at Angel Island. He was pooped.

Deadpan, Bette proposed, "Let's go to bed!"

When Bette told us about her late husband and his liquor store, she joked, "My husband sold liquor at a store. I drank it."

Tuesday, August 14: Margaret and Jeanne were dishing out the compliments last night. Margaret proclaimed, "Scott is so lucky to have you visit him every day."

Then Jeanne confided, "When you're not here, people ask where you are and everyone really likes you and Scott."

I told them how sweet their words were. Then I thought, *Does Scott want me to be here all the time?* So I asked him and he quickly said yes. After a brief pause I said, "Right answer!" Even Scott laughed with that playful smile of his.

The chicken cordon bleu wasn't very good and Scott had a hard time chewing and swallowing it. As we waited in the hallway for a CNA to take Scott to bed, I overheard a gentleman in another room say, "Chicken Cordon Bleu…more like chicken cordon *blah*!"

Roberto was putting Scott to bed for a nap when he leaned over to me and whispered, "The menu was being passed out today, but instead of *pork carnitas* it said *porn carnitas*." And laughter abounds.

Monday, August 20: Grandbaby Tatum was born on August 14 weighing in at 7 lbs. 15 oz and is 19 1/2 inches long. Of course, she is absolutely beautiful.

I didn't visit Scott at all yesterday as I didn't get to sleep until 5:00 in the morning. Deciding to give myself a break, I stayed home all day, took a shower, ate, read, slept, then repeated as necessary. I needed this!

This morning I went to the Monday ALZ support group to talk about my nursing home experiences. I created a handout with information on Medi-Cal including funny quips by Scott, Bette, and Roberto. My goal was to show that this experience can be filled with compassion and love for everyone you meet, and that even though it's scary, you can transform the scary part into a healing experience.

When I visited Scott at lunch he asked, "Do you still want me?"

"Of course, I love you and always will."

"Are you sure?"

"Of course I'm sure. I wouldn't be here if I didn't love you." He then ate a hearty lunch of French Dip sandwich, tater tots, and pudding.

When Scott and I first met, I was jealous when he talked to any single woman. Scott was never jealous. He is the ultimate gentleman, treating all women with total respect. Now it seems the roles have been reversed, and Scott is the jealous one. I find it comforting in a sad sort of way. Maybe he doesn't know what he is saying, but I like to think he's trying to express his love for me in the only way he can.

After putting Scott's dirty clothes in the washing machine, I went over to Jonathan and Charlie's. As Killian ran around the room, I chased him like a big bad wolf. He was laughing and having a ball while baby Tatum was asleep in her swing. When she woke up, Killian was across the room taking a breather sitting in a big red wagon with his stuffed animals. He was talking to his mom when all of a sudden he said, "Grandma," then tried to tell me something. I couldn't understand him, but that was the first time he spoke directly to me. I was overjoyed!

Scott was still in bed at dinnertime. Sandy helped him get up and into the dining room. As we were passing Bette, she said very loudly, "There she is!"

As Lindsay came up behind Bette, she spoke into her radio, "Okay, we found Julie and she's on her way to the dining room." Lindsay turned Bette around to follow us. Thinking, *How cute was that*, I chuckled to myself.

Jeanne was waiting for us, but she was adamant that Bette not sit at our table. But Gil and Cynthia were visiting. We ended up putting Gil on Scott's left, then Jeanne and Cynthia, with Bette next to me. Otherwise, WWIII was going to erupt. Jeanne was so mad that Bette was at our table so I am considering having a talk with her.

Tuesday, August 21: Jeanne claimed she was upset that Bette keeps taking her stuff. I explained that Bette has dementia and doesn't always know what she is doing. I reminded Jeanne that Scott sometimes takes somebody else's drink, "and you know that Scott doesn't know what he's doing." She acknowledged that and seemed to understand. The next day, Jeanne sat with us and was nicer to Bette.

I could feel Bette watching me and Scott when Bette said, "You are so good."

I touched her arm and declared, "So are you!"

Bette said, "I've never had to be (good)."

I gave another short presentation to my original Tuesday ALZ support group and it went longer than the one on Monday. Since I didn't have to run off, I was able to answer some burning questions people had about Medi-Cal and nursing homes.

Thursday, August 30: Arriving late for dinner a few nights ago, I could tell that Scott was upset. Jeanne was sitting at our table. Trying to comfort Scott, she said, "Look, Julie's here. See? I told you she'd be here."

Looking at Scott, I knew it was me he was annoyed with. Several times I asked if something was wrong. When he finally spoke, it was in an accusatory tone.

"Where were you?" Not sure what was going on in his mind, I was confused about what he thought I had been doing. In a broken voice, he said, "I've been trying to help everyone, too."

"I know, and everyone appreciates your help," I said as I tried to comfort him. He must have thought I was wandering the halls helping everyone and anyone. What he can't grasp, though, is that he is my main concern.

Last night, Scott wouldn't look at me or respond—he was so mad again. No matter how often I asked what was wrong, he still wouldn't answer or look at me. Asking one last time if he was mad at me, he finally said, "Yes." I decided not to take it personally, didn't get upset, just kept helping him.

He must have remembered how he had treated me yesterday, as today he tried to explain that he didn't mean it, that it wasn't me, it was him.

Friday, September 14: Scott has been at Sunnybrook for six months. No one thought he would live this long, not even me. Today at lunch Bob visited. Scott really enjoys these times. I'm not sure how much of the conversation Scott can follow, but I've learned to stop talking if he needs to say something. Most times what he says doesn't make sense, but on the rare occasion his response shows he's following along.

After Bob left, I wheeled Scott to his room. Erika was his CNA and while we were talking, Scott said something about me being his mom. And he seemed dead serious. Does everyone think I look older than I am? Ugh!

At dinner, we talked about the spelling of the TV show *I Dream of Jeannie*. Jeanne kept saying it was spelled Genie, like Genie in a bottle, so I looked it up on my iPhone and showed her the correct spelling. "That was not how Jeannie was spelled back when I watched the show," Jeanne insisted rather tersely.

A new resident named Keith who appears to be in his later 60's or a bit older is the sweetest man (later I found out he is 87). He'll call me over to ask how he can get something done, how does he order something else if he doesn't like the meal, or how does he get back to his room? Sometimes he tries to stand up on his own because he's tired of waiting for someone to take him back to his room.

Like all the residents I've gotten to know, I try to help Keith in any way I can. One day this week at dinnertime, Keith stood up attempting to wheel his chair out of the room. The CNA was very thankful that I got her attention. The biggest worry is that someone might fall. She thanked me so many times I felt uncomfortable.

I know that they are overworked and underpaid and most of the staff have hearts of gold, so if I can help in my own way when I see something that's not quite right, why shouldn't I? It may not be kosher and the State would probably tell me to stop, but I would tell the State that they should make nursing homes pay the staff a decent salary, with a lower resident-to-staff ratio. Who is responsible for regulating nursing homes so that money isn't the main focus? Money should never be the main focus. Making sure residents get the care they need and having consistency with the CNAs is what's important.

I can't tell you how many times I've wheeled Scott to his room and waited 15 minutes for someone to put him to bed. By the time a CNA walks in, Scott is too tired to stand up on his own, and it takes two CNAs to help him stand to change his brief and put him to bed. I don't blame the CNAs at all for these fixable and humane issues. I blame the staffing shortage, the greed of the owners, and the low wages.

Saturday, September 15: I was in a deep sleep when I heard a text come in. It was Charlie saying, *How are you and Scott doing? Killian is playing with the elephant you got him with your recording and he's asking for you. Tatum is old enough now that we might be able to visit Scott. Maybe we can plan something?*

She texted a video of Killian playing with the elephant, listening to a recording of me saying, "Killian, it's Grandma Julie, peek-a-boo, I see you, peek-a-boo, I see you." He was holding the elephant and twirling it around in his arms while the recording played. And of course, it made my heart leap with joy.

That would be great. Scott and I would love it, I responded. *We'll have to maneuver around everyone's nap, including Scott's.* That didn't work out today, but hopefully soon.

Gloria and Geoffrey visited Scott at lunchtime. We were already sitting with Keith and Jeanne, but we were able to rearrange so everyone fit comfortably. When lunch was over, Keith asked me how he could find out what therapy he needed for the day.

We found the printout for his PT in his room. After reading it, he asked to go to the nurses' station to double check. As I pushed Keith to the nurses' station and Gloria pushed Scott, one of the male CNA's said, "Are you trying to get a job here?"

Keith was confused about how to let the PT person know where he would be at 2:00 p.m. I assured Keith that he didn't need to do anything because the PT person would find him. Somewhat relieved, we got Keith situated in front of the TV with the other residents. The rest of us then went outside to sit in the shade and visit. Soon it was time for Gloria and Geoff to leave and I took Scott to his room for a nap.

Scott was awake tonight when I arrived. Marc the CNA quickly got him up and into the wheelchair then pushed him to the dining room. On the way, I heard a woman calling out, "Somebody help me." She said it a couple of times as I walked past her room. I know that the staff gets upset when I step in where I shouldn't, but I felt compelled to go back to see what I could do. Her call light was on and soon Marc walked in, so I knew she would be in good hands. Then I heard someone yell, *Hi Julie.* It was one of my favorite nurses. As I yelled back, *Hi Isabelle,* there was a spring to my step.

At the table, Scott grabbed my hand. "We need to talk about the money you're taking," He exclaimed. He seems to believe that I'm cleaning out our bank account. I swear I don't know where he comes up with these ideas. When he was recovering from aspergillus pneumonia in the hospital in 2007, he thought I was selling the house. Then he thought I was remodeling the kitchen, and now he thinks I'm spending the little savings we have.

"I know everyone loves you here, but..." He couldn't finish the sentence, but I was starting to wonder if he was jealous of all the attention I give to other residents.

Trying to ease his mind, I insisted, "Every resident needs help and if I can bring some joy into their lives, then that is what I need to do. And besides, if I were taking all the money you think we have, I wouldn't be coming here twice a day to make sure you are taken care of."

Later Bette wheeled up to our table. After she was settled, I asked her to tell Scott that I am here twice a day and wouldn't take any money. She told Scott this, but he still didn't believe it. So I texted Charlie about the situation. We FaceTimed with Killian and Tatum, which just made my day as I was missing them all so much. Charlie told Scott that I would never spend all the money, yet he still wasn't buying it. Jonathan came on and I asked him to tell Scott that I wouldn't spend all our money. Scott believed Jonathan. After we hung up, Scott was more relaxed, but I was unsettled. It's annoying that he'll believe Jonathan but not his own wife.

When I got home to my empty abode, I fixed a salad and poured myself a glass of merlot to help me relax. Scott's accusation left me feeling like I had been run over. Before Alzheimer's, Scott agreed with and trusted every single purchase I suggested. Making the decision together was important. Before I purchased the new Honda in June, I thought about what Scott would want me to do about the expensive repairs looming over our old car. Without a doubt, he would have told me to buy a new one. Maybe I should have talked to him about it, but I didn't think he would understand anything I said. Was I wrong? Would he have understood?

Note to Caregivers:

Responding to Scott's hurtful comments is a struggle for me. I try to give as much of me as I can and he responds with an accusation. Some of us will instinctively know what to do or say, but not me. My instincts don't usually kick in the first or even the second time. I suppose, regarding the money issue, I could have asked him more questions as to his thoughts. At this point in the disease, though, I just didn't think he could grasp anything, much less talk about it. Now I wonder if his brain could hear and decipher what I said, but just didn't allow him to respond in a coherent way. Such a complicated and sad illness for everyone involved.

Another tough issue is when to tell the truth and when to tell a little white lie. Telling the truth is very important for me, yet sometimes the truth is not appropriate for someone with Alzheimer's. Their reality is not our reality. For instance, if your loved one says she sees her deceased mother, the appropriate response is to acknowledge what they are seeing and let them feel their mother's presence. Who are we to know whether it is a hallucination or other worldly visit? And why should we ruin a perfectly innocent supposed sighting that lifts up their spirit? Go with the flow and be gentle with your charge.

31

I See You

Sunday, September 23, 2018: Alyssa the nurse was almost out the door when she turned around to give me a report.

"Julie, today at breakfast Bette was seriously cutting Scott's donut," she confided in me. "I asked Bette if she was going to eat his donut and she said, *Oh no. Julie isn't here and I wanted to make sure that he could eat the donut, so I was cutting it up for him.*"

I shared that Bette had once told me that she wished she could help Scott in the morning like I do at lunch and dinner. "I let her know that she didn't need to worry about him and that one of the CNA's would help him," I told Alyssa. "She really wants to help." Between Bette and Jeanne, I never worry too much when visiting isn't possible.

Scott was sitting up in bed when I arrived, while Anna attempted to get him up and into the wheelchair. He was not happy and I just didn't feel like trying to figure it out.

Once he was eating and drinking in the dining room, he became his comical self. It was nice *not* having Jeanne in the room because we were able to talk without interruptions. At one point, I was bringing the spoon up to Scott's mouth when he said, "What are you putting *that* into?"

"Your mouth."

Scott's reply, "Smart ass!" didn't even phase me.

After settling Scott in front of the TV with the other residents, I took the almost empty cup of water out of Scott's hand to put on a tray by the kitchen door. As I started walking back, I decided to sneak behind the nurses' station so Scott wouldn't see me leave. He was engrossed with the movie *Atypical*, so I felt it would be easier for everyone concerned. No complicated goodbyes, no fuss. But hey, I love this man.

Thursday, October 4: On Monday, Keith and his wife Mary, who had moved into Sunnybrook three weeks ago due to a fall, left quietly to go to their new home, wherever that will be. I noticed that they were not at dinner on Monday night. The bed in Mary's room was stripped and all of her things were gone. So were Keith's things. That night I realized that the Sunnybrook residents who have brought such joy into my life, will soon be a part of my past.

Tonight at dinnertime, Jeanne asked me what I had done today. I gave her the short version.

"I came to Sunnybrook at lunchtime, went to Trader Joe's for groceries, went home to do Scott's laundry, then came here," I announced.

Well, that woke Scott up. He looked at me all serious and said, "I can do my *own* laundry."

"I know," I said lovingly, "I just wanted to help you with it." He shrugged and continued eating his stir fried chicken, veggies, and rice as if we had never talked about laundry. (I tasted the stir fry and it was quite tasty. Kudos to the chef!)

Scott's comment made me realize that he still believes he can function on his own. The mind is a complicated and amazing phenomenon.

Tuesday, October 16: While I was telling Roberto about my planned trip to Modesto for my aunt's 90th birthday party, Jeanne suggested, "You should take Scott." Roberto gave a half gasp then laughed. I felt exactly the same as I attempted to explain that it would be cruel to take Scott on a two-and-a-half-hour drive—besides which, he couldn't get in and out of my car without lots of help.

Tonight at dinner, it was Bette, Jeanne, Scott and me. I don't know if Jeanne was upset that Bette was sitting with us or not, but Jeanne said, "Did Bette tell you what she did last night?"

I looked at Jeanne and said no.

"She told Scott you would be in any moment and he got very upset that you didn't come." Bette was oblivious to the conversation as her memory is getting worse. I tried to explain this to Jeanne, but she didn't get my drift.

At one point, Bette mouthed *I don't like her* to me. She wasn't eating so Lindsay brought her sherbet. Jeanne scolded Bette that she needed to eat her dinner first. Finally I told Jeanne, "Let her be. As long as she is eating something, everyone is happy."

Wednesday, October 24: Last Thursday night, we couldn't get Scott to open his eyes. The CNA and I kept repeating, "Scott, wake up. It's dinnertime." After the third or fourth time, Jack yelled out, "SCOTT, OPEN YOUR EYES!" Apparently, he was trying to sleep and we were waking him up. It's funny because he is hard of hearing, and yet he could hear that.

Last Saturday I drove to Modesto for my Aunt Rose Anne's 90th birthday party. Seeing cousins, especially my cousins Lynn and Rose Marie, was important to me as we try to stay in close contact. The highlight of the party was Aunt Rose Anne singing one of my favorite songs, *Edelweiss*. My mom loved that song, too, so it brought back many happy memories of her singing in her lilting soprano voice.

After the party, we went to Aunt Rose Anne and Uncle Jim's apartment at the retirement home. We visited for a while and I shared some of the comical sayings the residents come up with at Sunnybrook. Erik, married to my older cousin Brigitte, enjoyed the stories about Bette so much that he shared them with the next group that joined us a half hour later. The only awkwardness was that I think my relatives expected me to be a total mess and didn't know how to act around me. When someone asked about Scott, I think they expected me to break down and cry.

Maybe because I'm trying *not* to force feed Scott, it seems like he isn't eating as much. At lunch today I mixed up his cottage cheese and fruit and put the spoon in his hand so he could scoop it up by himself.

I was talking to Jeanne when I saw that he had turned the spoon upside down. As food fell on the plate, he put the inverted spoon in his mouth. So much for him eating alone.

After lunch, Mayra the CNA couldn't get him to stand up to change his brief. When another CNA Nancy arrived, they did it together. Nancy left thinking Mayra could get him into bed, but now Scott's brain wasn't telling his legs to sit down. When Mayra called Nancy back in, Scott finally sat down on the bed and lay down. He was asleep before I left the room.

When Bill delivered the mail yesterday (and yes, Bill Nasi is our mailman), he told me he was catching a cold and asked me what he should take since Marilyn is out of town. I gave him my last four 12-hour Allegra. Later he called to thank me and we talked a bit about Scott.

"I told Marilyn that if I ever get as bad as Scott, just give me something and let me go," Bill stated emphatically. Unfortunately, it's not that simple. I explained that when Scott starts pushing the food and meds away, that will be the time to stop his meds completely.

Tuesday, October 30: Sunnybrook had a Halloween Carnival this afternoon from 2:30 p.m. to 5:00 p.m. While Charlie stayed with Tatum in her stroller, I took Killian around to all the booths so he could play games to win toys and candy. Killian's favorite, though, was jumping in the bouncy house. Scott missed the fun because he was in bed taking a nap.

Sunday, November 11: Tonight I found Scott sitting by the nurses' station. He was mad! I cornered Roberto to wheel Scott to the dining room.

Rewind to last Monday. After visiting Scott, I made a trip to Trader Joe's. When I got home to get out of the car I felt a familiar pull on my left hip. I don't know how I was able to get the groceries and laundry put away, but I did—then iced my back. When I tried to stand up, it was like all the other times I've put my back out. At 5:00 p.m., I was still trying to figure out how I could go back to Sunnybrook, but finally accepted that that wasn't going to happen. I stayed home until Thursday, enjoying the time alone and trying not to worry about Scott.

So back to tonight. When Roberto had Scott set up at the table, I put my cushion on the chair and sat down. He still looked mad, so I asked him if there was something wrong. In an accusatory tone, he demanded, "Who's Steve?" (Maybe since I was out with my back he thought I was doing something untoward.)

Astonished, I countered with, "I don't know any Steve. Do you know someone named Steve?"

He didn't have an answer, but he was still mad. It made me feel like he thought I was having an affair. I truly believe that is what was going on in his feeble mind. Distrusting me seems to be his new thing. Is he having hallucinations? If this were a normal marriage, distrust and accusations like this would get us into counseling. But it's not normal for Scott, and there's no way I can ease his mind when doubts set in.

Scott smiled when he saw Matthew sit down next to him. The distraction helped get him out of his distrustful mood. It's just so sad that Scott and I can't have a normal conversation where I understand him and he understands me. All I can do is be there and not take his comments to heart.

Sunday, November 25: When I went to see Scott last night, I gave him a piece of a banana, placed the rest of the banana and peel out of his reach, then went to check his room for snacks. By the time I got back to the dining room, Scott was eating the banana...peel and all. Trying to get him to spit it out was not happening, so I pulled out my phone to check the Internet to see if it's okay to eat the banana peel. It is and I was so relieved.

It's a bit comical that Scott thinks he can help me with something. When I was leaving tonight, I explained that I was going home to ice my back as it had been bothering me all day.

"Is there something that you'd like me to do?" he asked with visible concern.

Yes, Scott, I thought, *I wish there was something you could do, and I wish you could still share in our day-to-day life. I miss you so much.*

At lunchtime today, Lindsay was wheeling Bette out the door. A CNA was standing there with a pillowcase draped over her shoulder filled with tablecloths and cloth napkins. It looked like a bag of goodies. As Bette was going by she exclaimed, "Hi, Santa!" It's amazing that someone who has dementia can think so quickly on her feet.

♡

Thursday, December 6: Last night I completed about half of my Christmas cards when I ran out. It may sound silly, but I'm excited that I'll be going to Corrick's Stationery tomorrow to check out all the Christmas cards and ornaments. These little things give me joy.

I've been helping out with the Alzheimer's Holiday Sing-along and Luncheon, picking up dessert paper plates and napkins, ordering cookies and cello baggies for the cookies. Last year's Christmas handouts with the lyrics will be used again this year, and Chloe's will be catering.

Three tables were pushed together making an intimate gathering for dinner tonight with Scott, me, Jeanne, Carol, Barbara, and Margaret. All the ladies stayed after they were done eating while Scott finished his food. Alicia the CNA kept asking each of them if they'd like to go to the front to watch TV, but no one wanted to leave. Alicia said it's because they want to sit with me, which gave me a feeling of so much love.

Tonight Scott was laughing and smiling with all the ladies. They get that he can't remember much anymore, so they give him a lot more slack than they give each other. Especially Bette and Jeanne. If Bette doesn't like someone, she completely ignores him or her. It's rude and comical at the same time.

Suddenly Margaret exclaimed, "Look at Scott, *LOOK AT SCOTT!*" Scott was getting ready to put the sharp end of a knife into his mouth. Scared silly, I grabbed it out of his hand before he got it all the way to his lips. Luckily, the knives at Sunnybrook are *not* sharp.

When I asked Scott if he wanted more to eat, he told me no then picked up something to eat. Thank goodness I have my wits about me or these interchanges would surely make me loony.

Monday, December 10: Sunnybrook has a new resident, a 35-year-old Hispanic man. His English is not particularly good, so Margaret interpreted tonight at dinner. His name is Benjamin, lives in Fresno, and he fell from a two-story building on a construction job, hurting his back, right arm, and leg. He has a radiant glow about him.

Tonight I took Scott's clean clothes to his room first. By the time I stepped into the dining room, everyone was situated with no place to squeeze in. Jeanne moved to Benjamin and Margaret's table, so I could sit next to Scott. I could hear Jeanne talking to Benjamin with Margaret interpreting. Pretty soon I was involved in the conversation as I recited one through ten in Spanish. Benjamin tried to recite one through ten in English, but he only got to five, skipping to eight. We were having fun trying to help each other with English and Spanish phrases.

Benjamin asked Margaret what was wrong with Scott. As I explained the physical and mental incapacities to Margaret, she repeated in Spanish. Benjamin told me how sorry he was for Scott's disease. In Spanish, he said, "I can see that your love for Scott is so real and beautiful," which of course made me cry. We talked back and forth sharing our lives, what we did when we worked, how old we are, and I shared family pictures of Matthew, Jonathan, Charlie, Killian, and Tatum.

When Scott was done with dinner, Anna wheeled him to the nurses' station where I helped find a movie for the residents to watch. They chose *Beethoven*, a Christmas story about a St. Bernard dog. Scott was mesmerized. As I was getting ready to head out, Isabelle sweetly declared, "Everyone just loves you." I told her that I loved all of them, too. "You should work here since you are so good with everyone." My thought was, *Uh…no thank you!*

Two nights later, our table consisted of Scott, Matthew, Barbara, and George. Scott kept giving Matthew strange looks. Then in a snappy voice asked, "Is that your boyfriend?" He was dead serious.

I explained to Scott that, "No, you are my boyfriend and my husband. Matthew is our son." Looking at Matthew again, he recognized him. What the brain of an Alzheimer's patient believes to be true is just crazy. Am I not reassuring him enough? What am I missing?

Sunday, December 23: Friday was the Alzheimer's Holiday Sing-along and Luncheon. Counting caregivers and those with dementia, 52 people sang holiday songs with much enthusiasm. The food from Chloe's was delicious as always and the centerpieces Lauren and Shelley (employees of the Alzheimer's Association) purchased helped to set the mood for the holidays. The person with a round sticker on the bottom of their placemat took the centerpiece home. All of us got a bag of cookies to enjoy later. We thanked Shawna, our pianist, with a beautiful holiday plant.

One caregiver mentioned to Diane that she just couldn't get into the mood for Christmas, but the singing and luncheon did the trick. For this I am thankful that all of our effort made for a wonderful celebration.

Yesterday at dinnertime, Scott wasn't talking much. He wouldn't respond to me, so I looked at my Facebook page. There was Bob Kat, in a Facebook memory from 2013. It took my breath away when I saw her photo. I was already feeling the loss of my husband, my friend. Seeing Bob Kat in her red Christmas basket looking right at me was too much. In my mind, I started looking back at the years since Scott was diagnosed with Alzheimer's. So many upheavals we went through and losing Bob Kat in the middle of it all. Looking back, I can't believe we survived it all.

The biggest reason for the tears and sense of complete loss was realizing that this Christmas will be the first one without Scott at our Christmas dinner celebration. This Christmas day, Jonathan, Charlie, Killian, Tatum, Matthew, Gloria, Bill, Marilyn, Janice, Olga Lee, Karen and I will gather, but Scott and Geoffrey will not be present. (Geoffrey is now in a residential care facility.) I will visit Scott at noon at Sunnybrook as usual, but he is unaware that it's Christmas.

Sunday, December 30: Last Friday, I noticed Ken watching Scott. Ken then looked at me and said, "He is seriously disabled and he is so lucky he has you taking care of him. Come here and give me a hug. I love you." I told Ken I loved him, too, and decided that Ken was being very sweet and loving. As I moved in for the hug, I told Ken not to touch me anywhere inappropriately as he has been known to do. He was a complete gentleman. What Ken said made me choke up as sometimes I forget how disabled Scott really is.

Last night Gloria made lobster with fettuccine and mushrooms and I brought a salad with Litehouse Ranch dressing. We drank a red wine blend and visited for three hours. Even though most of the dialogue was about our spouses, we had a wonderful time sharing our frustrations and fears along with the funny incidents that happen. Gotta laugh.

A few weeks ago I decided to stop bringing Scott's soiled clothes home to wash and dry. It was becoming an almost daily chore and Sunnybrook provides laundry services. But ever since, his sweatpants and sweatshirts have gone missing. They finally turned up in his roommate Jack's closet. Hallelujah!

Friday night and tonight were special. There seemed to be this feeling of camaraderie among everyone from the nurses and CNAs, to the residents and to me. Both nights had us sitting with Jeanne and Bette at dinner. Tonight, after Jeanne ate all of her chicken sandwich, potatoes, and dessert, she wanted Scott's meal. They put Scott's ground up chicken on regular bread, but the bread was soaked in gravy. Jeanne ate Scott's entire sandwich, using her fingers to wipe up the gravy on her plate.

Bette told me her Aunt Virginia was coming to pick her up. Since she is 84, I am pretty certain her aunt is no longer alive. Thinking a little white lie was the most humane response, I comforted her by saying, "The nurses at the front desk will find you when your aunt arrives, so you don't need to worry."

Sunday, January 13, 2019: Bob visited Scott last Friday at lunchtime. Bob was in a great mood as he had just come from a meeting with his Purple Heart group. When Scott saw Bob he got a big smile on his face. When Bob made a comment, Scott's response didn't make any sense, so Bob would look my way to interpret. I just shrugged my shoulders and mouthed, "I don't know."

Last night Scott wouldn't talk to me again and I couldn't get him to eat or drink. I tried for an hour. Although he wouldn't answer my questions, he shook his head that he didn't want me to leave. I finally couldn't handle it anymore, so told him I loved him but that I was going home. I let him know that Roberto would help him from here.

This morning, he was still upset. He did, however, drink the water I brought him. I wasn't sure if he was going to eat while I was there, but when Bette told him how adorable he was, his face lit up. From that point on he was fine. He ate his lunch and drank his orange juice.

Jeanne told me that after I left last night, Scott said he hadn't wanted me to leave and that he would try not to be mean to me anymore. Apparently he's aware of his attitude towards me. He just can't express his feelings. I can't blame him for being angry when he thinks I have abandoned him.

Sunday, January 27: Even though Scott continues to be angry, at least he is eating. I've tried to let him do as much as possible without interfering, but it's hard not to. He will pick up the fork or spoon and then just sit there. I'll push the utensil towards his mouth and sometimes he will eat, but usually he'll put it back on his plate. When I feel myself getting annoyed and frustrated, it's time for a break.

Last night, Anna wheeled Scott up to the front. She started to park him at the end where he couldn't see the TV, so at my request she moved him to the other side. Then she wheeled Bette down the center aisle to the front. When Bette saw me, she started yelling, "No…NO!" Then she planted both feet down hard to make Anna stop. I chuckled as I watched this unfold, knowing that she wanted to see me. When Anna brought her over, she had to maneuver everyone around so Bette could sit next to Scott. Who would have thought that I would feel so much love for these beautiful souls and receive so much love in return.

Friday, February 1: Last night took a lot of patience. At our table sat Scott, me, Bette, Jeanne, and a new resident named Sue.

Starting off, Sue asked me, "Do you live here?"

"No, I live about five minutes away."

Bette looked at Sue and asked, "Who is she?"

"That's Sue."

"Who?"

Moving closer to Bette's ear, I said louder, "Her name is Sue!"

"This food is so good tonight," Jeanne said.

"It is…I tasted Scott's meatloaf." It was the second best meatloaf I've ever had!

Pointing to Scott, Sue asked me, "Are you his caregiver?"

"That's my husband, Scott, and yes, I am his caregiver."

"Does he live here?" Sue asked.

"Yes."

"What's wrong with him?"

"He has Alzheimer's."

"He doesn't talk much."

"No, he doesn't," and my short responses would make it seem that I don't talk much either.

Looking at Sue again, Bette asked, "Who's that?"

"That's Sue."

"Who?"

Closer to her ear again, I said even louder, "HER NAME IS SUE!"

"Oh."

"Wow, this food is so good," Jeanne said as I ignored her.

"Do you work?" Sue asked.

"No."

"What did you do when you worked?"

"I worked in the health insurance industry all my life."

Jeanne piped up, "I love this food. The meatloaf is so good. Look, I've almost eaten it all."

"Yes, I see that Jeanne."

Pointing to Scott, Sue asked, "What's wrong with him?"

"Look, I've eaten all my food," Jeanne interrupted. "Aren't I good?"

"Yes Jeanne, you did really well."

"Where do you live?" Sue asked.

"About 5 minutes away."

"Do you work?"

"No," I stated again.

"What did you do when your worked?"

"Who is that woman over there?" Bette questioned again. And on it went while Scott sat there in his own little world.

Wednesday, February 13: One morning mid-January as I was lying on the floor doing my back exercises, an earsplitting sound began. It seemed to be coming from outside and it was killing my ears. I kept thinking that whoever was causing this dreadful noise was awfully rude.

Off and on through the following weeks I heard this annoying humming sound while at home. I was wondering why none of my neighbors ever came over to complain. When it stopped three weeks later, I was so relieved. But then it would come back at odd times, day or night, just driving me crazy. I finally started asking neighbors and friends to come over to listen, but only one neighbor could hear it. *Okay, good,* I thought, *I'm not going crazy.*

I was so stressed about the humming in the house that I contacted my plumber, Jeremy Gardea, thinking it had something to do with the water pipes under the house. Before he came out, he suggested that I tighten all the water hook ups in and outside the house. After adjusting the faucets, the humming was only at night, then stopped completely last Saturday. My ears have been hurting ever since, but at least the sound seems to be gone. So whether it was tightening the plumbing or God's intervention, my ears are starting to feel better.

I've been trying to figure out why Scott has been refusing to eat. One day, I thought he said, "Stop beating me," then realized he said, "Stop feeding me." To get around this issue, I'll put food on the fork or spoon then slip the utensil into his fingers. Because he thinks that *he* is the one putting food on the utensil, he will put it in his mouth.

After everyone has eaten and left the dining room, I turn Scott's wheelchair towards me so that we are facing each other. He seems to respond better and I am able to spoon feed the remainder of his meal without issue.

Today one of the residents was playing the piano and, may I add, not very well. Roberto came up to me to share that he had overheard Annie and his Aunt Julia (both residents), "This place is a freaking insane asylum!" referring to the woman playing the piano. We were in stiches.

Friday, February 15: Last night I dreamed that Scott was ahead of me as we were walking down a boardwalk. When Scott turned the corner, I didn't think I'd have to hurry because he was only a couple of feet in front of me. But when I turned to follow him, he was nowhere to be seen. Frantic, I was running around calling his name. As in all my dreams with cell phones, I couldn't get mine to work. The phone looked funny and the buttons on the keypad were all mixed up. Terrified and feeling completely alone, I attempted to call 911. My only thoughts were to reach a dispatcher to explain, *My husband is missing and has Alzheimer's... please hurry.* I woke up in a panic until I realized it was only a dream.

Tuesday, March 5: After Diane, Gloria, and I ate lunch at Tomatina's, we browsed a couple stores to enjoy some girl time. Gloria and I made plans to go to the YMCA at 4:00 p.m. for an exercise class and Matthew was coming over afterwards to watch *The Wizard of Oz.*

I arrived at Sunnybrook around 3:00 p.m., but Scott was fast asleep in his room. Wanting to tell someone I wouldn't be in at dinnertime, I found Erika sitting at the nurses' station. Before I could say a word she announced, "Do I have a story for you!"

Apparently at lunchtime Bette and Margaret were trying to help Scott eat. First Margaret got out of her chair to spoon feed Scott. When Erika told her the CNAs were watching him, Margaret exclaimed, "But no one is helping him eat." Erika told her it was because he eats very slowly, but not to worry as the CNAs would take care of him. Then Bette reached way over to put food on his fork trying to help too. Thinking the CNAs were *NOT* doing their job, Bette and Margaret became so agitated that Erika had to get one of the nurses to calm them down.

The YMCA event was cancelled, but Matthew and I had a great time eating pizza and salad. An intense conversation followed the movie. It felt good having a day to connect with my son outside of the nursing home. *(It sure sounds like I eat a lot of pizza. Must be my comfort food.)*

Wednesday, March 6: At dinner tonight, I pulled Scott's wheelchair over to me. He put his hand on my leg and squeezed it. While looking into his deep brown eyes, I said, "I see you." Scott looked deep into my eyes and said, "I see you, too!" I'm going to miss him so much!

Recently when Alicia was walking Scott in the hallway, someone said, "How are you doing, Scott?" Scott's response, "She didn't give me a choice," was priceless.

Sunday, March 10: Today I spoke with Mike, one of the nurses, about having Scott evaluated for hospice again. He assured me that he would talk to the doctor to set up a consultation.

At lunchtime, Scott was staring at me suspiciously. "Do you know who I am?" I asked. He shook his head no. I was devastated and thankful that I've had all this time with him knowing me. "That's okay," I said, "because I know who you are and I'm here to take care of you."

Marilyn and Bill visited Scott for about a half hour at dinnertime. Scott wouldn't eat the ravioli or salad, so Roberto brought an egg salad sandwich and chocolate pudding. Since Scott was keeping his mouth closed like a child refusing to eat, I turned my chair and his wheelchair so we were facing each other. He drank some milk and I spoon-fed him bits of sandwich. After he ate half the sandwich, he picked up a piece and ate it on his own. After that, though, I was back to spoon feeding him. I noticed that his fingernails were getting long again, so once he was done eating and everyone had left the room, I got out my clippers to trim his nails.

The last time Scott told me he loved me was only two weeks ago, and now he doesn't know who I am.

After dinner, the dining room was quiet and empty. Recently, Scott has begun staring at the person in his vision of sight and right then it was me. As Scott observed me, he lifted up his right arm, which made me wonder what he would do next. I stayed as quiet and still as possible. With his right hand he reached towards me and very gently touched my face. I was shocked and intrigued. As he massaged my left cheek, I held my breath so as not to break the spell.

Roberto entered and sat down at the desk. Not wanting this precious moment to end, I didn't glance over, but I could feel Roberto watching. Scott seemed so sweet and loving when all of a sudden he took his right index finger and put it in my mouth, pulling on it like a fishhook. OMG! I didn't know what to do, but I certainly didn't like the feel of that finger in my mouth. As I gently removed his finger, I tried hard not to laugh.

A few minutes later, I placed his hand on my cheek to rub my face. "Soft, huh?" I asked. He nodded. Then I took my hand and rubbed his cheek saying, "Your face is rough 'cuz you're a boy. My face is soft 'cuz

I'm a girl." He agreed with another nod. Then Lindsay walked into the room and the spell was broken.

Sharing the story with Lindsay, Roberto said, "It was so sweet seeing Scott touch Julie's face, but when he put his finger in her mouth, I didn't know if I should laugh or cry." We all broke out laughing, which made Scott laugh too.

Tuesday, March 12. Scott was placed on hospice through Memorial Hospice of St. Joseph Health. I already feel grateful that I will have another set of eyes on Scott's care.

Note to Caregivers:

John's wife Marilyn was in a skilled nursing facility (SNF). When John, a member of my ALZ support group, felt it was time for hospice services, he asked Marilyn's doctor to set up an evaluation. The doctor didn't feel she was ready. Unfortunately by the time the doctor agreed to an evaluation, John's wife was just two weeks away from dying. John's only regret was that he didn't call hospice when he felt it was necessary.

As the caregiver, *you have the right* to call a hospice at any time to ask questions. You do not need your doctor's approval for a phone call. The hospice agency will determine if a consultation is appropriate and contact your doctor to set up that consult. If you remember, I had three hospice consultations for Scott: one at home, and two at the nursing home.

Some of the key signs that your loved one may qualify for hospice are as follows: regular trips to the emergency room, chronic and difficult-to-treat pain, breathing difficulties, rapid decrease in appetite and/or weight loss, sudden mental impairment, and increased sleep. Each situation is different and your observations are valid.

To qualify for hospice care, a hospice doctor and your loved one's doctor will, to the best of their knowledge, certify that your loved one is terminally ill, meaning he or she has a life expectancy of six months or less. The extra care your loved one *and you* receive from hospice is well worth that phone call…so don't wait. And if for any reason your loved one doesn't qualify for hospice yet, you will have gained some valuable information to prepare yourself for the future. Best of all, you as a caregiver may be able to receive counseling services from hospice even before your loved one passes away.

To find hospice care, check out local listings on the Internet under hospice agencies.

Scott and Julie's Wedding Reception and
Open House – November 30, 1991

Matthew, Scott, Julie, and Jonathan – August 25, 2002

Jonathan, Scott, and Charlie - August 11, 2013

Julie and Scott – June 13, 2015

Bob Kat on Scott's lap – July 17, 2015

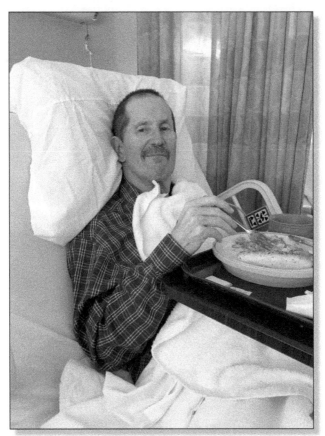

Scott – March 10, 2018

Matthew and Scott – May 16, 2018

Jonathan, Killian, Scott, Tatum, Julie, and
Charlie – September 16, 2018

Julie, Tatum, and Scott – February 24, 2019

32

I Don't Know
What I Need

Thursday, March 14, 2019: Matthew and I sat with Sue, the resident mentioned in the February 1 dialogue. She asked Matthew three times if he knew about Friend's House, a senior retirement community. The first two times Matthew said no. She explained to him that she had been on the Board of Directors and that her parents had lived there. Another resident mentioned that Friend's House is a Quaker religious community where there is no minister, everyone is considered equal, and when someone is saved they quake with joy. What a wonderful description of this Christian faith.

The third time Sue asked Matthew if he knew about Friend's House, he announced, "Yes, I do. Weren't you on the Board?"

"Oh, yes," she said, "Did you know some of the members?" *Aha, she got you, Matthew!* He told her no and that was that.

While I was feeding Scott, he picked up my right hand with his right hand. Keeping as still as possible, I watched him tenderly. Matthew also watched closely as Scott put his thumb in the palm of my hand and rubbed it lovingly. He really doesn't know who I am, but he must feel the love emanating from my heart.

The humming sound is back and hasn't relented since last Monday. During the night I started wondering whether the humming could be in my ears. I went to Gloria's the next day to see if I could hear it in her house…which I did. An appointment has been scheduled with the audiologist to check my hearing, but first I have an appointment with my PCP to check for wax buildup.

Monday, March 25: The diagnosis is Tinnitus with significant hearing loss in my left ear. But if I am unable to hear as well, why do I hear a high pitched sound? It's a mystery and I am totally baffled! Admittedly, I was driving my family, friends, and yes, even the plumber Jeremy crazy complaining about the humming sound. Jeremy asked me a few times if I thought it could be Tinnitus. I couldn't believe he would ask me *that*, like wouldn't I know if the humming was *in* my ear? Apparently not and what a relief to finally figure this out. Thank you, Jeremy!

Tonight when I pulled Scott's wheelchair so we were facing each other, Ken said, "You should feed him like he was an animal in the zoo."

"What animal would he be?"

"A monkey," Ken said.

I told Scott he was an orangutan. He just stared at me and laughed when I laughed. Then Ken said, "Be sure to feed the monkey. He needs the food."

When I looked up at Scott, I found him staring into my eyes. Choking up I said, "I love you."

I was surprised when he quietly said, "I know!" and the tears came.

Monday, April 8: About a week ago, I asked the dietician to put Scott on pureed foods. He'll eat it at first then just stops and sits there. Tonight, I turned him towards me to see if he would eat a sandwich, but he must not have liked the taste *and* he kept chewing and chewing. He was able to swallow the chocolate pudding and drank two MightyShakes, but he was upset that I was pushing him to eat. When I knew he had had enough of me and the food, Nancy the CNA wheeled him to the front and I pushed Bette. As I reached over Scott trying to get my bag from behind his seat, I accidentally scratched his face. Before I could say *I'm sorry*, he looked at me with such venom and said, "Are you crazy?"

I was shocked and upset and said right back, "Do I look crazy?" That was when I realized that he really doesn't know who I am—he was no longer the man I love. The man I married would have never said that to me, especially with such animosity. My heart has been hurting ever since and I don't know what to do. Part of me wants to stop visiting and the other part wants to see this to the end. How much emotional pain must a caregiver go through each and every day while taking care of the person they love? Maybe it's the emotional pain that takes so many caregivers before the patient.

Monday, April 22: Last Thursday, Lisa, the nurse from Memorial Hospice, left me a phone message. She said that after seeing Scott and reviewing his chart, she thought it would be best if we stopped all his medications except for the Sandimmune and CellCept (the immunosuppressive drugs that keep him alive) and Noxafil (for aspergillus). Apparently, Scott sometimes refuses his meds and has been refusing the immunosuppressive drugs every other day. Not good.

I left Lisa a message this morning saying that Jonathan, Matthew and I agreed that we are ready to stop these other meds. Lisa called back after she spoke with Dr. Jaffe. Together they went through his medication list and will stop everything except the three above plus Omeprazole (Prilosec) for his stomach. I expected to be heartbroken, but I was relieved. It will be good for Scott not to be subjected to a slew of drugs and vitamins anymore.

I went over to Jonathan and Charlie's new place yesterday for an Easter Egg hunt. After the hunt, Killian sat with me so I could help him open the colorful plastic eggs and find the tasty treats and toys inside. He was having so much fun sitting with me. Maybe he was overwhelmed with the excitement of the egg hunt, but I like to think he liked being with his Grandma Julie.

Sunday, April 28: Bill and Marilyn visited Friday night and Matthew came last night. All were good visits, but none of them included Scott... at least not really. He can't respond to their questions and doesn't look at them. I can see the sadness on their faces.

When Allison the nurse looked up Scott's medication record two nights ago we realized he hadn't received his CellCept for four days last week. This is a really bad sign. So tonight I asked Isabelle, another nurse, what I need to be concerned about from here on out. For example, if Scott were to break a leg, would he be taken to Kaiser for treatment? Isabelle tried to help me understand that if he went to Kaiser, surgery would be performed on his leg, he probably wouldn't make it through the surgery, and if he did, what would his quality of life be like? Would I want him to go through that?

So I asked her what would happen if we didn't want him to have surgery, thinking this option would be cold and heartless and maybe even cruel. But Isabelle assured me that with comfort care through hospice, he would be given Ativan to keep him calm, morphine to keep him out of pain, *and* he would probably go quickly. It was good to hear that—as Scott's Durable Power of Attorney for Health Care—I can refuse this type of treatment and that will be my choice when the time comes. I feel like I'm finally getting that being on hospice means this really is the end of Scott's life.

Gloria and Geoffrey visited today at lunchtime. Even though their last visit was some time ago, it still shocked me when Gloria told me how much Scott had declined. I see him getting worse every day, but to hear someone else voice those words made it very real. I was worried about how Geoffrey would react to Scott, and almost told Gloria not to bring him. Gloria said Geoff didn't remember that Scott had Alzheimer's and later told her that Scott looked really bad.

Monday, April 29: Scott wasn't eating much, so I asked Lindsay to bring me some chocolate ice cream and a MightyShake. Once he began eating the ice cream and drinking the shake, I slipped him a bit of egg salad sandwich. He ate it so I gave him more ice cream and shake, then slipped in another piece of the sandwich.

At one point, he raised his hand to massage my face while looking into my eyes. I like to think he was trying to tell me he loved me and that this was the only way he could express it. Maybe a part of him is recognizing a part of me.

The last couple of days Scott's been telling me *Thank you* when I help him. It surprises me when I hear his voice.

Monday, May 6: Last night at dinnertime, Scott was asleep in his wheelchair. Before I arrived, I stopped at Phyllis Burgers for a chocolate shake—and had a banana in my purse. As I've done many times before, I put the straw up to his mouth to drink the shake and he downed three-fourths before eating some banana. Lindsay brought me a tuna sandwich and I was able to get one bite down when I noticed he was forgetting to swallow. Mind you, he was doing all this with his eyes closed.

Roberto was walking behind Scott and his face told me that I shouldn't be feeding him. "I guess I shouldn't be trying to get him to eat or drink?" I asked.

"Not really, but we let the family do what they feel they need to do," he responded. In that moment I realized Scott's body was beginning to shut down.

After the CNAs got him into bed, I felt his hands and they were warm. As I felt his forehead, I could tell he was running a fever. Allison thought he had a fever, too. When leaving, I asked one of the nurses, Denise, to have Allison call me if I needed to come back.

I went home to fix dinner and play Mahjong. As I was brushing my teeth, Denise called to confirm that Scott was running a fever of 101.1 degrees. They gave him a Tylenol enema and put him on oxygen. She was going to call hospice and we could connect in the morning.

When I arrived at Sunnybrook this morning, I couldn't find Scott in his room or the dining room. At the front desk I learned that the hospice aide, Anne, was giving him a shower. He was getting the best shower ever, although he was confused. He looked at me as if to say, *Finally someone who will save me from all of this.* I stayed with him even though both Anne and the CNA Felicitas were doing such a wonderful job. Once he was almost completely dressed, they attempted to stand him up. He had no energy, so they brought in a mechanical lift to move him to the wheelchair. In his room, they needed to use the mechanical lift again. Worried that he hadn't eaten this morning, I was able to get a bit of chocolate pudding and MightyShake into him before the lift was ready to put him in bed.

Once he lay down, it was lights out. He hasn't opened his eyes since, except to take some meds. I left to get lunch and call hospice to make sure they knew Scott was declining. I spoke with a woman who seemed to know, and told me that Lisa would be at Sunnybrook this afternoon. I was glad that I hadn't missed her. When I got back, Scott was still asleep. Gil and Cynthia were sitting by his bed, so we visited while waiting for Lisa.

After examining Scott, Lisa seemed to agree with me that he was declining from not eating or drinking *and* refusing his meds. When I asked Lisa if we needed to start an IV so he could get fluids, she said, "Only if you want to stop hospice services."

"No, that is not an option," I said. I still didn't get how this all worked. The one thing I did get, though, was that Scott was ready to go home.

Lisa eased my mind by describing the end of life in this beautiful way: "When someone is dying, their body has the wisdom to know what to do. It's as if this wisdom is there to protect them as they ease onto the other side. They don't feel hunger or thirst like we do. Their body is getting ready for the shutdown if you will." As she was talking, I realized that putting him on hospice a few months ago was one of the best things I've ever done. Hospice support is needed to help him die comfortably and lovingly through the end of life. Doctors and nurses keep him alive and CNAs assist with activities of daily living, but hospice is there to help him live comfortably and free of pain at the end. Having these wonderful people help Scott ease from this life into the beautiful life waiting for him is essential for me and Scott.

Lisa commented that Scott looked really good, comfortable, and it helped that he had such a great shower that morning. She said he looked really tired, though. Then she looked at me to ask, "How are you doing?"

"I'm okay," I muttered.

"You must also feel really tired."

All I could say was, "Yes, I am very tired." And scared.

After Gil and Cynthia left, I gave Roberto an update. He told me he was there for me anytime I needed him, and came in a few times to check in on us. Since Scott was running a fever and couldn't be roused, I thought something I fed him went into his lungs. But that was not the case—refusing his immunosuppressive drugs was causing his heart to reject his body.

I texted Jonathan, Matthew, and Gloria with updates. When I got home to fix dinner, I called Janice, who met me at Sunnybrook that evening. At 4:00 p.m. Scott's heart rate was 120, which is considered high. His fever has been stable at 99.1 degrees. Jonathan is going to visit tomorrow morning and Matthew will visit tomorrow night.

Tuesday, May 7: This day is a complete blur. I believe Janice came over to sit with me. Bill and Marilyn were out of town and Gloria left for a trip back east.

Scott hasn't eaten or received liquids since Sunday night. He started coughing yesterday right after the shower and is on oxygen and inhalation therapy. Today, hospice put him on morphine. I am happy that Scott will be going home to family and friends who have passed before. He's been through so much since his heart transplant and if he woke up now, he wouldn't know what was going on.

Wednesday, May 8: I was just getting out of the shower when Lisa called to say she felt Scott was ready to pass in a few days, if not today. She asked me if I needed anything and I said no. On the way to Sunnybrook, I started crying, and called Janice to tell her about my conversation with hospice. Still driving and not sure what to do, I left Lisa an incoherent message saying, "I don't know what I need, but I need something." Then I called Janice again and said I would like her to come down. When Lisa came in shortly after I arrived, I realized what I needed: my family and friends sitting vigil with me.

The first to arrive was Bob, then Jonathan, Janice, Charlie, Olga Lee, Gil, Cynthia, and Matthew. We sat there telling stories about Scott and keeping watch.

From around 11:00 a.m. on, the staff and residents came in to tell Scott farewell. Staff people spoke directly into Scott's ear to tell him how much they loved him and will miss him. Jonathan couldn't believe how many caring people made an effort to say goodbye and profess their love for a man who had been living at Sunnybrook for just over a year.

Roberto came in off and on throughout the day. Alyssa, my sweet earth angel, kept constant vigil until 2:30 p.m. when Allison took over. The care they gave him was incredible, constantly checking on him, making sure he wasn't in pain or uncomfortable. Lisa peeked in every so often to examine Scott, and explained the dying process and how to tell when death is near.

Jonathan was the last to leave and it was now 10:00 p.m. Feeling confident Scott would not leave his body until I returned, I left too. At home, I ate some oatmeal, watched some TV, and tried to relax.

I'm not sure why Scott is hanging on, but he is. His heart rate is 140 and his breathing is steady but rapid. Maybe his dementia has him scared and he's not able to break free of his body. I've asked God and his angels to help him go home, but I'm not feeling their presence. It doesn't matter, though, as long as Scott is feeling a spiritual presence. After all he is the one going home.

Thursday, May 9: At 2:30 a.m. a male nurse called to ask me to come back to Sunnybrook. At 4:00 Scott's breathing was still regular so I spoke to Scott telepathically that I was going home to get a few hours of sleep, thinking, *Please hang on until I get back.* I was in the shower when Lisa called to say it was going to be any moment now. Somehow I was back by his side by 8:15.

Scott passed away at 9:20 a.m. this morning. We were alone together, and that was important to me. It looked like he was struggling, but since Lisa and the nurses had explained the dying process, I felt prepared. At the end, I was timing his breaths and could tell that it was going to happen any moment. I was texting Jonathan as his breathing slowed down: 5 seconds, 7 seconds, 12 seconds, back to 2 seconds when Roberto came in.

While the two of us watched Scott, I heard, then saw, a landscaper with a leaf blower going full blast right outside Scott's window. I couldn't hear Scott's breathing and thought, *And life goes on.* I said as much to Roberto and he said, "I was thinking the same thing."

After Roberto left, Scott's breaths started slowing down to 5 seconds, 7, 10, back to 5, 8, 11, 20, and when he got to 30 seconds I thought, *The next breath will be his last.* He took one more breath…and it *was* his last. It was a beautiful experience and I will miss Scott for the rest of my life. After all, he is *my* Phoenix Man.

Epilogue

When Scott passed away that Thursday morning in May, I thought I would be devastated. But what I felt was relief for him and a bit of euphoria knowing he was with the angels, receiving their love and comfort as he acclimated himself to his spiritual body. Before allowing the CNA to clean his human body, I gave his hand one more goodbye squeeze. Immediately I pulled back when I felt how disfigured and sweaty his fingers had become. In that moment I understood we really are *not* our bodies. Jonathan had just arrived and we left knowing Scott was gone this time—The Phoenix Man had gone home.

Grief is its own phenomenon. You can't just hold it awhile then let it go. No…you have to stare grief in the face and feel its fury until it dissipates, rolling away like a wave only to come back harder and stronger the next time. Each wave takes more of you, leaving pain and sadness in its wake.

The day Scott passed, I made arrangements to meet with the funeral home, to order necessary paperwork from Scott's retirement office, and to book the room for the Celebration of Life. When I look back at my notes, I can't believe I was able to do that!

After breakfast Friday morning, I went to the funeral home to complete the paperwork for Scott's body to be cremated and to order death certificates. I was amazingly calm, talking to the funeral service worker as if nothing in my life had changed. Crying on the drive down may have helped. That night while out for a walk it hit me that Scott was gone and the word *widow* came into my mind. I felt like a marked woman and decided that word was not for me.

On Saturday, I halfheartedly took myself over to Sunnybrook to pick up Scott's belongings. When I walked into his old room, I said *Hi* to Ron, Jack was asleep, and Ken wasn't around. There was someone new in Scott's bed. Ron was crying as I left with Scott's clothes, so I asked Angie to make sure someone checked in on him.

When I got home I noticed the humming sound in my left ear was practically gone. Was it caused by stress or the noises at Sunnybrook? Later, sitting on my bed, I noticed the alarm clock said 6:13 p.m. Scott's birthday is June 13. Out loud I said, "Okay, I know you are here and giving me a sign. Thanks, honey."

June 2019: A month after Scott's death, as a small group headed back to the dock on Lake Sonoma in Jonathan and Charlie's boat, I told a story that included Scott. First using the words my ex-husband, I thought, *Wait—Scott's not my ex-husband.* When I said husband, I knew that wasn't right either. I was baffled about what to call him. Tonight, while out walking I figured it out: he is my late husband.

Even though Scott had passed away, I was able to attend one more caregiver retreat at The Bishop Ranch. This last one just happened to be on Scott's birthday. Staying busy was my goal. Later that night, Jon, Charlie, Matthew, and the grandkids met me at Tomatina's for dinner. Getting together on Scott's special day was necessary for all of us.

After a few weeks of mourning, I began writing thank you cards to the staff at Sunnybrook. This was a difficult yet necessary task. As I created the cards and typed the notes on my computer, I was surprised at how easily the words flowed as I expressed each person's impact on both of us. It was as if Scott were right there helping me along. If not Scott, then an angel was whispering the right words.

Once the cards were done and sent, Sunnybrook's activity director Angie and I planned a June 19 memorial service for Scott and another long-term resident. It was beautifully done. Jonathan, Matthew, Marilyn, Shirley, and Bob attended. Everyone loves dessert, so I made 48 chocolate and white cupcakes and oatmeal chocolate chip cookies for the staff and residents, decorating the table with rainbow napkins. A poster board with photos of Scott, family, and friends was on display. Angie provided drinks and fresh fruit to keep it a bit healthier. A chaplain from Memorial Hospice conducted the service.

Wanting to stay busy, I signed up for any class that sounded interesting—I did *not* want to be alone. The day after the Sunnybrook memorial, I was scheduled for a class called Aging Gayfully. In my mind I thought, *Wow, I can't believe there is a class to help us age gayfully*, you know like joyfully or cheerfully.

At the Senior Center, there was a line to sign in and pay for the class. I couldn't tell if everyone was checking in for Aging Gayfully, but I did hear some talk about a class for LGBTQ people. After signing in, I headed upstairs where I encountered another line. The seats were almost filled. An acquaintance from my HICAP days was the facilitator, and that was a plus. But as I started looking around, something seemed off to me. Feeling like the people were there to meet other people, I began to feel uncomfortable. That was when it finally dawned on me that *Aging Gayfully* was a class for LGBTQ people.

With so many people standing in line behind me, it was difficult to leave. A few people said, "No, it's okay, you're in the right room." But at this point, I knew that I was *not* in the right room, got through the crowd, and back downstairs.

Back at the front desk, I asked if there was any way I could get my fee back since I didn't realize the true gist of the class. The woman at the desk and I laughed at my total ineptitude, as I really *wasn't* thinking straight, if you'll pardon the pun. Who knows, maybe in my next life.

August 2019: For two months I put my whole being into planning the Celebration of Life to be held on August 11 (Matthew's birthday) at Legends Banquet Hall at the Bennett Valley Golf Course. I needed the celebration to be special. While gathering photos to create a bookmark, I was in full-blown mourning. This I did not expect, yet I knew that these feelings of desperation, sadness, and uncertainty were a necessary part of the healing process.

Wanting a video of Scott's life, I asked Patti, who took over the ALZ sing-along for Diane and me, to come over to my place so we could play around with PowerPoint until I felt comfortable continuing on my own. Janice copied songs onto a CD. Then Lauren spent a long afternoon and evening teaching me how to insert and time the songs into the PowerPoint program. Matthew suggested on which photos to add in, take out, or move around. His recommendations added enormously to the perfect PowerPoint presentation.

On the day of the celebration, Penny showed up early to make floral arrangements out of the bouquets I bought from Trader Joe's. The pale yellow roses, pink carnations, golden sunflowers, statuesque lilies, and greenery were artfully displayed in the vases I had collected from my special friends before the event. These stunning bouquets were then placed on the long tables that surrounded the event, and each friend left with their vase full of colorful blooms.

Jan Fichter, a dear friend, was a huge help setting up the round tables where guests would sit, while I arranged the framed photos of Scott with family and friends. Marilyn and Shirley had guests sign in so I could concentrate on greeting everyone.

In the center of each guest's table we placed a centerpiece of either baby roses in red and yellow, or other colorful arrangements of plants and flowers. Later other family and friends took one home when it was over.

Jonathan played the PowerPoint of Scott's life, which began with the song *Celebrate Good Times, Come On* by Kool and the Gang and ended with *One Day Less* by John Michael Montgomery. You could hear a pin drop when it was over. The tears flowed freely.

Gil was the Emcee and gave a talk about his younger brother. The scheduled speakers were me, Bill, Jonathan, Bob, Matthew, and RPJ; Doug, Wally Cox, and Mike O'Brien added a few words at the end. The hors d'oeuvres were delicious. Jonathan raved about the stuffed mushrooms and made sure I got a few before they were all gone. Dede, a friend of Marilyn's, made raspberry, chocolate, and vanilla cheesecake cupcakes that were a hit. When the celebration was over and everyone had left, Matthew, RPJ, and I sat in the bar reflecting on a very difficult yet perfect day.

The next morning was a complete let down. *Now what?* I wondered. *I'm all alone, now what do I do?* I hadn't a clue.

September 2019: It's been four and a half months since Scott passed away. As I backed out of the garage this afternoon, all of a sudden the song *Could It Be I'm Falling in Love* came on. When I heard *And darling you'll always be, the only one for me, heaven made you specially,* I started crying. Then I noticed it was 3:13 p.m. It seems that when Scott wants my attention the number 13 or 613 comes up somewhere.

I haven't been remembering my dreams much since Scott passed. But one morning right before I woke up, I was talking to a few people outside a restaurant when I glanced past them and saw Scott standing there staring at me. I woke up longing to see him.

Grieving is a lonely process. I thought about it a lot when Scott was sick. I wondered how I would feel when he was gone. The interesting thing is that it hits me at the oddest moments and takes my breath away. If I let the feelings flow through me, it is a powerful pain of sorrow and sadness. I feel guilty because if I had had the money, I would have kept Scott at home with round-the-clock care. And yet if that had happened, I would never have met all the wonderful people at Sunnybrook and they would have never met The Phoenix Man.

I began attending a grief support group with Memorial Hospice. Eight of us were going through our own sorrow. With two facilitators, we met once a week for eight weeks. Five of us continue to meet and have become fast friends: Jules (Julie), Kathi, Lynn, Lou Ann, and me. Since we didn't want to call ourselves the Grief Support Group, Kathi dubbed us *The Feisty Five.*

October 2019: The HICAP Girls (Mary, Joyce, Eileen, and me) met for lunch on Friday, October 25 at Sea Thai Bistro to celebrate Mary's birthday. One member Toni was home on hospice services. We planned to see her the next day but the Kincade Fire began. This was just two years after the Tubbs Fire. Toni was evacuated to a nursing home in Petaluma and we were unable to see her before she passed away. We will miss her beautiful and resilient spirit.

The Kincade Fire started northeast of Geyserville on October 23, 2019, burning 77,758 acres until the fire was fully contained on November

6. The fire prompted a massive mandatory evacuation stretching from the vineyards of Sonoma County to the coastal communities of Geyserville, Healdsburg, Windsor, Sebastopol, Bodega Bay, and parts of Santa Rosa. The firefighters worked tirelessly to stop the oncoming avalanche of fire. Fortunately my sons and I lived in areas that were not evacuated.

Saturday, December 25, 2019: Christmas dinner turned out better than I thought. Everyone but Gloria and RPJ gathered at my place: Jon, Charlie, Killian, Tatum, Matthew, Janice, Olga Lee, Karen, Bill, and Marilyn. We missed RPJ's deep voice for the Christmas carols. I also invited John from the ALZ transition group, whose wife died last July. I was worried about him being alone and assured him that he would feel comfortable in our mix of family and friends.

Remembering how much Jonathan loved the stuffed mushrooms at the Celebration of Life, I decided to surprise him by finding a recipe for parmesan-stuffed mushrooms. Yesterday, I prepared all the mushrooms by removing the stems then washing and patting them dry. Was I glad I did! As the ham was baking in the oven this afternoon, I prepared the stuffing mix for 40 mushrooms. Wanting everything ready at the same time, I kept watching the clock—but stuffing the mushrooms took longer than I would have thought. Fifteen-minute prep time kiss my sweet a*s! This was not a job that should be taken lightly and I certainly won't for next year.

We started eating before Jon, Charlie, and the grandkids arrived as they were running a bit late. Luckily I had asked everyone to leave some stuffed mushrooms for Jon. Jonathan took three of the five that were left and then someone got up quickly to finish them off. Who was that sly person??? When Jonathan got up again, he was *extremely* disappointed that they were all gone—I mean he cried like a baby! Next year I'll need to make at least 60.

Before we started eating, I thanked everyone for coming and for the food that they brought to share. We toasted both Scott and John's Marilyn for wherever they are in the afterlife. This was a good day.

January 2020: The New Year began without a hitch and I began the process of piecing together this book from emails and writings done in the last 12 years. At the same time, I continued my classes of Tai Chi and Mindful Meditation, lunch with the HICAP Girls, dinners with The Feisty Five, the ALZ Transition Group, and began facilitating a new ALZ support group. Staying busy was still a priority so I met with friends and family when I wasn't working on this book. I felt a newness to my life and I knew the hard part of mourning was behind me.

But wait! I'm not sure I thought this through. Each email and personal writing brought back difficult times and sad memories of my life with Scott. Yet mixed in with the tears were also happy remembrances of the joys and blessings Scott gave to me these last 12 years. There were times when I wasn't sure this manuscript was going anywhere. I questioned whether anyone would be interested in our story or if anything I had to share would help other caregivers. *Come on angels and guides I need your help,* I thought many a time.

Of course, the COVID-19 pandemic of 2020 shifted my life online. Both Alzheimer's support groups use Google Hangouts Meet. My meditation class and the Feisty Five meet on Zoom.

Tuesday, April 28, 2020: As I write this, almost a year has gone by since Scott passed away and I still think about him all the time. A few weeks ago I dreamt that Scott and I were in the bathroom at Target and he wasn't sure what to do. As I was helping him pull up his pants, someone knocked on the door. Opening the door just wide enough, I could see a woman wanting to come in. I whispered that I was helping my husband who has Alzheimer's and she seemed to understand. When I woke up I could feel the sadness of the disease, but also felt the happiness of being with him again. It's a paradox how these feelings of sorrow and loss can also bring me joy, because they remind me of our love for each other.

Tonight I was out walking on the trail close to my place heading north. Jonathan had promised he would FaceTime. When my phone rang, Jonathan and Tatum were smiling at me. Tatum threw me kisses and I teased her by saying I was going to tickle her feet. Jon put me up on the TV screen, so Tatum could watch me on TV *and* the iPhone.

"Now I wish I had fixed my hair today," I told Jon, as Charlie laughed in the background. As I talked and walked, a beautiful gray cat that I've encountered before walked towards me wanting some pets. I turned the phone towards the cat and Tatum screeched with excitement.

I wanted to talk to Killian but he wouldn't come out of his bedroom. Killian was upset because he wanted to talk to Grandpa Scott, so Jonathan took the phone into Killian.

"I hear you want to talk to Grandpa Scott," I said. "Grandpa's in heaven sweetie and we can't see him or talk to him anymore. He can see us, though, and watches over you and loves you."

"Grandpa had a bad heart and died," Killian responded.

"Yes, Grandpa used to have a bad heart, but then he got a new heart. What happened then was that Grandpa's brain…" and I couldn't think of the words that would help him understand.

"Grandpa's brain didn't work anymore?" Killian asked.

"Yes, that's right. His brain stopped working and he went to heaven, but he's watching over you and he loves you."

As we were talking, I turned the phone so Killian could see the footbridge and the creek below. He was enthralled with all that I was seeing on the trail. Then Tatum said goodnight and threw me more kisses. She was fussy because she wanted to keep talking to Grandma. I was thrilled.

As I got closer to home, I turned my phone so Killian could see the two elderly ladies waving to him as they walked their dogs. When I was ready to turn into my cul-de-sac, the orange tabby that lives across the street sauntered over. While I petted the cat, Killian was cooing to her in his baby voice. All of it gave me so much joy.

It was time for Killian to go to bed, so we threw each other lots of kisses. I kept saying, "I love you. Sweet dreams! I love you!"

And this beautiful life goes on.

Note to All Those Who Are Grieving:

As I was editing this book, I realized that it would be incomplete without addressing the elephant in the room: widowhood, grieving, and a new life. And although this note is addressing those who have lost a partner, the same suggestions apply to anyone who is going through the grieving process.

The death of a significant other is its own kind of mourning. It's an ending of your old life and the beginning of a new one. Whether you were a longtime caregiver or lost your partner quickly, learning to adjust is a challenge. Grieving is a lonely road, but there are ways to help you adapt while going through the mourning process. There is no time requirement that says you must be done mourning by such and such a date. Each person has their own timeline and grieves in their own way. And mourning your significant other, who was the most important person in your life, takes time and brings a new set of adjustments. Learning to be single again is also tough.

Don't wait for your friends to call or text. Unless they have lost a spouse or partner, they can't understand what you are feeling and may need your guidance. Let them know you are hurting and that you need a listening ear. What I found interesting was that some friends believed that I had already mourned Scott through all the years of caregiving. So in the first few months of being a widow, I felt deserted. Soon realizing that my friends didn't know what to say or how to react around me, I began to broach the subject by bringing Scott into the conversation. Once I confessed the pain I was feeling, it became easier to get together. My friends didn't have to wonder if it was okay to talk about Scott. Because I opened up, they felt comfortable talking about Scott and we were able to grieve his loss together. After all, they were missing him, too.

Make plans and stay active. Reach out to the community for activities that will make you feel happy and brings you joy.

Counseling: If you haven't already, contact hospice or another counseling service to get one-on-one or group counseling.

Enroll in classes: Check out your local junior college, senior centers, or other outlets. If one class doesn't work, try another.

Volunteer: Find an organization where you can volunteer; someplace that will help heal your heart. For me it was through the Alzheimer's Association. If you like being around animals, try an animal shelter; if you'd rather help the elderly, a nursing home or senior center; if you enjoy being around children, look up volunteering for kids.

My sons didn't talk much about Scott after he passed and I didn't know why. When we were able to get together, I made a point of sharing stories about our life together, which included them, letting them know I could handle this. Even if one of us broke down, it was healing to open up and feel Scott's presence.

And I do feel Scott's presence with me through the days, weeks, and yes, now almost two years. He is still a big part of my life in wonderful ways I would have never imagined. Feeling blessed!

Index

Tracheotomy 60, 61, 77
Tubbs Fire 148, 149, 150, 257

U

Uncle Johnny (Father John Houle)
        41, 44
Urinary Tract Infection (UTI) 162

V

Vascular Dementia 146
Vertigo 88, 89
Veterans 90, 124
Virtue 124, 131
Voriconazole 71

W

Waiting Game 6, 24, 30
What ifs 141, 151, 153, 158
Worst-case scenario 53, 83

X

Xanax (brand-name for alprazolam)
        98, 99, 100, 101

Y

You have the right 72, 90, 239

Scott Joseph Bennett
Spring Lake, Santa Rosa, CA
January 3, 2010

9 781982 268732